PLANT-BASED
DIET COOKBOOK FOR
BEGINNERS

1000 Days of Quick and Healthy Recipes to Enjoy Sustainable Living and Take Care of Your Well-Being Without Sacrificing Taste

Allison Lawrence

Table of Contents

Introduction 11

What to Eat and What to Avoid 12

Measurement Conversion Table 16

Breakfast..................................... 18

1. Chocolate Peanut Butter Protein Shake 18

2. Turmeric Tofu Scramble.................. 18

3. Banana–Nut Butter Boats 18

4. Tahini Braised Greens 18

5. Spicy Oats................................. 19

6. Chia Seed Pudding 19

7. Tofu Fries.................................. 19

8. Berries with Cream 20

9. Chocolate Strawberry Milkshake 20

10. Apple Cinnamon Smoothie.............. 20

11. Peanut Butter Protein Smoothie 20

12. Breakfast Burritos........................ 20

13. Pomegranate Smoothie 21

14. Berry Ginger Zing Smoothie............. 21

15. Cauliflower Oatmeal 21

16. Protein Bars.............................. 21

17. Zucchini Oatmeal........................ 22

18. Chocolate Zucchini Bread 22

19. Corn Griddle Cakes with Tofu Mayonnaise 22

20. High Protein Toast....................... 23

21. Avocado Miso Chickpeas Toast.......... 23

22. Berry Compote Pancakes................ 23

23. Chickpeas Spread Sourdough Toast 24

24. Eggplant Sandwich 24

25. Amaranth Banana Porridge 24

26. Quinoa Porridge with Amaranth........ 24

27. Cinnamon and Almond Porridge........ 25

28. Apple Porridge 25

29. Pumpkin Spice Granola Bites.............. 25

Lunch..26

30. Hot Roasted Peppers Cream 26

31. Quinoa and Parsley Salad 26

32. Lentil Vegetable Loaf....................... 26

33. Spicy Hummus Quesadillas................. 27

34. Tex-Mex Tofu & Beans 27

35. Chickpea Salad 27

36. Greek Salad with Tofu Feta................. 28

37. Plant-Strong Bowl.......................... 28

38. Cauliflower Fried Rice...................... 28

39. Brussels Sprouts & Cranberries Salad 28

40. Coconut Brussels Sprouts.................. 29

41. Sweet Potato Quesadillas 29

42. Tofu Cacciatore 29

43. Moroccan Eggplant Stew 30

44. Mushrooms and Chard Soup................ 30

45. Vegetable Tacos 30

46. Grilled Eggplant Roll-Ups.................. 31

47. Pasta with Olives and White Beans . 31

48. Bowl with Root Vegetables................. 31

49. Amaranth Polenta with Wild Mushrooms 32

50. Pasta with Mushroom Sauce............... 32

51. Spaghetti Squash With Peanut Sauce 32

52. Vegetable Fajitas Tacos.................... 33

53. Chickpea Flour Quiche 33

54. Nori Burritos 33

55. Roasted Brussel Sprouts with Parmesan 34

56. Kale and Black Olives 34

57. Baked Parsnip and Potato 34

58. Cheese Broccoli Pasta 34

59. Turmeric Zucchinis......................... 35

60. Eggplant Masala 35

126. Sweet Potatoes Vanilla Pudding..... 56

127. Vegetable Wontons 56

Vegetables And Sides 58

128. Steamed Broccoli with Sesame 58

129. Balsamic Zucchini Bowls 58

130. Vegan Fat Bombs 58

131. Carrot Cake Balls 58

132. Avocado and Tempeh Bacon Wraps 59

133. Peppers and Hummus 59

134. Mixed Vegetable 59

135. Indonesian-Style Spicy Fried Tempeh Strips........ 60

136. Pomegranate Flower Sprouts........... 60

137. Sherry Roasted King Trumpet........ 60

138. Garlic and Herbs Mushrooms Skillet 61

139. Baked Brussel Sprouts 61

140. 3-Ingredient Flatbread................ 61

141. Grape Tomatoes and Zucchini........ 61

142. Tofu & Asparagus Stir Fry 62

143. Asparagus Spears........................ 62

144. Oregano Tomato and Radish 62

145. Pepper & Tomato Bake................ 63

146. Red Rose Potato Toasts 63

147. Zucchini Fries......................... 63

148. Brussels Sprouts & Carrots............... 64

149. Tofu Curry 64

150. Rosemary Sweet Potato Chips........ 64

151. Sunflower Seed Bread 64

152. Cheesy Fennel 65

153. Sweetened Onions 65

154. Baked Vegetables with Cheese and Olives 65

155. Hasselback Zucchini..................... 66

156. Saffron Avocado Cream 66

157. Turmeric Artichokes 66

158. Garam Masala Asparagus.................. 66

159. Walnuts Allspice Bell Peppers.......... 67

160. Gold Potato Masala..................... 67

161. Coriander Broccoli and Onions........ 67

162. Cinnamon Potato..................... 68

163. Ginger Zucchinis and Carrots........ 68

164. Chinese Orange Tofu.................... 68

165. Baked Root Vegetables 69

166. Quinoa and Black Bean Lettuce Wraps 69

167. Pico de Gallo 69

Soups, Stews and Salads 70

168. Creamy Cauliflower Pakora Soup ... 70

169. Tomato Gazpacho 70

170. Cauliflower Asparagus Soup 70

171. Chickpea and Noodle Soup 71

172. Kale and Cauliflower Salad 71

173. Spinach Soup with Dill and Basil 72

174. Cauliflower Spinach Soup 72

175. Zucchini Soup........................ 72

176. Vegetable Stew 72

177. Egg Avocado Salad..................... 73

178. Marinated Veggie Salad 73

179. Southwest Style Salad 73

180. Arugula with Fruits and Nuts............ 74

181. Brussels Sprouts and Ricotta Salad 74

182. Endive Salad 74

183. Moroccan Leeks Snack Salad 74

184. Roasted Butternut and Chickpeas Salad 75

185. Sprouts and Apples Snack Salad 75

186. Avocado with Raspberry Vinegar Salad 75

187. Cannellini Pesto Spaghetti 75

188. Kale and Lemon Salad........................ 76

189. Cauliflower Carrot Soup........................ 76

61. Minty Masala Tomatoes 35

62. Coconut milk Rice 35

63. Cheese Pockets 36

64. Vegan Taco Bowls 36

65. Caprese Stuffed Avocado 36

66. Black and Veggie Tacos 37

67. Roasted Butternut Squash Pasta 37

68. Arugula Pesto Couscous 37

Dinner 38

69. Mexican Lentil Soup 38

70. Red Pepper and Tomato Soup 38

71. Tarragon Soup 38

72. Mushroom Soup 39

73. Pasta with Kidney Bean Sauce 39

74. Coconut Rice 39

75. Barley and Mushrooms with Beans . 39

76. Coconut Curry Lentils 40

77. Stuffed Peppers with Kidney Beans 40

78. Tempeh Tikka Masala 40

79. Caesar Vegan Salad 41

80. Emmenthal Soup 42

81. Vegetables with Wild Rice 42

82. Cheese Board 42

83. Mushroom Steaks 43

84. Sprout Wraps 43

85. Cauliflower Steaks 43

86. Dijon Maple Burgers 44

87. Cucumber Bites with Chive and Sunflower Seeds 44

88. Vegetable Fajitas 44

89. Veggie Balls in Tomato Sauce 45

90. Kale Wraps with Chili and Green Beans 45

91. Grilled Peaches 45

92. Sausage Links 46

93. Dinner Rolls 46

94. Roasted Bell Peppers with Spicy Mayonnaise 46

95. Bell Peppers and Masala Potatoes 47

96. Nutmeg Okra 47

97. Creamy Eggplants 47

98. Eggplant Stacks 47

99. Oil-Free Mushroom and Tofu Burritos 48

100. Brown Rice Lettuce Wraps 48

101. Cashew Mac and Cheese 48

102. Pineapple Tofu Kabobs 49

103. Smoky Red Pepper Hummus 49

Snacks and Appetizers 50

104. Basil Zucchini Noodles 50

105. Cauliflower Popcorn 50

106. Zucchini Chips 50

107. Chocolate Almond Bars 51

108. Strawberry Watermelon Ice Pops .. 51

109. Pineapple, Peach, and Mango Salsa 51

110. Buffalo Cauliflower Dip 51

111. Sweet 'n' Spicy Crunchy Snack Mix 52

112. Kale Spread 52

113. Fudgy Choco-Peanut Butter 52

114. Tofu Sandwiches on Multigrain Bread 53

115. Seed Crackers 53

116. Banana Curry 53

117. Pumpkin Orange Spice Hummus 53

118. Banana Chips 54

119. Sesame Seed Bread 54

120. Spelt and Raisin Cookies 54

121. Taro Chips 55

122. Caramel Popcorn 55

123. Spicy Beet Chips 55

124. Paprika Cucumber Chips 56

125. Coconut Banana Pot 56

190. Creamy Potato Soup 76

191. Lemony Capers, Kale and Nuts Salad 76

192. Chickpeas & Squash Stew 77

193. Quinoa & Veggie Stew 77

194. Millet Tabbouleh, Lime and Cilantro 77

195. Grilled Lettuce Salad 78

196. Scallion and Mint Soup 78

197. Rainbow Mango Salad 78

198. Dandelion Salad 79

199. Amaranth Tabbouleh Salad 79

200. Cherry Tomato & Kale Salad 79

201. Avocado Power Salad 79

202. Warm Kale Salad 80

203. Creamy Asparagus Soup 80

204. Apple & Kale Salad 80

205. Zucchini & Tomato Salad 80

206. Chickpeas & Quinoa Salad 81

207. Basil and Avocado Salad 81

208. Dandelion and Strawberry Salad ... 81

209. Mango Salad 82

210. Corn and Egg Salad 82

211. Noodle Vegetable Salad 82

212. Creamy Parsnip Soup 83

213. Mexican Bean Salad 83

214. Roasted Potato Salad 83

215. Avocado Salad 84

216. Cabbage Mango Slaw 84

217. Kohlrabi Slaw with Cilantro 84

218. Butternut Squash Chickpea Stew .. 84

Legumes, Grains, Beans and Rice 86

219. Brown Lentil Bowl 86

220. Mom's Chili 86

221. Middle Eastern Chickpea Stew 86

222. Middle Eastern Za'atar Hummus 87

223. Anasazi Bean and Vegetable Stew 87

224. Black Bean and Corn Salad with Cilantro Dressing 87

225. Pecan Rice 88

226. Lentil and Wild Rice Soup 88

227. Broccoli and Rice Stir Fry 88

228. Balsamic Black Beans with Parsnip 88

229. Beluga Lentils with Lacinato Kale .. 89

230. Black Beans with Lime 89

231. Coconut Tofu Curry 89

232. Green Beans with Balsamic Sauce . 90

233. Cilantro and Avocado Lime Rice 90

234. Sweet Coconut Pilaf 90

235. Millet Fritters 91

236. Amaranth Porridge 91

237. Millet Porridge with Sultanas 91

238. Bulgur Wheat Salad 91

239. Aromatic Rice 92

240. Sweet Maize Meal Porridge 92

241. Sweet Oatmeal 92

242. Green Lentil Salad with Vinaigrette 92

243. Black Bean Taquitos 93

244. Lima Bean Casserole 93

245. Bean Bolognese 94

246. Rice and Vegetables 94

247. Black Bean Dip 94

248. Capers, Green Beans and Herbs Mix 94

249. Chickpeas Curry 95

250. Wild Rice and Black Lentils Bowl 95

251. Spanish-Style Saffron Rice with Black Beans 96

252. Green Beans 96

253. Squash Risotto 96

254. Zucchinis Cardamom Rice 97

255. Green Beans & Orange Sauce 97

256. Refried Beans 97

257. Spanish Rice 97

258. Chickpea Salad (2nd Version) 98

259. Cannellini Bean and Bell Pepper Burger 98

260. Chickpea Nuggets 98

Sauces and Condiments 100

261. Green Cilantro Sauce 100

262. Tartar Sauce 100

263. Sambal Sauce 100

264. Piri Sauce 100

265. Hemp Falafel with Tahini Sauce ... 101

266. Cranberry and Orange Sauce 101

267. Alfredo Sauce 101

268. Coriander Tahini Sauce 102

269. Tofu Hollandaise 102

270. Cranberry Sauce 102

271. Homemade Trail Mix 102

272. Mushroom Sauce 103

273. Quinoa with Mushroom 103

274. Vegetable Chili 103

275. Mushroom Dip 104

276. Cilantro, Lime Quinoa 104

277. Mushroom Gravy 104

278. Spicy Tomato Chutney 105

279. Lemon Avocado Salad Dressing 105

280. Red Salsa 105

Gluten-Free Recipes 106

281. Peach Mango Crumble (Pressure Cooker) 106

282. Ginger Spice Brownies 106

283. Cauliflower Wings 106

284. Eggplant Parmesan 107

285. Portobello Mushroom Stew 107

286. Barley and Chickpea Soup 107

287. Chili with Tofu 108

288. Pineapple and Mango Oatmeal 108

289. Slow Cooker Butternut Squash Oatmeal 109

290. French Toast 109

Dessert and Smoothie 110

291. Chocolate Peanut Butter Bars 110

292. Apple Crumble 110

293. Chocolate and Peanut Butter Smoothie 110

294. Lime and Cucumber Drink 111

295. Beet and Clementine Smoothie 111

296. Hazelnut and Chocolate Milk 111

297. Sweet and Sour Juice 111

298. Banana Walnut Bread 112

299. Cranberry and Almond Muffins 112

300. Pineapple Coconut Macaroons 112

301. Chocolate Chip Banana Cookies 113

302. Watermelon Strawberry Ice Pops 113

303. Raspberry Muffins 113

304. Chocolate Cake 113

305. Banana Muffins 114

306. Baked Apples 114

307. Banana Coconut Cookies 115

308. Butter Carrots 115

309. Parsley Potatoes 115

310. Tomato Kebabs 115

311. Fried Mustard Greens 116

312. Mushroom Stuffed Tomatoes 116

313. Banana Walnut Muffins 117

314. Protein Fat Bombs 117

315. Chocolate Mint Grasshopper Pie ... 117

316. Cold Lemon Squares 118

317. Green Tea and Vanilla Cream 118

318. Strawberries Cream 118

319. Power Smoothie 118

320. Pink Panther Smoothie 118

321. Tropical Smoothie 119

322. Pumpkin Smoothie 119

323. Banana and Chia Smoothie 119

324. Pineapple, Banana & Spinach Smoothie 119

325. Pumpkin Chia Smoothie 120

326. Green Mango Smoothie 120

327. Overnight Oatmeal 120

328. Almond Flour Muffins 120

329. Strawberry Ice Cream 121

330. Blackberry Pie 121

331. Cardamom Pears Smoothie 121

332. Pineapple Pudding 121

333. Indian Almond Kulfi 122

334. Wheat Cashew Kheer 122

335. Saffron Zucchini Pudding 122

336. Raisins Rice 122

337. Carrots Sugary Pudding 123

338. Saffron Coconut Cream 123

339. Masala Grapes and Bananas 123

340. Sugary Orange Cream 123

341. Rhubarb Coconut Milk Quinoa 124

342. Almond Chia Pudding 124

343. Strawberry and Banana Smoothie 124

344. Banana Shake 124

345. Easy Brownies 125

Recipe Index.............................126

Introduction

When it comes to plant-based nutrition, there is often the impression that you have to eat salad for the rest of your life. Yes, salad is always a good choice and can be very delicious if prepared in the right way; but it will not be your only source of food.

A plant-based diet is based on eating plant foods and whole foods. This means that you will have to eliminate all highly refined foods such as refined sugar and bleached flour. You will also start by minimizing or excluding the amount of eggs, dairy products, and meat. Instead, you will enjoy whole grains, vegetables, fruits, and legumes.

But keep in mind that "Plant-based" does not mean that a person's diet should be free of animal products such as meat or seafood. However, it is highly recommended not to eat these types of foods. In fact, many people prefer not to eat meat and wish to consume dairy products and/or eggs; or consume only vegetables, fruits and legumes.

The key to a successful plant-based diet is to give yourself a varied diet. Leafy greens are important, but they alone are not enough to get enough calories! If you think about it, you would have to consume pounds and pounds of kale to reach your calorie goal. Calories are essential because if they are not enough, you will feel depleted and exhausted. For this reason, the plant-based diet is full of delicious foods to try!

Why should most of what we eat come from the primary source?

Eating more vegetables constitutes the first nutrient known to man to counteract the incessant diseases that assail our population. Vegetables and greens offer, and in large quantities, micronutrients that give our bodies everything they need for a healthy and productive life. Eating regular vegetable meals and munching on foods grown directly from the earth will improve your well-being and life.

Most common health problems can be reduced with this simple approach.

Plant-based foods are broken down by the human digestive system differently than foods high in fat and protein. A diet rich in plant foods provides more fiber than a diet rich in animal and refined foods; these fibers absorb fats in the digestive tract, reducing the likelihood of being retained as body fat.

A plant-based diet not only works wonders for your body, but it also allows you to transform into a better version of yourself, providing your body with the most flawless fuel it can have.

What to Eat and What to Avoid

When it comes to a plant-based diet, you are never short of options. There is a wide range of foods that all come from plants. Below is a list of foods that can be eaten freely on a plant-based diet.

Vegetables

A person can survive just fine without animal meat, but he cannot live a healthy life without the consumption of vegetables in his life. It is said that a person's plate should be full of colorful vegetables to ensure good health. Listed below are the most common vegetables to use in a plant-based diet:

- Broccoli

- Cauliflower

- Beets

- Asparagus

- Carrots

- Zucchini

- Butternut squash

- Black cabbage

- Tomatoes

- Bell peppers

- Potatoes

- Sweet potatoes

Fruits

There is no restriction on fruit consumption. As we know, fruits are our primary source of fiber, carbohydrates, and vitamins and can ensure good health and active metabolism. The most commonly consumed fruits are:

- Grapes

- Apples

- Berries

- Melons

- Citrus fruits

- Bananas

- Avocados

Whole grains

Whole grains are another essential food group for the plant-based diet, as they are the primary energy source. The most commonly used grains are as follows:

- Brown rice

- Barley

- Buckwheat

- Quinoa

- Oats

- Spelt

- Whole meal bread

- Rye

Like grains, all products extracted from them are also fully permitted in this diet, such as wheat-based flours, chickpea or rice flours, etc.

Legumes

Legumes are another group of plant-based items that should be added to the diet to increase protein content. In addition, they are a rich source of carbohydrates and vital minerals:

- Chickpeas

- Kidney beans

- Black beans

- Lentils

- Peas

Seeds and nuts

Seeds and nuts are energy and nutrient bombs; their consistent use in foods increases the nutritional value of the diet:

- Chia seeds

- Pumpkin seeds

- Almonds

- Cashews

- Hemp seeds

- Flaxseed

- Pecans

- Brazil nuts

- Macadamias

- Pistachios

Healthy fats

Since animal fats cannot be consumed in a plant-based diet, all that remains is to choose from healthy vegetable oils. Olive oil is commonly used for cooking, while others can be used occasionally for salad dressing, etc.:

- Avocado oil

- Chia seed oil

- Walnut oil

- Canola oil

- Hemp seed oil

- Sesame oil

- Flaxseed oil

- Olive oil

Plant-Based Milk

Commonly used plant-based milk are as follows:

- Rice milk

- Coconut milk

- Almond milk

- Soy milk

- Oat milk

- Hemp coconut milk

"Recommended" foods to avoid

- Meat: poultry, red meat, pork, seafood, lamb, and seitan.

- Dairy products: yogurt, cheese, butter, half-and-half, cream, whey

- Eggs: chicken, duck, quail, ostrich

Foods to avoid

- butter, ghee, and other solid animal fats

- Refined sugar: white sugar, barley malt, beet sugar, brown sugar, fructose, powdered sugar, juice crystals, brown sugar, brown rice syrup, corn syrup

- Refined grains: white flour, white rice, quick-cooking oatmeal

- Sugary foods: cakes, cookies, and pastries

- All refined white carbohydrates

- All processed foods

- Excessive salt

 - Fried foods

- Processed vegan and vegetarian alternatives (which may contain salt or sugar)

- Beverages: fruit juices, soft drinks, sports drinks

.

Measurement Conversion Table

VOLUME EQUIVALENTS(DRY)

US STANDARD	METRIC (APPROXIMATE)
1/8 teaspoon	0.5 mL
1/4 teaspoon	1 mL
1/2 teaspoon	2 mL
3/4 teaspoon	4 mL
1 teaspoon	5 mL
1 tablespoon	15 mL
1/4 cup	59 mL
1/2 cup	118 mL
3/4 cup	177 mL
1 cup	235 mL
2 cups	475 mL
3 cups	700 mL
4 cups	1 L

VOLUME EQUIVALENTS(LIQUID)

US STANDARD	US STANDARD (OUNCES)	METRIC (APPROXIMATE)
2 tablespoons	1 fl.oz.	30 mL
1/4 cup	2 fl.oz.	60 mL
1/2 cup	4 fl.oz.	120 mL
1 cup	8 fl.oz.	240 mL
1 1/2 cup	12 fl.oz.	355 mL
2 cups or 1 pint	16 fl.oz.	475 mL
4 cups or 1 quart	32 fl.oz.	1 L
1 gallon	128 fl.oz.	4 L

TEMPERATURES EQUIVALENTS

FAHRENHEIT(F)	CELSIUS(C) (APPROXIMATE)
225 °F	107 °C
250 °F	120 °C
275 °F	135 °C
300 °F	150 °C
325 °F	160 °C
350 °F	180 °C
375 °F	190 °C
400 °F	205 °C
425 °F	220 °C
450 °F	235 °C
475 °F	245 °C
500 °F	260 °C

WEIGHT EQUIVALENTS

US STANDARD	METRIC (APPROXIMATE)
1 ounce	28 g
2 ounces	57 g
5 ounces	142 g
10 ounces	284 g
15 ounces	425 g
16 ounces (1 pound)	455 g
1.5 pounds	680 g
2 pounds	907 g

Breakfast

1. Chocolate Peanut Butter Protein Shake

Preparation Time: 5 minutes   **Servings: 1**

Ingredients:
- 2 tbsps. hemp hearts
- 1 cup chocolate almond milk
- ¼ cup peanut butter
- 2 bananas, frozen and finely minced

Directions: Get a blender and throw all the ingredients listed above in it. Blend well until smooth.

Nutrition: Calories: 395.1; Carbs: 67.9g; Protein: 14.2g; Fats: 10.8g

2. Turmeric Tofu Scramble

Preparation Time: 10 minutes   **Cooking Time: 15 minutes**
Servings: 4

Ingredients:
- 2 tbsps. Vegetable Broth or water
- 1 cup diced yellow onion
- ½ cup diced carrot
- ½ cup diced celery
- 1 (14 oz.) block extra-firm tofu, pressed & drained
- 1 tsp. ground turmeric
- ½ tsp. smoked paprika
- ½ tsp. chili powder
- 2 cups tightly packed chopped kale
- ½ tsp. salt or Spicy Umami Blend

Directions: Warm your broth on medium-high heat in a large skillet. Add the onion, carrot, and celery, and sauté until the onion begins to soften for about 3 minutes.
Crush the tofu with your hands into the skillet. Add the turmeric, smoked paprika, and chili powder, stir well and cook for 5 minutes.
Add the kale and stir well. Cover the skillet, adjust the heat to medium-low, and cook for 5 minutes more. Stir in the salt and serve.

Nutrition: Calories: 122.8; Fats: 5.9g; Protein: 11.3g; Carbs: 8.7g

3. Banana–Nut Butter Boats

Preparation Time: 5 minutes   **Cooking Time: 5 minutes**
Servings: 2

Ingredients:
- 4 large bananas, peeled
- ½ cup natural or homemade peanut butter
- 1 tbsp. unsweetened cocoa powder
- 1 to 2 tbsps. unsweetened soy milk
- ¼ tsp. ground cinnamon

Directions: Cut bananas in half lengthwise. Process cocoa powder, 1 tablespoon of soy milk and the peanut butter, in a blender until thick.
If necessary, increase the amount of soy milk to obtain the right consistency. Set aside.
Warm a large frying pan over medium-high heat. When the water boils, put the cut banana halves down into the pan and cook for about 1 minute, then turn and cook for 1 minute more.
Put 4 banana halves on each of both plates with cut side up. Pour about half of the sauce onto each plate. Sprinkle with a pinch or two of ground cinnamon and serve.

Nutrition: Calories: 634.8; Fats: 33.7g; Protein: 18.2g; Carbs: 77.9g

4. Tahini Braised Greens

Preparation Time: 5 minutes   **Cooking Time: 15 minutes**
Servings: 2

Ingredients:

- 2 tbsps. tahini
- 2 tsps. rice vinegar
- 1 small onion, halved and sliced
- 3 garlic cloves, minced
- ¾ cup Vegetable Broth
- 1 lb. kale or Swiss chard, leaves stemmed and cut into 2-inch pieces

Directions: Whisk the tahini and vinegar together in a measuring cup or small bowl. Set aside. Heat a large skillet over high heat. Put the garlic and onion, lower the heat to medium-high heat, and cook for about 1 minute. (Add a teaspoon or two of broth if it begins to stick.)

Add the greens and cook for 1 minute. Add the broth and tahini-vinegar mixture and stir to combine. Adjust the heat to medium, cover, then cook until the greens are soft, about 10 minutes, then serve.

Nutrition: Calories: 153.8; Fats: 8.7g; Protein: 7.2g; Carbs: 15.7g

5. Spicy Oats

Preparation Time: 15 minutes
Servings: 4

Cooking Time: 30 minutes

Ingredients:

- 1 large jalapeño, seeded and minced, divided
- 1 small yellow onion, diced
- 1 large red bell pepper, seeded & diced
- 1 cup steel-cut oats
- 2 cups Vegetable Broth
- 2 tbsps. nutritional yeast
- ½ tsp. salt, or 1 tsp. Spicy Umami Blend
- 8 oz. fresh baby spinach
- 1 large tomato, chopped
- 1 tsp. lemon juice

Directions: In a large saucepan, dry sauté half the jalapeño, the onion, and the bell pepper over medium-high heat for 5 minutes. Add the oats and broth and bring to a boil.

Adjust the heat to low, then simmer, occasionally stirring, until the oats are tender, about 25 minutes. Remove from the heat. Stir in the nutritional yeast, salt, spinach, cover, and let sit for 5 minutes.

In a small bowl, mix the tomato, remaining jalapeño, and lemon juice. Serve the savory oats with a couple of tablespoons of salsa over the top.

Nutrition: Calories: 201.8; Fats: 1.9g; Protein: 8.1g; Carbs: 38.7g

6. Chia Seed Pudding

Preparation Time: 15 minutes

Servings: 4

Ingredients:

- ¼ tsp. cinnamon
- 15 drops liquid stevia
- ½ tsp. vanilla extract
- ½ cup chia seeds
- 2 cups unsweetened coconut milk

Directions: Put the ingredients into the glass jar and mix well. Close jar with lid and place in the refrigerator for 4 hours. Serve chilled and enjoy.

Nutrition: Calories: 346.8; Fats: 32.9g; Carbs: 9.6g; Protein: 6.1g

7. Tofu Fries

Preparation Time: 15 minutes
Servings: 4

Cooking Time: 20 minutes

Ingredients:

- 15 oz firm tofu, drained, pressed, and cut into long strips
- ¼ tsp. garlic powder
- ¼ tsp. onion powder
- ¼ tsp. cayenne pepper
- ¼ tsp. paprika
- ½ tsp. oregano
- ½ tsp. basil
- 2 tbsps. olive oil
- Pepper
- Salt

Directions: Warm oven to 375°F. Mix all ingredients into the large mixing bowl and toss well. Place marinated tofu strips on a baking tray and bake in a preheated oven for 20 minutes.

Turn tofu strips to the other side and bake for another 20 minutes.

Nutrition: Calories: 136.8; Fats: 11.2g; Carbs: 2.1g; Protein: 9.1g

8. Berries with Cream

Preparation Time: 15 minutes   Servings: 1

Ingredients:
- ½ cup coconut cream
- 1 oz strawberries
- 1 oz raspberries
- ¼ tsp. vanilla extract

Directions: Add all fixings into the blender and blend until smooth. Pour in a serving bowl and top with fresh berries.

Nutrition: Calories: 302.8; Fats: 28.5g; Carbs: 11.8g; Protein: 3.5g

9. Chocolate Strawberry Milkshake

Preparation Time: 5 minutes   Servings: 2

Ingredients:
- 1 cup of ice cubes
- ¼ cup unsweetened cocoa powder
- 2 scoops of vegan protein powder
- 1 cup strawberries
- 2 cups unsweetened coconut milk

Directions: Add all fixings into the blender and blend until smooth and creamy. Serve immediately.

Nutrition: Calories: 220.8; Fats: 5.4g; Carbs: 14.8g; Protein: 27.9g

10. Apple Cinnamon Smoothie

Preparation Time: 5 minutes   Servings: 1

Ingredients:
- 1 tbsp. flaxseed, ground
- 8 oz coconut water
- ½ tbsp. protein powder, unsweetened
- 4 raw almonds
- 1 cup apple, diced
- 1 tsp. vanilla extract
- 1 tsp. ground cinnamon

Directions: In your blender, add all fixings. Puree for 15 seconds. Pour into a cup and add 3 cubes of ice.

Nutrition: Calories: 237.9; Carbs: 37.2g; Protein: 15.9g; Fats: 4.9g

11. Peanut Butter Protein Smoothie

Preparation Time: 3 minutes   Servings: 1

Ingredients:
- Granola of your preference
- ¾ cup almond milk, unsweetened
- 1 tbsp. protein powder
- 1 tbsp. peanut butter
- 6 ice cubes
- ½ cup blueberries, frozen

Directions: Except for the granola, add every ingredient in order into a blender and puree until smooth. Pour the blended mixture into a bowl. Add the granola as a topping.

Nutrition: Calories: 282.7; Carbs: 20.9g; Protein: 22.3g; Fats: 12.8g

12. Breakfast Burritos

Preparation Time: 10 minutes   **Cooking Time: 20 minutes**
Servings: 1

Ingredients:
- 4 tortillas, large or burrito size
- 1 cup sliced potatoes
- ½ cup salsa of choice
- 1 cup nopales, minced
- 1 cup black beans, rinse and drain them
- 1 cubed avocado
- 12 oz tofu, extra firm
- Pepper, freshly ground
- Garlic
- Sea salt
- 1 tsp. ground cumin

20

Directions: You'll need two saucepans. Set to medium-high heat and add equal amounts of coconut oil to both pans (1 tablespoon) to let them heat.

To one pan, add slices of potatoes. Into the other, put the minced nopales. Sauté both.

The potatoes should turn a golden color, while the nopales become dry, tender, and turn a brownish color.

Shift your nopales to a side of the pan and add tofu. Break the tofu down using a potato masher and keep cooking. You want the tofu to turn brown too.

You can add the sautéed potatoes to the pan of nopales now. Also, add black beans, pepper, cumin, salt, and garlic to the pan. Stir and let the mixture cook for 5 minutes.

Warm your salsa of choice and tortillas. Cover the mixture in your pan, alongside your salsa and avocado with the tortillas.

Nutrition: Calories: 410.8; Carbs: 50.9g; Protein: 20.3g; Fats: 13.7g

13. Pomegranate Smoothie

Preparation Time: 5 minutes   **Servings: 2**

Ingredients:

- 2 cups almond milk, unsweetened
- 2 medium apples, cored, sliced
- 2 bananas, peeled
- 2 cups frozen raspberries
- 1 cup pomegranate seeds
- 4 tsps. agave syrup

Directions: Place all the fixings into the jar of a high-speed food processor or blender in the order stated. Pulse for 1 minute until smooth, and then serve.

Nutrition: Calories: 141.2; Fats: 0.8g; Protein: 4.5g; Carbs: 30.2g

14. Berry Ginger Zing Smoothie

Preparation Time: 5 minutes   **Servings: 2**

Ingredients:

- 2 cups almond milk, unsweetened
- 1 cup frozen raspberries
- 1 cup of frozen strawberries
- 1 cup cauliflower florets
- 2 1-inch pieces of ginger

Directions: Place all the fixings into the jar of a high-speed food processor. Pulse for 1 minute until smooth, and then serve.

Nutrition: Calories: 299.8; Fats: 7.9g; Protein: 8.2g; Carbs: 29.7g

15. Cauliflower Oatmeal

Preparation Time: 15 minutes   **Cooking Time: 15 minutes**
Servings: 2

Ingredients:

- 1 cup cauliflower rice
- ½ cup unsweetened almond milk
- ½ teaspoon cinnamon
- 1 tablespoon honey
- ½ tablespoon peanut butter
- 1 strawberry, sliced

Direction: Mix milk with cauliflower rice, honey and cinnamon in a saucepan.

Cook the rice mixture to a boil then reduce the heat to low. Now cook the mixture for 10 minutes on a simmer.

Allow the oatmeal to cool, then garnish it with a strawberry. Serve.

Nutrition: Calories: 233.8; Fats: 4.2g; Carbs: 17.9g; Fiber: 6.8g; Sugar: 3.1g; Protein 6.2g

16. Protein Bars

Preparation Time: 10 minutes   **Cooking Time: 20 minutes**
Serving: 6

Ingredients:

- 1½ cup quick-cooking oats
- ½ cup almond meal
- ½ cup flaxseed meal
- 2 teaspoons cinnamon
- ½ teaspoon salt

- 4 tablespoons vegan protein powder
- 1 teaspoon pure vanilla extract
- 2 bananas, ripe and mashed
- ½ cup applesauce
- ¼ cup creamy peanut butter
- 2 tablespoons honey

Direction: Preheat your oven to 350 F.
Layer an 8x8 square baking dish with cooking spray. Mix all the ingredients in a large bowl.
Spread this mixture in the prepared pan. Bake the batter for 20 minutes in the oven.
Allow the mixture to cool, then slice. Serve.

Nutrition: Calories: 247.9; Fats: 11.9g; Carbs: 25.8g; Fiber: 3.8g; Sugar: 7.9g; Protein: 7.8g

17. Zucchini Oatmeal

Preparation Time: 15 minutes
Servings: 4

Cooking Time: 4 minutes

Ingredients:
- 2 cups rolled oats
- 6 tablespoons pea protein
- 2 teaspoons cinnamon
- 1 teaspoon nutmeg
- 2 ¼ cups almond milk
- 1 cup zucchini, grated
- ¼ cup maple syrup
- 1 teaspoon vanilla extract
- Toppings
- Banana
- Nuts
- Seeds
- Sugar-free chocolate chips
- 1 teaspoon coconut oil, melted

Direction: Sauté oats with coconut oil in an Instant Pot for 2 minutes on Sauté mode.
Combine the remaining ingredients, cover and close the cover.
Cook for 2 minutes on high pressure. When done, release all the pressure and remove the lid.
Allow the oatmeal to cool and garnish with desired toppings. Serve.

Nutrition: Calories: 231.8; Fats: 11.9g; Carbs: 25.8g; Fiber: 3.8g; Sugar: 7.9g; Protein 7.5g

18. Chocolate Zucchini Bread

Preparation Time: 15 minutes
Servings: 6

Cooking Time: 55 minutes

Ingredients:
- 1 ¼ cup whole wheat flour
- ¾ cup coconut sugar
- ½ cup raw cacao powder
- 3 teaspoons baking powder
- 2 teaspoons baking soda
- 1 cup zucchini, shredded
- ½ cup almond milk
- 1/3 cup unsweetened applesauce
- 1/3 cup coconut oil, melted
- 2 teaspoons vanilla extract
- 2/3 cup sugar-free chocolate chip

Direction: Preheat your oven to 350 F and layer a 9-inch loaf pan with wax paper.
Pat dry the shredded zucchini and keep it aside. Mix flour with baking soda, baking powder, cacao powder, coconut sugar and flour in a bowl. Stir it with vanilla, applesauce, milk, and peanut butter, then mix until smooth.
Fold in sugar-free chocolate chips and zucchini shreds.
Spread this batter in the prepared loaf pan. Bake this bread for 55 minutes in the oven. Allow the bread to cool, then slice. Serve.

Nutrition: Calories: 217.9; Fats: 21.6g; Carbs: 21.7g; Fiber: 0.6g; Sugar: 0.9g; Protein: 2.5g

19. Corn Griddle Cakes with Tofu Mayonnaise

Preparation Time: 15 minutes
Servings: 1

Cooking Time: 35 minutes

Ingredients:
- 1 tbsp flax seed powder + 3 tbsp water
- 1 cup water or as needed
- 1 cup yellow cornmeal
- 1 tsp salt
- 1 tsp baking powder
- 1 tbsp olive oil for frying
- 1 cup tofu mayonnaise for serving

Directions: Take a medium bowl, mix the flax seed powder with water and allow thickening for 5 minutes to form the flax egg.
Mix in the water and then whisk in the cornmeal, salt, and baking powder until soup texture forms but not watery.

Warm 1/4 of the olive oil in a griddle pan and pour in a quarter of the batter. Cook until set and golden brown beneath, 3 minutes. Flip the cake and cook the other side until set and golden brown too.
Plate the cake and make three more with the remaining oil and batter.
Top the cakes with some tofu mayonnaise before serving.

Nutrition: Calories: 895.9; Fats: 50.1g; Carbs: 91.2g; Proteins: 17.6g

20. High Protein Toast

Preparation Time: 30 minutes   **Cooking Time: 15 minutes**
Servings: 1

Ingredients:
- White bean: 1 drained and rinsed
- Cashew cream: ½ cup
- Miso paste: 1 ½ tbsp

- Toasted sesame oil: 1 tsp
- Sesame seeds: 1 tbsp
- Spring onion: 1 finely sliced

- Lemon: 1 half for the juice and half wedged to serve Rye bread: 4 slices toasted

Directions: In a bowl add sesame oil, white beans, miso, cashew cream, and lemon juice and mash using a potato masher. Make a spread
Spread it on a toast and top with spring onions and sesame seeds Serve with lemon wedges

Nutrition: Calories: 331.8; Carbs: 44.1g; Proteins: 14.8g; Fats: 9.1g

21. Avocado Miso Chickpeas Toast

Preparation Time: 30 minutes   **Cooking Time: 15 minutes**
Servings: 1

Ingredients:
- Chickpeas: 400g drained and rinsed
- Avocado: 1 medium
- Toasted sesame oil: 1 tsp

- White miso paste: 1 ½ tbsp
- Sesame seeds: 1 tbsp
- Spring onion: 1 finely sliced

- Lemon: 1 half for the juice and half wedged to serve Rye bread: 4 slices toasted

Directions: In a bowl add sesame oil, chickpeas, miso, and lemon juice and mash using a potato masher
Roughly crushed avocado in another bowl using a fork Add the avocado to the chickpeas and make a spread.
Spread it on a toast and top with spring onion and sesame seeds Serve with lemon wedges

Nutrition: Calories: 455.8; Carbs: 33.1g; Proteins: 14.9g; Fats: 26.1g

22. Berry Compote Pancakes

Preparation Time: 30 minutes   **Cooking Time: 30 minutes**
Servings: 1

Ingredients:
- Mixed frozen berries: 200g
- Plain flour: 140 g
- Unsweetened almond milk: 140ml

- Icing sugar: 1 tbsp
- Lemon juice: 1 tbsp
- Baking powder: 2 tsp
- Vanilla extract: a dash

- Salt: a pinch
- Caster sugar: 2 tbsp
- Vegetable oil: ½ tbsp

Directions: Take a small pan and add berries, lemon juice, and icing sugar Cook the mixture for 10 minutes to give it a saucy texture and set aside Take a bowl and add caster sugar, flour, baking powder, and salt and mix well
Add in almond milk and vanilla and combine well to make a batter Take a non-stick pan, and heat 2 teaspoons oil in it and spread it over the whole surface
Add ¼ cup of the batter to the pan and cook each side for 3-4 minutes Serve with compote

Nutrition: Calories: 462.8; Carbs: 91.8g; Proteins: 9.8g; Fats: 4.8g

23. Chickpeas Spread Sourdough Toast

Preparation Time: 30 minutes
Servings: 1

Cooking Time: 15 minutes

Ingredients:
- Chickpeas: 1 cup rinsed and drained
- Pumpkin puree: 1 cup
- Vegan yogurt: ½ cup
- Salt: as per your need
- Sourdough: 2 slices toasted

Directions: In a bowl add chickpeas and pumpkin puree and mash using a potato masher Add in salt and yogurt and mix. Spread it on a toast and serve

Nutrition: Calories: 186.9; Carbs: 33.2g; Proteins: 8.7g; Fats: 2.1g

24. Eggplant Sandwich

Preparation Time: 30 minutes
Servings: 1

Cooking Time: 30 minutes

Ingredients:
- 1 eggplant, sliced
- 2 teaspoons parsley, dried
- Salt and black pepper to the taste
- 1/2 cup vegan breadcrumbs
- 1/2 teaspoon Italian seasoning
- 1/2 teaspoon garlic powder
- 1/2 teaspoon onion powder
- 2 tablespoons almond milk
- 4 vegan bread slices
- Cooking spray
- 1/2 cup avocado mayo
- 3/4 cup tomato sauce
- A handful basil, chopped

Directions: Season eggplant slices with salt and pepper, leave aside for 30 minutes and then pat dry them well. In a bowl, mix parsley with breadcrumbs, Italian seasoning, onion and garlic powder, salt and black pepper and stir. In another bowl, mix milk with vegan mayo and also stir well.
Brush eggplant slices with mayo mix, dip them in breadcrumbs mix, place them on a lined baking sheet, spray with cooking oil, introduce baking sheet in your air fryer's basket and cook them at 400 degrees F for about 15 minutes, flipping them halfway.
Brush each bread slice with olive oil and arrange 2 of them on a working surface.
Add baked eggplant slices, spread tomato sauce and basil and top with the other bread slices, greased side down. Divide between plates and serve.

Nutrition: Calories: 323.8; Fats: 15.8g; Fibers: 3.8g; Carbs: 18.7g; Proteins: 12.3g

25. Amaranth Banana Porridge

Preparation Time: 10 minutes
Servings: 8

Cooking Time: 25 minutes

Ingredients:
- 2 cups amaranth
- 2 cinnamon sticks
- 4 bananas, diced
- 2 tablespoons chopped pecans
- 4 cups water

Directions: Combine the amaranth, water, and cinnamon sticks, and banana in a pot.
Cover and let simmer around 25 minutes.
Remove from heat and discard the cinnamon. Places into bowls, and top with pecans.

Nutrition: Calories: 210, Fats: 5 g, Carbs: 38 g, Protein: 10 g, Fiber:6g

26. Quinoa Porridge with Amaranth

Preparation Time: 5 minutes
Servings: 2

Cooking Time: 15 minutes

Ingredients:
- ½ cup amaranth, cooked
- 2 tablespoons agave syrup
- ½ cup black quinoa, cooked
- ½ cup soft-jelly coconut milk
- 2 cups spring water

Directions: Take a medium saucepan, place it over medium heat, add cooked quinoa and amaranth, pour in the water, stir until mixed, and then bring it a boil.
Switch heat to the low level and then simmer for 10 to 25 minutes until grains have absorbed all the liquid.

Pour in the coconut milk, add agave syrup, stir until mixed, and then simmer for another 5 minutes until thoroughly cooked and slightly thickened.

Nutrition: Calories: 203.8; Fats: 3.8g; Proteins: 8.2g; Carbs: 32.8g

27. Cinnamon and Almond Porridge

Preparation Time: 10 minutes   **Cooking Time: 30 minutes**
Servings: 4

Ingredients:
- 2 cups almond coconut milk
- 2 cups water
- 2 teaspoons agave syrup
- 2 cups amaranth
- ¼ teaspoon vanilla extract
- ½ cup almonds
- ½ teaspoon ground cinnamon
- ¼ teaspoon salt

Directions: Add all Ingredients: except almonds and cinnamon to a pan and heat over medium heat, and stir well. Bring the mixture to a simmer. Cook for 5 minutes, stirring often.
Add almonds and cinnamon on top. Once done, serve.

Nutrition: Calories: 107.6; Fats: 7.6g; Carbs: 7.9g; Protein: 7.2g

28. Apple Porridge

Preparation Time: 10 minutes   **Cooking Time: 5 minutes**
Servings: 4

Ingredients:
- 2 cups unsweetened hemp coconut milk
- 3 tablespoons walnuts, chopped
- 3 tablespoons sunflower seeds
- 2 large apples; peeled, cored, and grated
- Pinch of ground cinnamon
- ½ small apple, cored and sliced

Directions: Take a large skillet and stir in the coconut walnuts, sunflower seeds, milk, grated apple, vanilla, and cinnamon over medium-low heat and cook for about 3–5 minutes.
Remove from the heat and transfer the porridge into serving bowls.
Top with remaining apple slices and serve.

Nutrition: Calories: 146.8; Fats: 0.6g; Carbs: 16.9g; Protein 3.5g

29. Pumpkin Spice Granola Bites

Preparation Time: 2 hours   **Servings: 2**

Ingredients:
- Pumpkin Pie Spice (.50 t.)
- Old-fashioned Rolled Oats (.75 C.)
- Medjool Dates (15)
- Pumpkin Puree (.33 C.)
- Granola (.50 C.)

Directions: To start off, go ahead and place the oats into a food processor and process until it becomes flour. Once this is done, add in the spice, pumpkin, and dates. Puree everything again until you get a dough. From this dough, use your hands to take small bits and roll into ten balls. Place the balls into the fridge for two hours and allow to firm up. Finally, roll the balls in your favorite granola and then enjoy.

Nutrition: Calories: 99.5; Proteins: 10.3g; Carbs: 24.8g; Fats: 9.7g

Lunch

30. Hot Roasted Peppers Cream

Preparation Time: 10 minutes
Servings: 4

Cooking Time: 30 minutes

Ingredients:
- 1 red chili pepper, minced
- 4 garlic cloves, minced
- 2 lbs. mixed bell peppers, roasted, peeled, and chopped
- 4 scallions, chopped
- 1 cup coconut cream
- Salt and black pepper to the taste
- 2 tbsps. olive oil
- ½ tbsp. basil, chopped
- 4 cups vegetable stock
- ¼ cup chives, chopped

Directions: Warm-up a pot with the oil on medium heat, put the garlic and the chili pepper, and sauté for 5 minutes.
Add the peppers and the other ingredients, toss, bring to a simmer and cook over medium heat for 25 minutes. Blend the soup using an immersion mixer, divide it into bowls and serve.

Nutrition: Calories: 139.8; Fats: 1.8g; Carbs: 4.9g; Protein: 8.2g

31. Quinoa and Parsley Salad

Preparation Time: 15 minutes

Servings: 2

Ingredients:
- ½ cup quinoa, uncooked
- 1 cup water
- ¾ cup parsley leaves
- ½ cup celery, sliced
- ½ cup green onions, sliced
- 3 tbsps. fresh lemon juice
- ½ cup dried apricots, chopped
- 1 tbsp. agave syrup
- 1 tbsp. olive oil
- ¼ cup unsalted pumpkinseed kernels, toasted
- ¼ tsp. salt
- ¼ tsp. black pepper

Directions: Add quinoa and water to a pan and bring to boil. Cover, reduce heat, and simmer for 20 minutes. Add to a bowl and fluff with a fork. Add celery, parsley, onions, and apricots.
Whisk olive oil, lemon juice, syrup, salt, and black pepper. Add to quinoa mixture and toss well. Top with seeds and serve.

Nutrition: Calories: 237.9; Fats: 8.2g; Carbs: 34.8g; Protein: 6.3g

32. Lentil Vegetable Loaf

Preparation Time: 15 minutes
Servings: 4

Cooking Time: 55 minutes

Ingredients:
- 2 cups cooked lentils, drained well
- 1 tbsp. olive oil
- 1 small onion, diced
- 1 carrot, finely diced
- 1 stalk celery, diced
- 1 package (8 oz.) white or button mushrooms, cleaned and diced
- 3 tbsps. tomato paste
- 2 tbsps. soy sauce
- 1 tbsp. balsamic vinegar
- 1 cup old-fashioned oats, uncooked
- ½ cup almond meal
- 1 ½ tsps. dried oregano
- ⅓ cup ketchup
- 1 tsp. balsamic vinegar
- 1 tsp. Dijon mustard

Directions: Warm your oven to 400°F and grease a 5" x 7" loaf tin, then pops to one side. Add olive oil to a skillet and pop over medium heat.
Add the onion and cook for five minutes until soft. Add the mushrooms, celery, and carrots and cook until soft.
Grab your food processor and add the lentils, tomato paste, soy sauce, vinegar, oats, almond, and oregano. Whizz well until combined, then transfer to a medium bowl.
Pop the veggies into the food processor and pulse until combined. Transfer to the bowl. Stir everything together.
Move the mixture into the loaf pan, press down, and pop into the oven. Cook for 35 minutes, add the topping, and then bake again for 15 minutes. Remove from the oven and allow about10 minutes to cool.

Nutrition: Calories: 225.8; Carbs: 24.8g; Fats: 5.9g; Protein: 12.3g

33. Spicy Hummus Quesadillas

Preparation Time: 5 minutes   **Cooking Time: 15 minutes**
Servings: 4

Ingredients:
- 4 x 8" whole grain tortilla
- 1 cup hummus
- Fillings: spinach, sundried tomatoes, olives, etc.
- Extra-virgin olive oil for brushing

To serve:
- Extra hummus
- Hot sauce
- Pesto

Directions: Put your tortillas on a flat surface and cover each with hummus. Add the fillings, then fold over to form a half-moon shape.
Pop a skillet over medium heat and add a drop of oil. Add the quesadillas and flip when browned. Repeat with the remaining quesadillas, then serve and enjoy.

Nutrition: Calories: 255.9; Carbs: 24.7g; Fats: 11.9g; Protein: 7.2g

34. Tex-Mex Tofu & Beans

Preparation Time: 25 minutes   **Cooking Time: 12 minutes**
Servings: 2

Ingredients:
- 1 cup dry black beans
- 1 cup dry brown rice
- 1 14-oz. package firm tofu, drained
- 2 tbsps. olive oil
- 1 small purple onion, diced
- 1 medium avocado, pitted, peeled
- 1 garlic clove, minced
- 1 tbsp. lime juice
- 2 tsp. cumin
- 2 tsp. paprika
- 1 tsp. chili powder
- Salt and pepper to taste

Directions: Cut the tofu into ½-inch cubes. Heat the olive oil in a skillet. Put the diced onions and cook until soft, for about 5 minutes.
Add the tofu and cook for 2 minutes, flipping the cubes frequently. Meanwhile, cut the avocado into thin slices and set them aside.
Lower the heat and add in the garlic, cumin, and cooked black beans. Stir until everything is incorporated thoroughly, and then cook for an additional 5 minutes.
Add the remaining spices and lime juice to the mixture in the skillet. Mix thoroughly and remove the skillet from the heat.
Serve the Tex-Mex tofu and beans with a scoop of rice and garnish with the fresh avocado. Enjoy immediately, or store the rice, avocado, and tofu mixture separately.

Nutrition: Calories: 314.8; Carbs: 27.3g; Fats: 16.2g; Protein: 13.2g

35. Chickpea Salad

Preparation Time: 5 minutes   **Servings: 3**

Ingredients:
- 1 (14 oz.) can chickpeas, drained and rinsed
- 2 celery stalks, finely chopped
- 2 scallions, coarsely chopped
- 2 tbsps. vegan mayonnaise
- Juice of ½ lemon
- 2 tsps. capers and brine
- 1 tsp. dried dill or 1 handful fresh dill, chopped
- ½ tsp. Dijon mustard
- ¼ tsp. kelp flakes
- ¼ to ½ tsp. salt
- Freshly ground black pepper

Directions: In a medium bowl, mix the lemon juice, celery, chickpeas, mayo, scallions, dill, capers, mustard, kelp flakes, salt, and pepper.
Mix and mash everything together using a potato masher. Taste then flavor with additional salt, pepper, or lemon, if desired. Enjoy on its own, on top of a romaine or endive leaf, or with rice cakes.

Nutrition: Calories: 192.6; Fats: 3.8g; Carbs: 32.8g; Protein: 7.2g

36. Greek Salad with Tofu Feta

Preparation Time: 15 minutes   Servings: 6

Ingredients:

- 1 green bell pepper, coarsely chopped
- 1-pint cherry or grape tomatoes halved
- 1 small red onion, chopped
- 1 cucumber, chopped
- 1 (14 oz.) can butter beans, drained and rinsed
- ½ bunch parsley, coarsely chopped
- ½ cup pitted kalamata olives
- 1 garlic clove, minced
- Juice of 1 lemon
- 3 tbsps. red wine vinegar
- 3 tbsps. olive oil
- Tofu Feta
- 1 tsp. salt
- Freshly ground black pepper

Directions: In a medium bowl, combine the bell pepper, tomatoes, onion, cucumber, beans, parsley, olives, and garlic. Next, add the lemon juice, vinegar, and oil. Mix well.
Add the tofu feta (and any of the tofu marinade) to the salad. Season with salt and as much pepper as you would like, and then mix again.

Nutrition: Calories: 141.8; Fats: 7.9g; Carbs: 13.7g; Protein: 4.2g

37. Plant-Strong Bowl

Preparation Time: 25 minutes   Servings: 4

Ingredients:

- 2 cups white or brown rice, cooked
- 1 (14 oz.) can of black beans, drained and rinsed
- 1 (14 oz.) can chickpeas, drained and rinsed
- 4 cups spinach, chopped
- 1 cucumber, chopped
- Microgreens, for garnish

Directions: Divide the rice evenly among 4 food storage containers, and then add to each container ¼ cup of black beans, ¼ cup of chickpeas, 1 cup of spinach, and ¼ of the chopped cucumber.
Garnish each container with a small handful of microgreens. Serve.

Nutrition: Calories: 513.8; Fats: 21.9g; Carbs: 69.8g; Protein: 14.3g

38. Cauliflower Fried Rice

Preparation Time: 15 minutes   **Cooking Time: 15 minutes**
Servings: 6

Ingredients:

- 1 head cauliflower
- 1 tbsp. sesame oil
- 1 white onion, finely chopped
- 1 large carrot, finely chopped
- 4 garlic cloves, minced
- 2 cups frozen edamame or peas
- 3 scallions, sliced
- 3 tbsps. Bragg liquid aminos or tamari
- Salt
- Freshly ground black pepper

Directions: Trim the cauliflower into florets and put them to a food processor. Process the cauliflower using the chopping blade and pulsing until the cauliflower has the consistency of rice. Set aside.
Heat a skillet over medium-high heat. Drizzle in the sesame oil and then add the onion and carrot, cooking until the carrots begin to soften for about 5 minutes. Stir in the garlic and cook within another minute.
Add the cauliflower and edamame or peas. Heat until the cauliflower softens and the edamame or peas cook for about 5 minutes. Then add the scallions and liquid aminos or tamari. Mix well. Add in black pepper if desired.

Nutrition: Calories: 116.8; Fats: 2.9g; Carbs: 18.7g; Protein: 7.2g

39. Brussels Sprouts & Cranberries Salad

Preparation Time: 10 minutes   Servings: 6

Ingredients:

- 3 tbsps. lemon juice
- ¼ cup olive oil
- Salt and pepper to taste
- 1 lb. Brussels sprouts, sliced thinly
- ¼ cup dried cranberries, chopped
- ½ cup pecans, toasted and chopped
- ½ cup Parmesan cheese shaved

Directions: Mix the olive oil, lemon juice, pepper, and salt in a bowl. Add cranberries, pecans and the Brussels sprouts in this mixture. Sprinkle the Parmesan cheese on top.

Nutrition: Calories: 244.8; Fats: 18.3g; Carbs: 15.6g; Protein: 6.5g

40. Coconut Brussels Sprouts

Preparation Time: 15 minutes   **Cooking Time: 10 minutes**
Servings: 4

Ingredients:

- 1 lb. Brussels sprouts, trimmed and sliced in half
- 2 tbsps. coconut oil
- ¼ cup of coconut water
- 1 tbsp. soy sauce

Directions: Place the coconut oil in a pan over medium heat, and cook the Brussels sprouts for 4 minutes then pour in the coconut water and cook for 3 minutes. Combine the soy sauce and cook for another 1 minute and serve.

Nutrition: Calories: 113.8; Fats: 6.8g; Carbs: 10.8g; Protein: 4.2g

41. Sweet Potato Quesadillas

Preparation Time: 15 minutes   **Cooking Time: 1 hour & 9 minutes**
Servings: 3

Ingredients:

- 1 cup dry black beans
- ½ cup dry rice of choice
- 1 large sweet potato, peeled and diced
- ½ cup of salsa
- 3-6 tortilla wraps
- 1 tbsp. olive oil
- ½ tsp. garlic powder
- ½ tsp. onion powder
- ½ tsp. paprika

Directions: Preheat the oven to 350°F. Line a baking pan with parchment paper. Drizzle olive oil on the sweet potato cubes. Transfer the cubes to the baking pan. Bake the potatoes in the oven until tender, for around 1 hour. Allow about 5 minutes for the potatoes to cool, and then add them to a large mixing bowl with the salsa and cooked rice. Use a fork to mash the fixings into a thoroughly combined mixture.
Warm a saucepan over medium-high heat and add the potato/rice mixture, cooked black beans, and spices to the pan. Cook everything for about 5 minutes or until it is heated through.
Take another frying pan and put it over medium-low heat. Place a tortilla in the pan and fill half of it with a heaping scoop of the potato, bean, and rice mixture.
Fold the tortilla halfway to cover the filling and cook until both sides are browned—about 4 minutes per side.
Serve the tortillas with some additional salsa on the side.

Nutrition: Calories: 328.7; Carbs: 54.1g; Fats: 7.2g; Protein: 10.9g

42. Tofu Cacciatore

Preparation Time: 45 minutes   **Cooking Time: 35 minutes**
Servings: 3

Ingredients:

- 1 14-oz. package extra-firm tofu, drained
- 1 tbsp. olive oil
- 1 cup matchstick carrots
- 1 medium sweet onion, diced
- 1 medium green bell pepper, seeded, diced
- 1 28-oz. can dice tomatoes
- 1 4-oz. can tomato paste
- ½ tbsp. balsamic vinegar
- 1 tbsp. soy sauce
- 1 tbsp. maple syrup
- 1 tbsp. garlic powder
- 1 tbsp. Italian seasoning
- Salt and pepper to taste

Directions: Chop the tofu into ¼- to ½-inch cubes. Heat the olive oil on medium-high heat in a large skillet. Add onions, garlic, bell peppers, and carrots; sauté until the onions turn translucent, around 10 minutes while stirring frequently.
Now add the balsamic vinegar, soy sauce, maple syrup, garlic powder, and Italian seasoning.
Stir well while pouring in the diced tomatoes and tomato paste; mix until all ingredients are thoroughly combined. Add the cubed tofu and stir one more time.
Cover the pot, turn the heat to medium-low, and allow the mixture to simmer until the sauce has thickened, for around 20-25 minutes.
Serve the tofu cacciatore in bowls and top with salt and pepper to taste, or store for another meal.

Nutrition: Calories: 273.1; Carbs: 33.2g; Fats: 9.2g; Protein: 13.7g

43. Moroccan Eggplant Stew

Preparation Time: 45 minutes
Servings: 4

Cooking Time: 32 minutes

Ingredients:
- 1 cup dry green lentils
- 1 cup dry chickpeas
- 1 tsp. olive oil
- 1 large sweet onion, chopped
- 1 medium green bell pepper, seeded, diced
- 1 large eggplant
- 1 cup vegetable broth
- ¾ cup tomato sauce
- ½ cup golden raisins
- 2 tbsps. turmeric
- 1 garlic clove, minced
- 1 tsp. cumin
- ½ tsp. allspice
- ¼ tsp. chili powder
- Salt and pepper to taste

Directions: Warm-up the olive oil in a medium skillet on medium-high heat. Add the onions and cook until they begin to caramelize and soften in 5-8 minutes.

Cut the eggplant into ½-inch eggplant cubes and add it to the skillet along with the bell pepper, cumin, allspice, garlic, and turmeric.

Stir the ingredients to combine everything evenly and heat for about 4 minutes; then add the vegetable broth and tomato sauce.

Now cover the skillet, lower the heat, and let the ingredients simmer until the eggplant feels tender, or for about 20 minutes.

Uncover and mix in the cooked chickpeas and green lentils, as well as the raisins and chili powder. Simmer the ingredients until all the flavors have melded together, or for about 3 minutes.

Store the stew for later, or serve in a bowl, top with salt and pepper to taste, and enjoy!

Nutrition: Calories: 416.8; Carbs: 80.2g; Fats: 2.3g; Protein: 17.9g

44. Mushrooms and Chard Soup

Preparation Time: 10 minutes
Servings: 4

Cooking Time: 30 minutes

Ingredients:
- 3 cups Swiss chard, chopped
- 6 cups vegetable stock
- 1 cup mushrooms, sliced
- 2 garlic cloves, minced
- 1 tbsp. olive oil
- 2 scallions, chopped
- 2 tbsps. balsamic vinegar
- ¼ cup basil, chopped
- Salt and black pepper to the taste
- 1 tbsp. cilantro, chopped

Directions:
Heat-up a pot with the oil over medium-high heat, add the scallions and the garlic, and sauté for 5 minutes. Add the mushrooms and sauté for another 5 minutes.

Add the rest of the ingredients, stir, bring to a boil and cook over medium heat for 20 minutes more. Ladle the soup into bowls and serve.

Nutrition: Calories: 139.8; Fats: 3.9g; Carbs: 3.7g; Protein: 8.3g

45. Vegetable Tacos

Preparation Time: 20 minutes
Servings: 6

Cooking Time: 35 minutes

Ingredients:
- 1 head of cauliflower
- 1 sweet potato
- 1 onion
- 2 tbsp. olive oil
- 1/ tsp. Himalayan Sea salt
- 1/ tsp. black pepper
- 1 can chickpeas
- ½ cup BBQ

Directions: Preheat your oven to 425°F and put a sheet of parchment paper on a large baking tray.

Chop the cauliflower into small florets, the sweet potato into inch sized cubes, and dice the onion into small pieces.

Evenly place the cauliflower, sweet potato, and onion across the baking tray. Sprinkle oil, salt, and pepper across and mix to coat. Cook in the oven for about 10-15 minutes.

Take the tray out of the oven and dump the chickpeas on top. Pour ½ cup of BBQ sauce on top and stir to coat. Bake for another 8 minutes, or until the vegetable are soft.

Nutrition: Protein: 13.2g; Fats: 45.8g; Carbs: 40.8g

46. Grilled Eggplant Roll-Ups

Preparation Time: 5 minutes   **Cooking Time: 8 minutes**
Servings: 8

Ingredients:

- Olive oil, two tablespoons
- Basil, fresh, chopped, two tablespoons
- Onion, one half sliced paper-thin
- Bell pepper, one half sliced paper-thin
- Tomato, one large
- Eggplant, one medium

Directions: After cutting off both of the ends of the eggplant, slice it into strips the long way that is about a quarter-inch thick. Slice the onion, bell pepper, and the tomato very thinly and set to the side.
Brush the olive oil onto the slices of eggplant and grill them in a skillet for three minutes on each side. When both sides are grilled, lay the slices of eggplant on a plate and lay a slice each of tomato, onion, and bell pepper on each zucchini slice. Sprinkle all with the black pepper and the basil.
Carefully roll each slice as far as it will roll.

Nutrition: Calories: 179.9, Fats: 2.9g; Carbs: 27.9g; Protein: 4.2g; Fiber:11.9g

47. Pasta with Olives and White Beans

Preparation Time: 30 minutes   **Servings: 2**

Ingredients:

- Ziti or rigatoni, whole-wheat, four ounces
- Nutritional yeast, one half cup
- Cannellini beans, one fifteen ounce can drain and rinse Black pepper, one half teaspoon
- Basil, ground, one quarter cup
- Black olives, two tablespoons chopped
- Tomatoes, two medium-sized diced
- Garlic, minced, two tablespoons
- Olive oil, one tablespoon

Directions: Cook the pasta per the package instructions.
Cook the beans and garlic in the hot oil for five minutes.
Take the pan from the heat. Add in the olives, pepper, basil, and tomatoes and mix well. Place the pasta on two plates, evenly divided and top with the tomato bean mix.
Sprinkle on the nutritional yeast and serve.

Nutrition: Calories: 339.9; Fats: 7.9g; Carbs: 54.8g; Protein: 10.2g; Fiber: 11.8g

48. Bowl with Root Vegetables

Preparation Time: 15 minutes   **Cooking Time: 35 minutes**
Servings: 1

Ingredients:

- ½ cup cubed beets
- ½ cup cubed carrots
- ½ cup cubed yams
- Pinch garlic powder
- Pinch onion powder
- Pinch freshly ground black pepper
- ½ cup Flavorful Brown Rice Pilaf
- ½ cup mixed greens
- ¼ cup Sweet Peanut Butter Dipping Sauce
- 1 tablespoon sunflower seeds
- ¼ cup Smoked Cashew Cheese Spread (optional)

Directions: Preheat the oven to 425°F.
Place the carrots, yams, and beets in a single tier on a baking sheet covered with non-stick foil. Sprinkle with the pepper, onion powder, and garlic powder. Cook for 35 minutes until the vegetables are tender, turning once halfway through.
In the microwave, heat the Flavorful Brown Rice Pilaf. Combine the mixed greens, roasted vegetables, warmed rice pilaf, in a bowl. Cover with the peanut butter sauce, then sprinkle with the sunflower seeds. Add the cashew cheese spread.

Nutrition: Calories: 448.7; Fats: 18.7g; Carbs: 69.9g; Fiber: 9.9g; Protein: 15.2g

49. Amaranth Polenta with Wild Mushrooms

Preparation Time: 10 minutes
Servings: 3

Cooking Time: 30 minutes

Ingredients:
- ½ ounce dried porcini
- 1 tablespoon olive oil
- ¼ cup shallots, chopped
- 1 cup amaranth
- ¼ teaspoon salt
- 1 teaspoon fresh thyme, chopped
- Ground pepper, to taste

Directions: Combine 1 ¾ cups boiling water and mushrooms. Leave for 10 minutes to soften.
In a saucepan, cook shallots in olive oil for 1 minute. Add amaranth, mushrooms, and soaking liquid. Simmer for 15 minutes. Add pepper, thyme, and salt. Simmer for another 15 minutes. Serve in small bowls.

Nutrition: Calories: 249.8; Fats: 6.9g; Carbs: 37.9g; Protein: 12.3g; Fiber: 8.8g

50. Pasta with Mushroom Sauce

Preparation Time: 15 minutes
Servings: 4

Cooking Time: 25 minutes

Ingredients:
- 12 ounces spelt pasta
- 4 tablespoons avocado oil
- 1 pound fresh white mushrooms, sliced
- 2 garlic clove, minced
- 2 cups homemade walnut coconut milk
- 2 tablespoons fresh parsley, chopped
- 1½ tablespoons fresh key lime juice
- Sea salt, as needed
- Pinch of cayenne powder

Directions: In a medium saucepan, add salted water and bring to a rolling boil.
Add pasta and cook for about 8–10 minutes or according to manufacturer's directions.
Warm 2 tbsp of the oil, in a skillet, over medium heat and sauté the mushroom and garlic for about 4–5 minutes.
With a slotted spoon, transfer the mushrooms onto a plate.
In the same skillet, heat the remaining oil over medium heat.
Slowly, add the flour, beating continuously. Cook for about 1 minute, stirring continuously.
Slowly, add the coconut milk, beating continuously until smooth.
Add the mushrooms, parsley, lime juice, salt, and cayenne powder and cook for about 1–2 minutes.
Divide the pasta onto serving plates. Top with mushroom sauce and serve.

Nutrition: Calories: 380.9; Fats: 0.6g; Carbs: 66.8g; Protein: 16.8g

51. Spaghetti Squash With Peanut Sauce

Preparation Time: 15 minutes
Servings: 4

Cooking Time: 15 minutes

Ingredients:
- 1 cup cooked shelled edamame; frozen, thawed
- 3-pound spaghetti squash
- ½ cup red bell pepper, sliced
- ¼ cup scallions, sliced
- 1 medium carrot, shredded
- 1 teaspoon minced garlic
- ½ teaspoon crushed red pepper
- 1 tablespoon rice vinegar
- ¼ cup coconut aminos
- 1 tablespoon maple syrup
- ½ cup peanut vegan butter
- ¼ cup unsalted roasted peanuts, chopped
- ¼ cup and 2 tablespoons spring water, divided
- ¼ cup fresh cilantro, chopped
- 4 lime wedges

Directions: Prepare the squash: cut each squash in half lengthwise and then remove seeds.
Take a microwave-proof dish, place squash halves in it cut-side-up, drizzle with 2 tablespoons water, and then microwave at high heat setting for 10–15 minutes until tender.
Let squash cool for 15 minutes until able to handle. Use a fork to scrape its flesh lengthwise to make noodles, and then let noodles cool for 10 minutes.
While squash microwaves, prepare the sauce: take a medium bowl, add vegan butter in it along with red pepper and garlic, pour in vinegar, coconut aminos, maple syrup, and water, and then whisk until smooth.
When the squash noodles have cooled, distribute them evenly among four bowls, top with scallions, carrots, bell pepper, and edamame beans, and then drizzle with prepared sauce.
Sprinkle cilantro and peanuts and serve each bowl with a lime wedge.

Nutrition: Calories: 418.7; Carbs:32.5g; Fats: 23.9g; Protein: 17.9g

52. Vegetable Fajitas Tacos

Preparation Time: 10 minutes   **Cooking Time: 8 minutes**

Ingredients:
- 2 Portobello mushroom caps, 1/3-inch sliced
- ¾ of red bell pepper, sliced
- ½ of onion, peeled, sliced
- ½ of key lime, juiced
- 2 spelt flour tortillas
- Extra:
- 1/3 teaspoon salt
- ¼ teaspoon cayenne pepper
- ¼ teaspoon onion powder
- 1 tablespoon grapeseed oil

Directions: Take a medium skillet pan, place it over medium heat, add oil and when hot, add onion and red pepper, and then cook for 2 minutes until tender-crisp.
Add mushrooms slices, sprinkle with all the seasoning, stir until mixed, and then cook for 5 minutes until vegetables turn soft.
Heat the tortilla until warm, distribute vegetables in their center, drizzle with lime juice, and then roll tightly.
Cool the wraps, cover with a plastic wrap and then with foil, and then store in the refrigerator for up to 5 days.
When ready to eat, reheat in the oven for 1 to 2 minutes until hot and then serve.

Nutrition: Calories: 336.8; Fats: 3.4g; Protein: 2.9g; Carbs: 72.9g

53. Chickpea Flour Quiche

Preparation Time: 10 minutes   **Cooking Time: 15 minutes**
Servings: 2

Ingredients:

For the Batter:
- 1 ½ tablespoon olive oil
- 1 ¼ cup chickpea flour
- 1 1/2cup spring water
- 1 teaspoon of sea salt

For the Filling:
- ½ cup chopped and cooked vegetables
- ½ teaspoon dried basil
- ½ teaspoon dried oregano

Directions: Switch on the oven, then set it to 500 degrees F and let it preheat.
Meanwhile, prepare the batter and for this, take a medium bowl, place all of its Ingredients: and then whisk until smooth batter comes together.
Add vegetables and herbs into the batter and then stir until combined.
Take six silicone muffin cups, grease them with oil, fill evenly with the prepared batter and then cook for about 15 minutes until firm and turn golden brown.

Nutrition: Calories: 181.9; Fats: 5.8g; Protein: 8.2g; Carbs: 24.9g

54. Nori Burritos

Preparation Time: 10 minutes   **Servings: 2**

Ingredients:
- 1 avocado, peeled, sliced
- 1 cucumber, deseeded, cut into round slices
- 1 zucchini, sliced
- 2 teaspoons sprouted hemp seeds
- 2 nori sheets
- Extra:
- 1 tablespoon tahini vegan butter
- 2 teaspoons sesame seeds

Directions: Working on one nori sheet at a Time, place it on a cutting board shiny-side-down and then arrange half of each avocado, cucumber and zucchini slices and tahini on it, leaving 1-inch wide spice to the right.
Then start folding the sheet over the fillings from the edge that is closest to you, cut into thick slices, and then sprinkle with 1 teaspoon of sesame seeds.
Repeat with the remaining nori sheet, and then serve.
Wrap the slices, one by one, in plastic wrap and foil and then refrigerate for up to 5 days.
When ready to eat, unwrap the slices, bring to room temperature and then serve.

Nutrition: Calories: 89.7; Fats: 1.2g; Protein: 1.8g; Carbs: 12.3g

55. Roasted Brussel Sprouts with Parmesan

Preparation Time: 10 minutes
Servings: 4

Cooking Time: 20 minutes

Ingredients:
- 453g fresh Brussels sprouts
- 1 tablespoon olive oil
- ½ teaspoon salt
- ⅛ teaspoon pepper
- 32 g grated Parmesan cheese

Directions: Set to 350 Roast. Cut the bottoms from the Brussels sprouts and pull off any discolored leaves. Toss with the olive oil, salt, and pepper, and place in the air fryer basket.
Roast for 20 minutes, shaking the air fryer basket twice during Cooking Time, until the Brussels sprouts are dark golden brown and crisp.
Transfer the Brussels sprouts to a serving dish and toss with the Parmesan cheese. Serve immediately.

Nutrition: Calories: 100.8; Fats: 1.2g; Carbs: 10.2g; Protein: 3.2g

56. Kale and Black Olives

Preparation Time: 5 minutes
Servings: 4

Cooking Time: 15 minutes

Ingredients:
- 1 and ½ kg kale, torn
- 2 tablespoons olive oil
- 1 tbsp Salt and black pepper to the taste
- 1 tablespoon hot paprika
- 2 tablespoons black olives, pitted and sliced

Directions: In a pan that fits the air fryer, combine all the ingredients and toss.
Put the pan in your air fryer, cook at 370 degrees F for 15 minutes, divide between plates and serve.

Nutrition: Calories: 36.8; Fats: 0.5g; Carbs: 2.3g; Protein: 6.8g

57. Baked Parsnip and Potato

Preparation Time: 15 minutes
Servings: 8

Cooking Time: 30 minutes

Ingredients:
- 280g potato, cubed
- 3 tbsp pine nuts
- 200g parsnips, chopped
- 100g Parmesan cheese, shredded
- 400g oz crème fraiche
- 1 slice bread
- 2 tbsp sage
- 4 tbsp vegan butter
- 4 tsp mustard

Directions: Prepare the Air Fryer to 360 F, and boil salted water in a pot over medium heat. Add potatoes and parsnips. Bring to a boil. In a bowl, mix mustard, crème fraiche, sage, salt and pepper. Drain the potatoes and parsnips and mash them with vegan butter using a potato masher. Add mustard mixture, bread, cheese, and nuts to the mash and mix. Add the batter to your cooking tray and cook for 25 minutes.

Nutrition: Calories: 209.9; Fats: 2.3g; Carbs: 9.7g; Protein: 1.8g

58. Cheese Broccoli Pasta

Preparation Time: 10 minutes
Servings: 2

Cooking Time: 10 minutes

Ingredients:
- 600ml water
- ½ kg pasta
- 800g cheddar cheese, grated
- 64 g broccoli
- 64 g half and half

Directions: Put the water and the pasta in your air fryer.
Add the steamer basket, add the broccoli, cover the cooker and cook on High for 4 minutes.
Drain pasta, transfer it as well as the broccoli, and clean the pot.
Set it on sauté mode, add pasta and broccoli, cheese and half and half, stir well, cook for 2 minutes, divide between plates and serve as a side dish.

Nutrition: Calories: 289.7; Fats: 4.5g; Carbs: 26.8g; Protein: 6.7g

59. Turmeric Zucchinis

Preparation Time: 10 minutes
Servings: 4

Cooking Time: 15 minutes

Ingredients:
- 4 zucchinis, sliced
- ½ teaspoon turmeric powder
- 1 teaspoon chili powder
- ¼ cup vegetarian stock
- 1 tablespoon chili powder
- ½ teaspoon cayenne pepper
- ½ teaspoon garam masala

Directions: In your instant pot, mix the zucchinis with the turmeric, the stock and the rest of the ingredients, place the cover on and cook on High for 15 minutes.
Release the pressure naturally for 10 minutes, divide the mixture among plates and serve.

Nutrition: Calories: 41.8; Fats: 0.8; Carbs: 8.1; Protein: 3.1

60. Eggplant Masala

Preparation Time: 5 minutes
Servings: 4

Cooking Time: 20 minutes

Ingredients:
- 1 pound eggplant, roughly cubed
- 1 yellow onion, chopped
- 2 garlic cloves, minced
- 1 tablespoon vegetable oil
- A pinch of salt and black pepper
- 1 tablespoon sweet paprika
- 1 teaspoon cumin, ground
- 1 teaspoon garam masala
- 2 black peppercorns, crushed
- 1 teaspoon mustard seeds
- 1 teaspoon turmeric powder
- 1 cup tomato sauce

Directions: Set the instant pot on Sauté mode, add the oil, heat it up, add the onion, garlic, cumin, garam masala, peppercorns and the mustard seeds, stir and cook for 5 minutes.
Add the eggplant and the rest of the ingredients, put the lid on and cook on High for 15 minutes.
Release the pressure fast for 5 minutes, divide the mix between plates and serve.

Nutrition: Calories: 98.7; Fats: 4.1g; Carbs: 14.5g; Protein: 3.1g

61. Minty Masala Tomatoes

Preparation Time: 10 minutes
Servings: 4

Cooking Time: 20 minutes

Ingredients:
- 1 tbsp sunflower oil
- 1 pound cherry tomatoes, halved
- 2 shallots, chopped
- 1 tablespoon lime zest, grated
- 1 teaspoon lime juice
- 1 teaspoon garam masala
- 1 teaspoon cumin, ground
- 1 teaspoon coriander, ground
- A pinch of salt and black pepper
- 1 cup vegetarian stock
- 2 tablespoons mint leaves, chopped

Directions: Set the instant pot on Sauté mode, add the shallots, garam masala, cumin and coriander, stir and sauté for 5 minutes.
Add the tomatoes and the rest of the ingredients, toss, put the lid on and cook on High for 15 minutes.
Release the pressure naturally for 10 minutes, divide between plates and serve.

Nutrition: Calories: 109.8; Fats: 3.5g; Carbs: 7.5g; Protein: 2.2g

62. Coconut milk Rice

Preparation Time: 10 minutes
Servings: 4

Cooking Time: 30 minutes

Ingredients:
- 1 cup white rice
- 2 cups coconut milk
- 1 teaspoon cardamom powder
- 3 tablespoons sugar
- 1 tablespoon ghee, melted
- 1 tablespoon cashews, chopped
- 1 tablespoon raisins, chopped

Directions: In your instant pot, combine the rice with the coconut milk, cardamom and the other ingredients, toss, cover and cook on Low for 30 minutes. Release the pressure naturally for 10 minutes, divide the mix into bowls and serve.

Nutrition: Calories: 311.8; Fats: 6.9g; Carbs: 54.2g; Protein: 7.9g

63. Cheese Pockets

Preparation Time: 8 hours
Servings: 6

Cooking Time: 15 minutes

Ingredients:

For the Dough:
- 96 g Almond Flour
- 64 g Coconut Oil
- ½ tsp Salt

For the Filling:
- 64 g Raw Cashews, soaked in water overnight
- 1 tbsp Nutritional Yeast
- ½ tsp Garlic Powder
- ¼ tsp Salt

Directions: All ingredients in a bowl combine it for the dough Knead into a smooth paste.
Mix the ingredients for the filling in a food processor. Blend until smooth.
Lightly dust your working counter with almond flour.
Roll out the dough into an 8"x12" rectangle. Cut the dough into six squares.
Fill each square with the cashew mixture. Fold the dough into triangles, pressing the sides to seal.
Lightly coat the frying basket with non-stick spray.
Arrange the cheese pockets inside and cook for 15 minutes at 380F.

Nutrition: Calories: 246.8; Fats: 9.1g; Carbs: 19.3g; Protein: 11.4g

64. Vegan Taco Bowls

Preparation Time: 15 minutes
Servings: 4

Cooking Time: 9 minutes

Ingredients:
- 2 (100g) packages frozen cooked brown rice
- 1 tablespoon olive oil
- 1 onion, chopped
- 3 garlic cloves, minced
- 1 (150g) can pinto beans, drained and rinsed
- 128 g frozen corn kernels
- ⅔ kgmild salsa, divided
- 42 g sour cream
- 2 tablespoons freshly squeezed lime juice
- 50g grated pepper Jack chees

Directions: Prepare the rice as directed on the package and set aside.
In a 6-inch metal bowl, drizzle the olive oil over the onion and garlic and toss to combine.
Set the air fryer to 375°F. Put the bowl into the air fryer basket. Cook for 3 to 4.
Take the basket out of the air fryer and add the beans, corn, and 42 g of salsa to the bowl; stir to combine.
Return the basket to the air fryer. Bake for another 5 minutes.
Meanwhile, combine the remaining 42 g of salsa, sour cream, and lime juice in a small bowl until well mixed.
Divide the rice equally among four bowls. Divide the bean mixture on top. Sprinkle with the sour cream mixture and sprinkle with the cheese. Serve.

Nutrition: Calories: 314.8; Fats: 10.2g; Carbs: 29.1g; Protein: 11.3g

65. Caprese Stuffed Avocado

Preparation Time: 5 minutes
Servings: 4

Cooking Time: 10 minutes

Ingredients:
- 1/2 cup cherry tomatoes
- 4 0z baby bocconcini balls
- 2 tablespoons basil pesto
- 1 tablespoon minced garlic
- 1/4 oil
- Salt and pepper to taste
- 2 ripe avocados
- 2 tablespoons balsamic glaze
- Basil for serving

Directions: In a mixing bowl, add cherry tomatoes, bocconcini balls, basil pesto, garlic, salt and pepper to taste.
Toss until well combined and all flavors have blended.
Half the avocados and arrange them on a platter.
Spoon the mixture in the avocado halves and drizzle with balsamic glaze. Top with basil and serve. Enjoy.

Nutrition: Calories: 340.8; Fats: 28.9g; Carbs: 14.7g; Protein: 8.2g

66. Black and Veggie Tacos

Preparation Time: 15 minutes
Servings: 4

Cooking Time: 10 minutes

Ingredients:

- 2 (15-ounce / 425-g) cans black beans, drained and rinsed ¼ cup ground flaxseeds
- 1 teaspoon paprika
- 1 teaspoon dried oregano
- 1 teaspoon ground cumin
- 1 teaspoon salt (optional)
- 1 teaspoon freshly ground black pepper
- 1 tablespoon coconut oil (optional)
- 4 (6-inch) corn tortillas
- 1 medium tomato, diced (about 7 ounces / 198 g in total) ¼ cup chopped cilantro
- ½ yellow onion, diced (about 3½ ounces / 99 g in total) 3 romaine lettuce leaves, sliced into thin ribbons 2 avocados, sliced
- 4 lime wedges

Directions: Pour the black beans in a food processor, then pulse to mash the beans until chunky.
Sprinkle the flaxseeds, paprika, oregano, cumin, salt (if desired), and ground black pepper over the mashed beans, then pulse to mix thoroughly.
Heat the coconut oil (if desired) in a skillet over medium heat.
Add the bean mixture to a single layer in the skillet and level with a spatula. Cook for 2-3 minutes. Flip the mixture and cook for 2 minutes to brown the other side. Turn off heat and let cool.
Unfold the tortillas among 4 plates, then divide the cooked bean mixture, tomato, cilantro, onion, lettuce, and avocado over the tortillas. Squeeze the lime wedges over and serve immediately.

Nutrition: Calories: 577.9; Fats: 21.8g; Carbs: 74.8g; Protein: 20.3g; Fiber: 19.9g

67. Roasted Butternut Squash Pasta

Preparation Time: 15 minutes
Servings: 4

Cooking Time: 35 minutes

Ingredients:

- ½ tablespoon olive oil
- 4 cups butternut squash, cubed
- 2 garlic cloves, unpeeled
- Salt and black pepper, to taste
- 8 ounces brown rice pasta
- 2 tablespoons vegan cream cheese
- 1 cup almond milk
- ½ cup frozen peas, thawed

Direction: Preheat your oven to 400 F.
Toss butternut squash with oil, black pepper and salt in a baking pan.
Add garlic and roast for 30 minutes. Cook the pasta as per the package's instruction then drain.
Peel the roasted garlic and add to a blender along with squash, salt, black pepper, almond milk and vegan cream cheese then blend until smooth. Add peas and squash sauce to the pasta and serve.

Nutrition: Calories: 448.7; Fats: 30.8g; Carbs: 31.8g; Fiber: 2.1g; Sugar 1.9g; Protein: 26.3g

68. Arugula Pesto Couscous

Preparation Time: 10 minutes
Servings: 4

Cooking Time: 20 minutes

Ingredients:

- 8 ounces Israeli couscous
- 3 large tomatoes, chopped
- 3 cups arugula leaves
- ½ cup parsley leaves
- 6 cloves of garlic, peeled
- ½ cup walnuts
- ¾ teaspoon salt
- 1 cup and 1 tablespoon olive oil
- 2 cups vegetable broth

Directions: Take a medium saucepan, place it over medium-high heat, add 1tablespoon oil and then let it heat.
Add couscous, stir until mixed, and then cook for 4 minutes until fragrant and toasted.
Pour in the broth, stir until mixed, bring it to a boil, switch heat to medium level and then simmer for 12 minutes until the couscous has been absorbed all the liquid and turn tender.
When finished, take the skillet off the heat, sprinkle it with a fork, and then set it aside until required.
While couscous cooks, prepare the pesto and for this, place walnuts in a blender, add garlic and then pulse until nuts have broken. Add arugula, parsley and salt, pulse until well combined, and then blend in oil until smooth.
Transfer couscous to a salad bowl, add tomatoes and the prepared pesto, and then toss until mixed.

Nutrition: Calories: 72.8; Fats: 3.9g; Protein: 2.1g; Carbs: 7.9g; Fiber: 1.9g

Dinner

69. Mexican Lentil Soup

Preparation Time: 5 minutes
Servings: 6

Cooking Time: 45 minutes

Ingredients:

- 2 cups green lentils
- 1 medium red bell pepper, cored, diced
- 1 medium white onion, peeled, diced
- 2 cups diced tomatoes
- 8 oz. diced green chilies
- 2 celery stalks, diced
- 2 medium carrots, peeled, diced
- 1 ½ tsps. minced garlic
- ½ tsp. salt
- 1 tbsp. cumin
- ¼ tsp. smoked paprika
- 1 tsp. oregano
- ⅛ tsp. hot sauce
- 2 tbsps. olive oil
- 8 cups vegetable broth
- ¼ cup cilantro, for garnish
- 1 avocado, peeled, pitted, diced, for garnish

Directions: Get a large pot over medium heat, add oil, and when hot, add all the vegetables, reserving tomatoes and chilies, and cook for 5 minutes until softened.
Then add garlic, stir in oregano, cumin, and paprika, and continue cooking for 1 minute.
Add lentils, tomatoes, and green chilies, season with salt, pour in the broth, and simmer the soup for 40 minutes until cooked.
When done, ladle soup into bowls, top with avocado and cilantro, and serve straight away

Nutrition: Calories: 234.9; Fats: 8.7g; Carbs: 31.9g; Protein: 9.2g

70. Red Pepper and Tomato Soup

Preparation Time: 10 minutes
Servings: 4

Cooking Time: 40 minutes

Ingredients:

- 2 carrots, peeled, chopped
- 1 ¼ lb. red bell peppers, deseeded, sliced into quarters
- ½ red onion, peeled, sliced into thin wedges
- 16 oz. small tomatoes, halved
- 1 tbsp. chopped basil
- ½ tsp. salt
- 2 cups vegetable broth

Directions: Switch on the oven, then set it to 450°F and let it preheat. Then place all the vegetables in a single on a baking sheet lined with foil and bake for 40 minutes until the skins of peppers are slightly charred.
When done, remove the baking sheet from the oven, let them cool for 10 minutes, then peel the peppers and transfer all the vegetables into a blender.
Add basil and salt to the vegetables, pour in the broth, and puree the vegetables until smooth. Serve straight away.

Nutrition: Calories: 77.2; Fats: 1.7g; Carbs: 14.2g; Protein: 3.6g

71. Tarragon Soup

Preparation Time: 15 minutes

Servings: 2

Ingredients:

- 2 tbsps. chopped fresh tarragon
- Celery stalk
- ½ cup raw cashews
- 1 tbsp. lemon juice
- 13 ½ oz full-fat coconut milk
- ½ tsp. pepper, divided
- ½ tsp. sea salt, divided
- 3 cloves crushed garlic
- ½ cup diced onion
- 1 tbsp. avocado oil

Directions: Add the oil to a medium pan and warm it up. Put in all the seasonings: pepper, salt, garlic bulbs, together with onion bulbs then prepare approximately five minutes.
Using a high-speed blender, add the onion mixture, tarragon, celery, cashews, lemon juice, and coconut milk.
Blend everything together until smooth. Taste and adjust the seasonings as you need to.
Divide into two bowls and enjoy. You can also add it back into a pot and heat through before serving.

Nutrition: Calories: 249.9; Carbs: 20.8g; Fats: 14.8g; Protein: 6.2g

72. Mushroom Soup

Preparation Time: 15 minutes   **Cooking Time: 10 minutes**
Servings: 2

Ingredients:
- 13 ½ oz Full-fat coconut milk
- 1 cup Vegetable broth
- ½ tsp. Pepper
- ¾ tsp. Sea salt
- 1 Crush garlic clove
- 1 cup Diced onion
- 1 cup Cut up cremini mushrooms
- 1 cup cut-up Chinese black mushrooms
- 1 tbsp. avocado oil
- 1 tbsp. coconut aminos
- ½ tsp. dried thyme

Directions: Warm up the grease in a very massive pan then put in all the seasonings: pepper, salt, garlic, onion bulb, and mushrooms.
Boil and prepare everything along for a few minutes, either that or till the onions turn soft. Mix in the coconut aminos, thyme, coconut milk, and vegetable broth.
Lower the fire down then allow the broth to boil for approximately a quarter-hour. Mix the broth from time to time. Taste and adjust any of the seasonings that you need to. Divide into two bowls and enjoy.

Nutrition: Calories: 128.9; Carbs: 3.8g; Fats: 9.9g; Protein: 2.1g

73. Pasta with Kidney Bean Sauce

Preparation Time: 5 minutes   **Cooking Time: 15 minutes**
Servings: 4

Ingredients:
- 12 oz. cooked kidney beans
- 7 oz. whole-wheat pasta, cooked
- 1 medium white onion, peeled, diced
- 1 cup arugula
- 2 tbsps. tomato paste
- 1 tsp. minced garlic
- ½ tsp. smoked paprika
- 1 tsp. dried oregano
- ½ tsp. cayenne pepper
- ⅓ tsp. ground black pepper
- ⅔ tsp. salt
- 2 tbsps. balsamic vinegar

Directions: Take a large skillet pan, place it over medium-high heat, add onion and garlic, splash with some water and cook for 5 minutes.
Then add remaining ingredients, except for pasta and arugula, stir until mixed and cook for 10 minutes until thickened.
When done, mash with the fork, top with arugula and serve with pasta. Serve straight away.

Nutrition: Calories: 235.9; Fats: 1.5g; Carbs: 45.9g; Protein: 12.3g

74. Coconut Rice

Preparation Time: 10 minutes   **Cooking Time: 25 minutes**
Servings: 7

Ingredients:
- 2 ½ cups white rice
- ⅛ tsp. salt
- 40 oz. coconut milk, unsweetened

Directions: Take a large saucepan, place it over medium heat, add all the ingredients in it and stir until mixed. Boil the mixture, then switch heat to medium-low level and simmer rice for 25 minutes until tender and all the liquid is absorbed. Serve straight away.

Nutrition: Calories: 534.9; Fats: 32.9g; Carbs: 56.8g; Protein: 8.3g

75. Barley and Mushrooms with Beans

Preparation Time: 5 minutes   **Cooking Time: 15 minutes**
Servings: 6

Ingredients:
- ½ cup uncooked barley
- 15 ½ oz. white beans
- ½ cup chopped celery
- 3 cups sliced mushrooms
- 1 cup chopped white onion
- 1 tsp. minced garlic
- 1 tsp. olive oil
- 3 cups vegetable broth

Directions: Put oil in your saucepan over medium heat, and when hot, add vegetables and cook for 5 minutes until tender.

Pour in broth, stir in barley, bring the mixture to boil, and then simmer for 50 minutes until tender.

When done, add beans into the barley mixture, stir until mixed and continue cooking for 5 minutes until hot. Serve straight away.

Nutrition: Calories: 201.8; Fats: 1.9g; Carbs: 38.7g; Protein: 9.4g

76. Coconut Curry Lentils

Preparation Time: 10 minutes　　　　　　　　　　　　　**Cooking Time: 40 minutes**
Servings: 4

Ingredients:

- 1 cup brown lentils
- 1 small white onion, peeled, chopped
- 1 tsp. minced garlic
- 1 tsp. grated ginger
- 3 cups baby spinach
- 1 tbsp. curry powder
- 2 tbsps. olive oil
- 13 oz. coconut milk, unsweetened
- 2 cups vegetable broth

For Servings:

- 4 cups cooked rice
- ¼ cup chopped cilantro

Directions: Put oil in your large pot over medium heat, and when hot, add ginger and garlic and then, cook for 1 minute.

Add onion, cook for 5 minutes, stir in curry powder, cook for 1 minute until toasted, add lentils, and pour in broth. Switch heat to medium-high level, bring the mixture to a boil, then switch heat to the low level and simmer for 20 minutes until tender and all the liquid is absorbed.

Pour in milk, stir until combined, turn heat to medium level, and simmer for 10 minutes until thickened.

Remove the pot, stir in spinach, and let it stand for 5 minutes until its leaves wilts and then top with cilantro. Serve lentils with rice.

Nutrition: Calories: 183.9; Fats: 3.2g; Carbs: 29.8g; Protein: 11.6g

77. Stuffed Peppers with Kidney Beans

Preparation Time: 5 minutes　　　　　　　　　　　　　**Cooking Time: 35 minutes**
Servings: 4

Ingredients:

- 3 ½ oz. cooked kidney beans
- 1 big tomato, diced
- 3 ½ oz. sweet corn, canned
- 2 medium bell peppers, deseeded, halved
- ½ of medium red onion, peeled, diced
- 1 tsp. garlic powder
- ⅓ tsp. ground black pepper
- ⅔ tsp. salt
- ½ tsp. dried basil
- 3 tsps. parsley
- ½ tsp. dried thyme
- 3 tbsps. cashew
- 1 tsp. olive oil

Directions: Switch on the oven, then set it to 400°F and let it preheat. Take a large skillet, place it over medium heat, add oil, and when hot, add onion and bake for 2 minutes until translucent.

Add beans, tomatoes, and corn, stir in garlic and cashews and cook for 5 minutes.

Stir in salt, black pepper, parsley, basil, and thyme, remove the pan from heat and evenly divide the mixture between bell peppers. Bake the peppers for 25 minutes until tender, then top with parsley and serve.

Nutrition: Calories: 138.8; Fats: 1.5g; Carbs: 17.9g; Protein: 5.3g

78. Tempeh Tikka Masala

Preparation Time: 15 minutes　　　　　　　　　　　　　**Cooking Time: 20 minutes**
Servings: 3

Ingredients:

Tempeh:

- ½ tsp. sea salt
- 1 tsp. garam masala
- 1 tsp. ginger, ground
- 1 tsp. cumin, ground
- 2 tsp. apple cider vinegar
- ½ cup vegan yogurt

- *8 oz. tempeh, cubed*

Tikka Masala Sauce:
- *2 cups frozen peas*
- *1 cup full-fat coconut milk*
- *1 cup tomato sauce*
- *¼ tsp. turmeric*
- *½ tsp. sea salt*
- *1 onion, chopped*
- *1 tsp. chili powder*
- *1 tsp. garam masala*
- *¼ cup ginger, freshly grated*
- *3 cloves garlic, minced*
- *1 tbsp. coconut oil*

Directions: Begin with making the tempeh by combining sea salt, garam masala, ginger, cumin, vinegar, and yogurt in a bowl. Add tempeh to the bowl and coat well; cover the bowl and refrigerate for 60 minutes.
In a pan big enough for 3 servings, add some coconut oil to heat using the medium setting, and begin preparing the sauce.
Sauté in the ginger, garlic, and onion for 5 minutes or until fragrant. Add the garam masala, chili powder, sea salt, and turmeric, and combine well.
Add the frozen peas, coconut, milk, tomato sauce, and tempeh, reducing the heat to medium. Simmer within 15 minutes Remove from the heat and serve with cauliflower rice.

Nutrition: Calories: 429.8; Carbs: 38.7g; Protein: 21.3g; Fats: 22.8g

79.Caesar Vegan Salad

Preparation Time: 15 minutes   **Cooking Time: 60 minutes**
Servings: 6

Ingredients:
- *5 cups kale, chopped*
- *10 cups romaine lettuce*

For the Cheese:
- *½ tsp. garlic*
- *1 tsp. extra virgin olive oil*
- *1 tsp. nutritional yeast*
- *1 garlic clove*
- *2 tbsps. hemp seeds, hulled*
- *⅓ cup cashews, raw*

Caesar Dressing:
- *½ tsp. sea salt*
- *½ tsp. garlic powder*
- *½ tsp. Dijon mustard*
- *2 tsp. capers*
- *½ tbsp. vegan Worcestershire sauce*
- *2 tbsps. olive oil (best if extra virgin)*
- *½ cup raw cashews, soaked overnight*
- *¼ cup water*
- *1 clove garlic, crushed*
- *1 tbsp. lemon juice*

Croutons:
- *⅛ tsp. cayenne pepper*
- *½ tsp. garlic powder*
- *½ tsp. sea salt*
- *1 tsp. olive oil, (best if extra virgin)*
- *14 oz. can chickpeas*

Directions: On the day before you plan to make this salad, in a little bowl, soak ½ c. of the raw cashews overnight then drain and rinse.
For the croutons, bring the oven to 400°F. Drain the chickpeas and rinse thoroughly. Using a tea towel or cheesecloth, rub the chickpeas so that the skins fall off.
Place those in a dish for baking. Spritz the chickpeas with oil and roll them around to coat. Season with cayenne, salt, and garlic powder.
Roast the chickpeas for approximately a quarter of an hour or until you are satisfied with the color. Remove from the oven, allowing it to cool and become firm.
For the dressing, combine everything but not the salt, either in a processor or blender. Blend until smooth liquid consistency.
If needed, add ½ tablespoon of water at a time until you have a dressing-like consistency. Season with salt to taste. Set to the side.
For the cheese, add garlic and cashews to a food processor, and process them until they reach a finely chopped consistency. Add hemp seeds, nutritional yeast, olive oil, and garlic powder and blend until combined. Season with salt to taste.
For the lettuce, after washing the kale, finely chop and set to the side. Chop the lettuce roughly into 2-inch pieces and toss with the kale in a bowl.
Pour some dressing and toss again to coat the greens fully. Sprinkle the cheese and croutons over the top. Serve cool and enjoy.

Nutrition: Calories: 283.9; Carbs: 25.1g; Protein: 8.9g; Fats: 18.2g

80. Emmenthal Soup

Preparation Time: 15 minutes   **Servings: 2**

Ingredients:
- Cayenne
- Nutmeg
- 1 tbsp. pumpkin seeds
- 2 tbsps. chopped chives
- 3 tbsps. cubed emmenthal cheese
- 2 cups vegetable broth
- 1 cubed potato
- 2 cups cauliflower pieces

Directions: Place the potato and cauliflower into a saucepan with the vegetable broth just until tender. Place into a blender and puree.

Add in spices and adjust to taste. Ladle into bowls, add in chives and cheese and stir well. Garnish with pumpkin seeds. Enjoy.

Nutrition: Calories: 379.9; Carbs: 0g; Fats: 27.9g; Protein: 27.3g

81. Vegetables with Wild Rice

Preparation time: 15 minutes   **Servings: 4**

Ingredients:
- Salt
- Basil
- Cilantro
- Juice of one lime
- 1 chopped chili pepper
- ½ cup vegetable broth
- 1 cup bean sprouts
- 2 cups chopped carrots
- 1 cup green beans, diced
- 1 cup broccoli, cleaved
- 1 cup Pak Choi
- 1 cup wild rice

Directions: Put all the chopped vegetables into a pan and add vegetable broth. Steam fry the vegetables until they are cooked through but still crunchy.

Using a mortar and pestle grind up the chili, basil, and cilantro until it forms a paste. Add in lime juice and mix well. Place the rice onto a serving platter. Add the vegetables on top and drizzle with dressing.

Nutrition: Calories: 375.9; Carbs: 54.9g; Fats: 14.8g; Protein: 0g

82. Cheese Board

Preparation Time: 10 minutes   **Cooking Time: 30 minutes**
Servings: 8

Ingredients:
- 2 cups almond flour
- 4 tbsp. onion powder
- Water
- 1 tsp. light soy sauce
- 1 tbsp. poppy seeds
- 5 tsp. agar powder
- ½ cup bell pepper
- ½ cup raw cashews
- 1 1/3 cup nutritional yeast
- 4 tbsp. lemon juice
- ½ tsp. mustard

Directions: reheat the oven to 350°F.

To make the crackers, mix together the flour, 3 tbsp. onion powder, 3 tbsp. water, soy sauce, and poppy seeds. Form into a ball.

Take a baking sheet and cover with baking paper and place the ball on top.

Press it down as flat as possible, then place another piece of parchment sheet on top.

On top of the second sheet of parchment, use a rolling pin to roll the cracker mix to about 1/4th inch thick.

Remove the second sheet of parchment and cook in oven for about 15 minutes.

When the crackers are done baking, let cool and cut into cracker-sized pieces. Store in an airtight container.

Put the agar and 1 ½ cups of water into a small pot over high heat. Wait for it to boil and whisk continuously until the mixture becomes thick like custard. Take off the heat and put into a blender.

Roughly chop pepper and add to the blender along with the cashews, nutritional yeast, lemon juice, 2 tsp. onion powder, and mustard. Pulse until smooth.

Pour the blended mix into a bread pan lined with parchment paper and refrigerate for at least 30 minutes before serving.

Nutrition: Protein: 27.3g; Fats: 39.8g; Carbs: 33.9g

83. Mushroom Steaks

Preparation Time: 20 minutes
Servings: 4

Cooking Time: 24 minutes

Ingredients:

- 1 tablespoon vegan butter
- ½ cup vegetable broth
- ½ small yellow onion, diced
- 1 large garlic clove, minced
- 3 tablespoons balsamic vinegar
- 1 tablespoon mirin
- ½ tablespoon soy sauce
- ½ tablespoon tomato paste
- 1 teaspoon dried thyme
- ½ teaspoon dried basil
- A dash of ground black pepper
- 2 large, whole portobello mushrooms

Directions: Warm butter in a pan over medium heat and stir in half of the broth.
Bring to a simmer then add garlic and onion. Cook for 8 minutes.
Whisk the rest of the ingredients except the mushrooms in a bowl.
Place this mixture to the onion in the pan and mix well.
Bring this filling to a simmer then remove from the heat.
Clean the mushroom caps inside and out and divide the filling between the mushrooms.
Take a baking sheet and put the mushrooms in it and top them with remaining sauce and broth.
Cover with foil then place it on a grill to smoke.
Cover the grill and broil for 16 minutes over indirect heat. Serve warm.

Nutrition: Protein: 13.1g; Fats: 60.8g; Carbs: 25.8g

84. Sprout Wraps

Preparation Time: 15 minutes

Servings: 2

Ingredients:

- Tortillas, whole-wheat, two large
- Parsley, one-half cup chopped
- Onion, green, two stalks
- Black pepper, one teaspoon
- Cucumber, one sliced thin
- Bean sprouts, one cup
- Salt, one half teaspoon
- Lemon juice, one tablespoon
- Olive oil, one tablespoon

Directions: Lay out each of the tortilla wraps on a plate. Divide evenly all of the ingredients between the two tortillas, leaving about two inches on either side for rolling the tortilla up.
When you have added all of the ingredients on the tortilla, then fold in the sides and roll the tortilla up into a cylinder shape.

Nutrition: Calories: 219.9; Fat: 2.8g; Carbs: 19.8g; Protein: 9.2g; Fiber:14.8g

85. Cauliflower Steaks

Preparation Time: 10 minutes
Servings: 4

Cooking Time: 20/25 minutes

Ingredients:

- ¼ Teaspoon black pepper
- ½ teaspoon sea salt, fine
- 1 tablespoon olive oil
- 1 head cauliflower, large
- ¼ cup creamy hummus
- 2 tablespoons lemon sauce
- ½ cup peanuts, crushed (optional)

Directions: Start by heating your oven to 425.
Cut your cauliflower stems, and then remove the leaves.
Put the cut side down, and then slice half down the middle.
Cut into ¾ inch steaks. If you cut them thinner, they could fall apart.
Place them in a single tier on a baking sheet, drizzling with oil.
Season with salt and pepper, and bake for twenty to twenty-five minutes.
They should be lightly browned and tender. Spread your hummus on the steaks, drizzling with your lemon sauce.
Top with peanuts if you're using it.

Nutrition: Calories: 159.8; Fats: 4.9g; Carbs: 18.8g; Protein: 6.2g; Fiber: 19.8g

86. Dijon Maple Burgers

Preparation Time: 10 minutes
Servings: 12

Cooking Time: 50 minutes

Ingredients:

- 1 red bell pepper
- 19 ounces can chickpeas, rinsed & drained
- 1 cup almonds, ground
- 2 teaspoons Dijon mustard
- 1 teaspoon oregano
- ½ teaspoon sage
- 1 cup spinach, fresh
- 1 – ½ cups rolled oats
- 1 clove garlic, pressed
- ½ lemon, juiced
- 2 teaspoons maple syrup, pure

Directions: Heat the oven to 350, and then get out a baking sheet. Line it with parchment paper.
Cut your red pepper in half and then take the seeds out. Place it on your baking sheet, and roast in the oven while you prepare your other ingredients.
Process your chickpeas, almonds, mustard and maple syrup together in a food processor.
Add in your lemon juice, oregano, sage, garlic and spinach, processing again.
Make sure it's combined, but don't puree it.
Once your red bell pepper is softened, which should roughly take ten minutes, add this to the processor as well.
Add in your oats, mixing well. Form twelve patties, cooking in the oven for a half hour. They should be browned.

Nutrition: Calories: 419.9; Fats: 8.8g; Carbs: 64.8g; Protein: 8.2g; Fiber: 11.8g

87. Cucumber Bites with Chive and Sunflower Seeds

Preparation Time: 5 minutes
Servings: 2

Cooking Time: 5 minutes

Ingredients:

- 1 cup raw sunflower seed
- ½ teaspoon salt
- ½ cup chopped fresh chives
- 1 clove garlic, chopped
- 2 tablespoons red onion, minced
- 2 tablespoons lemon juice
- ½ cup water (might need more or less)
- 4 large cucumbers

Directions: Place the sunflower seeds and salt in the food processor and process to a fine powder. It will take only about 10 seconds.
Add the chives, garlic, onion, lemon juice and water and process until creamy, scraping down the sides frequently.
The mixture should be very creamy; if not, add a little more water.
Cut the cucumbers into 1½-inch coin-like pieces.
Spread a spoonful of the sunflower mixture on top and set on a platter.
Sprinkle more chopped chives on top and refrigerate until ready to serve.

Nutrition: Protein: 13.2g; Fats: 62.8g; Carbs: 23.8g

88. Vegetable Fajitas

Preparation Time: 10 minutes
Servings: 2

Cooking Time: 8 minutes

Ingredients:

- 2 Portobello mushroom caps, 1/3-inch sliced
- ¾ of red bell pepper, sliced
- ½ of onion, peeled, sliced
- ½ of key lime, juiced
- 2 spelt flour tortillas

Extra:

- 1/3 teaspoon salt
- ¼ teaspoon cayenne pepper
- ¼ teaspoon onion powder
- 1 tablespoon grapeseed oil

Directions: Take a medium skillet pan, place it over medium heat, add oil and when hot, add onion and red pepper, and then cook for 2 minutes until tender-crisp.
Add mushrooms slices, sprinkle with all the seasoning, stir until mixed, and then cook for 5 minutes until vegetables turn soft. Heat the tortilla until warm, distribute vegetables in their center, drizzle with lime juice, and then roll tightly.

Nutrition: Calories: 336.9; Fats: 3.2g; Protein: 2.9g; Carbs: 72.9g

89. Veggie Balls in Tomato Sauce

Preparation Time: 20 minutes   **Cooking Time: 15 minutes**
Servings: 8

Ingredients:

- 1½ cups cooked chickpeas
- 2 cups fresh button mushrooms
- ½ cup onions, chopped
- ¼ cup green bell peppers, seeded and chopped
- 2 teaspoons oregano
- 2 teaspoons fresh basil
- 1 teaspoon savory
- 1 teaspoon dried sage
- 1 teaspoon dried dill
- 1 tablespoon onion powder
- ½ teaspoon cayenne powder
- ½ teaspoon ginger powder
- Sea salt, as needed
- ½–1 cup chickpea flour
- 6 cups homemade tomato sauce
- 2 tablespoons grapeseed oil

Directions: In a food processor, place the herbs, chickpeas, veggies, and spices and pulse until well combined.
Add the mixture into a large bowl with flour and mix until well combined.
Make desired-sized balls from the mixture.
Warm the grapeseed oil, in a pan, over medium-high heat and cook the balls in 2 batches for about 4–5 minutes or until golden-brown from all sides.
In a large pan, add the tomato sauce and veggie balls over medium heat and simmer for about 5 minutes.
Serve hot.

Nutrition: Calories: 246.8; Fats: 0.6g; Carbs: 38.1g; Protein: 12.2g

90. Kale Wraps with Chili and Green Beans

Preparation Time: 30 minutes   **Servings: 2**

Ingredients:

- 1 tablespoon fresh lime juice
- 1 tablespoon raw seed mix
- 2 large kale leaves
- 2 teaspoons fresh garlic (finely chopped)
- Half ripe avocado (pitted and sliced)
- 1 teaspoon fresh red chili (seeded & finely chopped)
- 1 cup fresh cucumber sticks
- Fresh coriander leaves (finely chopped)
- 1 cup green beans

Directions: Spread kale leaves on a clean kitchen work surface.
Spread each chopped coriander leaves on each leaf, position them around the end of the leaf, perpendicular to the edge. Spread green beans equally on each leaf, at the edge of each leaf, same as the coriander leaves.
Do the same thing with the cucumber sticks.
Cut the divide chopped garlic across each leaf, sprinkling it all over the green beans.
Cut and share the chopped chili across each leaf and sprinkle it over the garlic.
Now, divide the avocado across each leaf, and spread it over chili, garlic, coriander, and green beans.
Share the raw seed mix among each leaf, and sprinkle them over other ingredients.
Divide the lime juice across each leaf and drizzle it over all other ingredients.
Now fold or roll up the kale leaves and wrap up all the ingredients within them.

Nutrition: Calories: 279.7; Fats: 7.9g; Carbs: 7.9g; Protein: 6.3g

91. Grilled Peaches

Preparation Time: 10 minutes   **Cooking Time: 6 minutes**
Servings: 2

Ingredients:

- 2 large peaches, halved and pitted
- 1/8 teaspoon ground cinnamon
- 1 tablespoon walnuts, chopped

Directions: Preheat the grill to medium-high heat. Grease the grill grate.
Arrange the peach halves onto the prepared grill, cut side down and cook for about 3–5 minutes per side.
Remove the peach halves from grill and place onto serving plates.
Set aside to cool slightly. Sprinkle with cinnamon and walnuts and serve.

Nutrition: Calories: 82.9; Fats: 0.1g; Carbs: 14.2g; Protein: 2.6g

92. Sausage Links

Preparation Time: 10 minutes
Servings: 2

Cooking Time: 10 minutes

Ingredients:

- 1 cup cooked chickpeas
- 2 cherry tomatoes
- ½ cup sliced mushrooms
- ¼ cup chopped white onion
- ¼ cup chickpea flour
- Extra:
- ½ teaspoon basil
- ½ teaspoon oregano
- ½ teaspoon of sea salt
- ½ teaspoon cayenne powder
- ½ teaspoon dill
- 1 tablespoon grapeseed oil

Directions: Put the ingredients in a food processor except for chickpeas and then pulse until combined.
Add chickpeas, blend again until well combined, and then spoon the mixture into a piping bag.
Take a large skillet pan, place it over medium-high heat, add oil and then hot, squeeze chickpea mixture to make sausage links, and then cook for 3 to 4 minutes per side until nicely brown and cooked.

Nutrition: Calories: 186.9; Fats: 7.1g; Protein: 7.6g; Carbs: 23.8g

93. Dinner Rolls

Preparation Time: 20 minutes
Servings: 12

Cooking Time: 30 minutes

Ingredients:

- 128 ml coconut milk- 384 g plain flour
- 7½ tablespoons unsalted vegan butter
- 1 tablespoon coconut oil
- 1 tablespoon olive oil - 1 teaspoon yeast
- 1 teaspoon salt and black pepper, to taste

Directions: Preheat the Air fryer to 360 o F and grease an Air fryer basket.
Put olive oil, coconut milk and coconut oil in a pan and cook for about 3 minutes.
Remove from the heat and mix well.
Mix together plain flour, yeast, vegan butter, salt and black pepper in a large bowl.
Knead well for about 5 minutes until a dough is formed.
Cover the dough with a damp cloth and keep aside for about 5 minutes in a warm place.
Knead the dough for about 5 minutes again with your hands. Cover the dough with a damp cloth and keep aside for about 30 minutes in a warm place.
Divide dough into 12 even pieces and then, roll each into a ball. Arrange 6 balls into the Air fryer basket in a single layer and cook for about 15 minutes. Repeat with the remaining balls and serve warm.

Nutrition: Calories: 190.8; Fats: 2.1g; Carbs: 25.1g; Protein: 2.3g

94. Roasted Bell Peppers with Spicy Mayonnaise

Preparation Time: 10 minutes
Servings: 2

Cooking Time: 15 minutes

Ingredients:

- 4 bell peppers, seeded and sliced
- ½ teaspoon rosemary, dried
- 1 tablespoon olive oil
- 1 onion, sliced
- ½ teaspoon basil, dried
- 96 g mayo
- 1/3 teaspoon sriracha
- ¼ teaspoon black pepper, to taste
- 1 tbsp Kosher salt

Directions: Pre-heat your Air Fryer to 400 degrees F
Toss bell pepper and onion with olive oil, basil, salt, rosemary, salt, and black pepper
Place the peppers and onion to make a layer in the cooking basket. Cook for 12 to 15 minutes.
Make the sauce by whisking the mayonnaise and sriracha. Serve warm and enjoy!

Nutrition: Calories: 133.8; Fats: 2.3g; Carbs: 3.2g; Protein: 1.3g

95. Bell Peppers and Masala Potatoes

Preparation Time: 10 minutes   **Cooking Time: 20 minutes**
Servings: 4

Ingredients:
- 1 pound mixed bell peppers, cut into wedges
- 2 sweet potatoes, peeled and cut into wedges
- ½ cup vegetarian stock
- 1 teaspoon chili powder
- ½ teaspoon garam masala
- ½ teaspoon coriander, ground
- ½ teaspoon cumin, ground
- 1 tablespoon olive oil

Directions: In your instant pot, combine the bell peppers with the potatoes, the stock and the remaining of the ingredients, place the cover on and cook on High for 20 minutes.
Release the pressure naturally for 10 minutes, divide the mix between plates and serve.

Nutrition: Calories: 131.8; Fats: 3.8g; Carbs: 23.5g; Protein: 1.9g

96. Nutmeg Okra

Preparation Time: 10 minutes   **Cooking Time: 20 minutes**
Servings: 4

Ingredients:
- 1 pound okra, trimmed
- ½ cup vegetarian stock
- 1 tablespoon ghee, melted
- 1 red onion, chopped
- ½ teaspoon nutmeg, ground
- ½ teaspoon garam masala
- ½ teaspoon chili powder
- ½ teaspoon coriander, ground
- A pinch of salt and black pepper
- 1 tablespoon sweet paprika
- 2 tablespoon cilantro, chopped

Directions: Setting the instant pot on Sauté mode, add the ghee, heat it up, add the onion and sauté for 4 minutes.
Add the okra, the nutmeg and the rest of the ingredients, put the lid on and cook on High for 16 minutes.
Release the pressure naturally for 10 minutes, divide the mix between plates and serve.

Nutrition: Calories: 92.7; Fats: 3.5g; Carbs: 12.3g; Protein: 3.1g

97. Creamy Eggplants

Preparation Time: 10 minutes   **Cooking Time: 15 minutes**
Servings: 4

Ingredients:
- 2 eggplants, roughly cubed
- 1 cup coconut, shredded
- 1 cup coconut cream
- 2 tablespoons lime juice
- 1 bunch coriander, chopped
- ½ cup vegetarian stock
- 1 tablespoon ginger, grated

Directions: In your instant pot, combine the eggplants with the coconut, the cream and the remaining of the ingredients, place the cover on and bake on High for 15 minutes.
Release the pressure naturally for 10 minutes, divide the mix between plates and serve.

Nutrition: Calories: 125.7; Fats: 5.1g; Carbs: 11.2g; Protein: 2.8g

98. Eggplant Stacks

Preparation Time: 5 minutes   **Cooking Time: 15 minutes**
Servings: 4

Ingredients:
- 2 large tomatoes; cut into ¼-inch slices
- 32 g fresh basil, sliced
- 400g. Fresh mozzarella; cut into ½-oz. Slices
- 1 medium eggplant; cut into ¼-inch slices
- 2 tbsp. Olive oil

Directions: In a 6-inch round baking dish, place four slices of eggplant on the bottom. Put a slice of tomato on each eggplant round, then mozzarella, then eggplant. Repeat as necessary.
Sprinkle with olive oil. Cover with foil and place dish into the air fryer basket. Adjust the temperature to 350 degrees f and cook for 12 minutes. When done, eggplant will be tender. Garnish with fresh basil to serve.

Nutrition: Calories: 194.8; Fats: 5.1g; Carbs: 21.3g; Protein: 19.8g

99. Oil-Free Mushroom and Tofu Burritos

Preparation Time: 15 minutes　　　　　　　　　　　　**Cooking Time: 28 to 45 minutes**
Servings: 4

Ingredients:

- 1½ cups shiitake mushrooms, stemmed and sliced
- 2 large leeks, white and light green parts only, diced 1 medium red bell pepper, diced
- 3 cloves garlic, minced
- 3 tablespoons nutritional yeast
- 2 tablespoons low-sodium soy sauce
- 2 teaspoons ground coriander
- 2 teaspoons turmeric
- 2 teaspoons ground cumin
- Black pepper, to taste
- 1 pound (454 g) lite firm tofu, pressed and mashed ½ cup chopped cilantro
- 4 whole-wheat tortillas
- 1 cup salsa

Directions: Prepare the oven to 350ºF (180ºC). Line a baking pan with the parchment paper.
Add the mushrooms, leeks and red bell pepper to a saucepan over medium-high heat. Sauté for 8 to 10 minutes, or until the vegetables are softened.
Add the garlic, nutritional yeast, soy sauce, coriander, turmeric, cumin and black pepper to the saucepan. Reduce the heat to medium-low. Sauté for 5 minutes. Stir in the tofu mash.
Place the mixture in an even layer in the prepared pan. Bake for 25 to 30 minutes. Put the mixture to a large bowl and mix with the cilantro to combine well.
On a clean work surface, lay the tortillas. Spoon the mixture into the tortillas and spread all over. Drizzle the salsa over the filling. Roll up the tortillas tightly. Serve immediately.

Nutrition: Calories: 410.8; Fats: 14.9g; Carbs: 48.1g; Protein: 28.5g; Fiber: 12.3g

100. Brown Rice Lettuce Wraps

Preparation Time: 10 minutes　　　　　　　　　　　　**Cooking Time: 5 minutes**
Servings: 4

Ingredients

- 1 batch Potato Samosa Filling
- 8 romaine lettuce leaves
- 3 cups cooked brown rice
- Coriander Chutney

Directions: Place some of the samosa filling on the bottom of one of the lettuce leaves. Top with some brown rice and a spoonful of the coriander chutney.
Roll the leaf up around the filling. Repeat for the remaining lettuce leaves.

Nutrition: Calories: 283.9; Fats: 0.2g; Carbs: 64.1g; Protein: 7.8g

101. Cashew Mac and Cheese

Preparation Time: 15 minutes　　　　　　　　　　　　**Cooking Time: 10 minutes**
Servings: 4

Ingredients:

- 1½ cups raw cashews
- 2 garlic cloves
- ½ cup nutritional yeast
- 1¼ cups almond milk
- 1 jalapeño, chopped
- ¾ teaspoon ground turmeric
- ¾ teaspoon paprika
- ½ teaspoon onion powder
- 1 teaspoon Dijon mustard
- 1 teaspoon salt
- Black pepper, to taste
- 1-pound shell Conchiglie pasta

Direction: Soak cashews in 4 cups water in a bowl for 2 hours then drain.
Drain and blend the cashews with black pepper, salt, mustard, onion powder, paprika, turmeric, jalapeño, almond milk, yeast, and garlic in a blender until smooth.
Cook the noodles as per the package's instructions then drain.
Mix the noodles with the cashews sauce in a bowl. Garnish with black pepper. Serve warm.

Nutrition: Calories: 309.9; Fats: 5.8g; Carbs: 30.7g; Fiber: 2.1g; Sugar: 1.1g; Protein: 12.3g

102. Pineapple Tofu Kabobs

Preparation Time: 10 minutes   **Cooking Time: 10 minutes**
Servings: 4

Ingredients:
- 2 tablespoons tamari
- 1 teaspoon apple cider vinegar
- 2 tablespoons fresh pineapple juice
- 2 teaspoons ginger, grated
- 2 garlic cloves, minced
- ½ teaspoon ground turmeric
- 1 (14-ounce) package Nagoya extra firm tofu
- 2 cups fresh pineapple, cubed

Garnish
- Fresh chopped cilantro
- Diced onion
- Hot sauce

Direction: Pat dry the tofu block with a paper towel and cut into cubes.
Mix tamari, turmeric, garlic, ginger, pineapple juice, and apple cider vinegar in a large bowl.
Toss in tofu cubes then mix well and cover to marinate for 30 minutes.
Set a grill over medium high heat and grease its grilling grates.
Thread tofu and pineapple on the skewers and grill the skewers for 5 minutes per side.

Garnish with hot sauce, green onion and cilantro. Serve warm.

Nutrition: Calories: 303.8; Fats: 30.8g; Carbs: 26.8g; Fiber: 0.2g; Sugar: 0.3g; Protein: 4.8g

103. Smoky Red Pepper Hummus

Preparation Time: 5 minutes   **Servings: 4**

Ingredients:
- 1/4 cup roasted red peppers
- 1 cup cooked chickpeas
- 1/8 teaspoon garlic powder
- 1/2 teaspoon salt
- 1/8 teaspoon ground black pepper
- 1/4 teaspoon ground cumin
- 1/4 teaspoon red chili powder
- 1 tablespoon tahini
- 2 tablespoons water

Directions: Put the ingredients in the jar of the food processor and then pulse until smooth.
Tip the hummus in a bowl and then serve with vegetable slices.

Nutrition: Calories: 489 Fats: 30g Protein: 9g Carbs: 15g Fiber: 6g

Snacks and Appetizers

104. Basil Zucchini Noodles

Preparation Time: 10 minutes
Servings: 2

Cooking Time: 10 minutes

Ingredients:
- 1 zucchini, spiralized
- ¼ cup pine nuts
- 1/3 cup water
- 1¼ cup fresh basil
- ¾ cup cherry tomatoes, halved
- 1 avocado, chopped
- 2 tbsp fresh lemon juice
- Pepper
- Salt

Directions: Add zucchini noodles and tomatoes into the bowl.
Mix the rest of the ingredients in the blender and blend until smooth.
Pour blended mixture over zucchini noodles. Toss well. Serving Suggestion: Serve immediately.

Nutrition: Calories: 354.8; Fats: 31.2g; Carbs: 17.2g; Fiber: 9.5g; Sugar: 4.8g; Protein: 6.8g

105. Cauliflower Popcorn

Preparation Time: 10 minutes
Servings: 2

Cooking Time: 12 hours

Ingredients:
- 2 heads of cauliflower
- Spicy Sauce
- ½ cup of filtered water
- ½ teaspoon of turmeric
- 1 cup of dates
- 2-3 tablespoons of nutritional yeast
- ¼ cup of sun-dried tomatoes
- 2 tablespoons of raw tahini
- 1-2 teaspoons of cayenne pepper
- 2 teaspoons of onion powder
- 1 tablespoon of apple cider vinegar
- 2 teaspoons of garlic powder

Directions: Chop the cauliflower into small pieces.
Put all the ingredients for the spicy sauce in a blender and create a mixture with a smooth consistency.
Coat the cauliflower florets in the sauce. See that each piece is properly covered.
Put the spicy florets in a dehydrator tray. Add some salt and your favorite herb if you want.
Dehydrate the cauliflower for 12 hours at 115°F. Keep dehydrating until it is crunchy.
Enjoy the cauliflower popcorn, which is a healthier alternative!

Nutrition: Calories: 490.8; Fats: 12.8g; Carbs: 85.9g; Protein: 20.1g

106. Zucchini Chips

Preparation Time: 10 minutes
Servings: 5

Cooking Time: 2 hours

Ingredients:
- 1 large zucchini
- 2 tablespoons of olive oil
- Sea salt, to taste

Directions: Preheat your oven to 225ºF. Cover 2 baking sheets with a piece of parchment paper.
Slice zucchini on a mandolin (use medium thickness).
Place zucchini slices on a paper towel, cover them with another piece, and press. It will help you to squeeze extra water.
Spread zucchini slices on the covered baking sheets in a single layer. Brush each piece with olive oil by using a baking brush. Sprinkle salt on the top. Bake for about 2 hours until brown and crisp. Serve and enjoy!

Nutrition: Calories: 53.8; Fats: 4.8g; Protein: 0g; Carbs: 0.8g

107. Chocolate Almond Bars

Preparation Time: 10 minutes
Servings: 12

Cooking Time: 20 minutes

Ingredients:
- 1 cup Almonds
- 1 ½ cup Rolled Oats
- 1/3 cup Maple Syrup
- ¼ tsp. Sea Salt
- 5 oz. Protein Powder
- 1 tsp. Cinnamon

Directions: For making these delicious vegan bars, you first need to place ¾cup of the almonds and salt in the food processor.
Process them for a minute or until you get them in the form of almond butter.
Stir in the rest of the ingredients to the processor and process them again until smooth.
Next, transfer the mixture to a greased parchment paper-lined baking sheet and spread it across evenly.
Press them slightly down with the back of the spoon.
Chop down the remaining ¼ cup of the almonds and top it across the mixture.
Place them in the refrigerator for 20 minutes or until set.

Nutrition: Calories: 165.7; Fats: 5.9g; Carbs: 16.8g; Protein: 13.2g

108. Strawberry Watermelon Ice Pops

Preparation Time: 5 minutes + 6 hours to freeze

Servings: 6

Ingredients:
- 4 cups diced watermelon
- 4 strawberries, tops removed
- 2 tablespoons freshly squeezed lime juice

Directions: Mix the lime juice, watermelon, and strawberries in a blender. Blend for 2 minutes.
Pour evenly into 6 ice-pop molds, insert ice-pop sticks, and freeze for at least 6 hours before serving.

Nutrition: Calories: 60.8; Fats: 0g; Carbs: 14.8g; Protein: 1.2g

109. Pineapple, Peach, and Mango Salsa

Preparation Time: 15 minutes
Servings: about 6 cups

Cooking Time: 2 to 3hours on low

Ingredients:
- 1 medium onion, finely diced
- 2 garlic cloves, minced
- 1 medium orange, red, or yellow bell pepper, finely diced 1 (20-ounce) can crushed pineapple in juice
- 1 (15-ounce) can no-sugar-added mango in juice, drained and finely diced
- 1 (15-ounce) can no-sugar-added sliced peaches in juice, drained and finely diced
- ½ teaspoon ground cumin
- 1 teaspoon paprika
- Juice of 1 lime
- 3 to 4 tablespoons chopped fresh mint (about 10 to 15 leaves)

Directions: Put the onion, garlic, and bell pepper in the slow cooker. Add the pineapple and its juices, the mango, and the peaches. Sprinkle the cumin and paprika into the slow cooker. Put the lime juice and stir well to mix. Cover and cook on Low for 2 to 3 hours, or until the onion and peppers are cooked through and softened. Let the salsa cool slightly, then stir in the mint just before serving.

Nutrition: Protein: 22.1g; Fats: 38.7g; Carbs: 38.8g

110. Buffalo Cauliflower Dip

Preparation Time: 20 minutes
Servings: about 5 cups

Cooking Time: 2 hours on low

Ingredients:
- 1 cup water
- 1 cup raw cashews
- 2 tablespoons white vinegar
- ¼ teaspoon cayenne powder
- ½ cup unsweetened plant-based milk
- ¼ cup Low-Sodium Vegetable Broth or store-bought 1 (14.5-ounce) can cannellini or Great Northern white beans, drained and rinsed
- 3 tablespoons nutritional yeast
- ¼ cup diced onion
- 3 garlic cloves, minced
- 1 (12-ounce) package frozen riced cauliflower 1 recipe Shredded Tofu Meaty Crumbles (optional) Salt (optional)

- *12 celery stalks, cut into 3-inch-long sticks, for serving*

Directions: Boil the water and put the cashews in a medium bowl. Pour the hot water over the cashews and let soak to soften, at least 15 minutes. In a bowl, mix together the cayenne and vinegar.

Transfer the cayenne mixture to a blender or food processor, then add the milk, broth, beans, nutritional yeast, onion, and garlic. Drain the cashews and put them to the blender. Blend until creamy.

In the slow cooker, combine the cauliflower and tofu crumbles (if using). Season with salt (if using) and cover with the sauce. Mix well to combine. Cover and then, cook on Low for 2 hours. Serve with the celery sticks for dipping.

Nutrition: Calories: 67.9; Fats: 2.9g; Carbs: 6.8g; Protein: 4.2g; Fiber: 1.9g

111. Sweet 'n' Spicy Crunchy Snack Mix

Preparation Time: 5 minutes
Servings: 5½ cups

Cooking Time: 1½ hours on low

Ingredients:

- *1 cup raw cashews*
- *1 cup raw almonds*
- *1 cup raw pecan halves*
- *1 cup walnuts*
- *½ cup raw pepitas*
- *½ cup raw sunflower seeds*
- *¼ cup aquafaba*
- *¼ cup maple syrup*
- *1 teaspoon miso paste*
- *1 teaspoon garlic powder*
- *1 teaspoon paprika*
- *2 teaspoons ground ginger*

Directions: Put the cashews, almonds, pecans, walnuts, pepitas, and sunflower seeds in the slow cooker.

In a deep bowl, whisk or use an immersion blender to beat the aquafaba until foamy, about 1 minute. Add the maple syrup, miso paste, garlic powder, paprika, and ginger and whisk or blend to combine. Pour over the nuts in the slow cooker and gently toss, making sure all the nuts and seeds are coated.

Stretch a clean dish towel or several layers of paper towels over the top of the slow cooker, but not touching the food, and place the lid on top. Cook on Low for 1½ hours, stirring every 20 to 30 minutes to keep the nuts from burning. After each stir, dry any condensation under the lid and replace the towels before re-covering.

Line a rimmed baking sheet with parchment paper. Transfer the snack mix to the baking sheet to cool. Store in an airtight container for up to 2 weeks.

Nutrition: Calories: 181.9; Fats: 15.8g; Carbs: 7.9g; Protein: 5.2g; Fiber: 1.8g

112. Kale Spread

Preparation Time: 10 minutes

Servings: 2

Ingredients:

- *3 cups kale, chopped*
- *3 tbsps. tomato sauce*
- *¼ cup avocado mayonnaise*
- *Salt and black pepper to the taste*
- *1 tsp. mint, chopped*
- *1 tsp. turmeric powder*
- *½ tsp. garlic powder*

Directions: In a blender, mix the kale with the tomato sauce and the other ingredients, blend well and serve.

Nutrition: Calories: 99.8; Fats: 11.8g; Carbs: 0.9g

113. Fudgy Choco-Peanut Butter

Preparation Time: 15 minutes

Servings: 32

Ingredients:

- *4 oz. cream cheese (softened)*
- *2 tbsps. unsweetened cocoa powder*
- *½ cup butter*
- *½ cup natural peanut butter*
- *½ tsp. vanilla extract*
- *¼ cup powdered erythritol*

Directions: In a microwave-safe bowl, mix peanut butter and butter. Microwave for 10-second intervals until melted. While mixing every after sticking in the microwave.

Mix in vanilla extract, cocoa powder, erythritol, and cream cheese. Thoroughly mix. Line an 8x8-inch baking pan with foil and then distribute the mixture evenly.

Place in the fridge to set and slice into 32 equal squares. Storage in a tightly lidded container in the fridge and enjoy as a snack.

Nutrition: Calories: 64.8; Protein: 1.8g; Carbs: 0.8g; Fats: 5.8g

114. Tofu Sandwiches on Multigrain Bread

Preparation Time: 15 minutes   **Servings: 4**

Ingredients:

- 1 lb. extra-firm tofu, drained and patted dry
- 1 medium red bell pepper, finely chopped
- 1 celery rib, finely chopped
- 3 green onions, minced
- ¼ cup shelled sunflower seeds
- ½ cup vegan mayonnaise, homemade or store-bought
- ½ tsp. salt
- ½ tsp. celery salt
- ¼ tsp. freshly ground black pepper
- 8 slices whole-grain bread
- 4 (¼-inch) slices ripe tomato
- 4 lettuce leaves

Directions: Crumble your tofu then place it in a large bowl. Add the bell pepper, celery, green onions, and sunflower seeds. Stir in the mayonnaise, salt, celery salt, and pepper and mix until well combined.
Toast the bread, if desired. Spread the mixture evenly onto 4 slices of the bread. Put on top the tomato slice, lettuce leaf, and the remaining bread. Slice the sandwiches diagonally in half then serve.

Nutrition: Calories: 129.8; Carbs: 16.9g; Fats: 6.9g; Protein: 2.1g

115. Seed Crackers

Preparation Time: 5 minutes   **Cooking Time: 50 minutes**
Servings: 20

Ingredients:

- ¾ cup pumpkin seeds (pepitas)
- ½ cup sunflower seeds
- ½ cup sesame seeds
- ¼ cup chia seeds
- 1 tsp. minced garlic (about 1 clove)
- 1 tsp. tamari or soy sauce
- 1 tsp. vegan Worcestershire sauce
- ½ tsp. ground cayenne pepper
- ½ tsp. dried oregano
- ½ cup water

Directions: Preheat the oven to 325ºF. Prepare a rimmed baking sheet lined using parchment paper.
In a large bowl, combine the pumpkin seeds, sunflower seeds, sesame seeds, chia seeds, garlic, tamari, Worcestershire sauce, cayenne, oregano, and water.
Place on the prepared baking sheet and spread it out to all sides. Bake for 25 minutes. Remove the pan, then flip the seed "dough" over so the wet side is up.
Bake for another 20-25 minutes until the sides are browned. Cool completely before breaking up into 20 pieces. Divide evenly among 4 glass jars and close tightly with lids.

Nutrition: Calories: 338.7; Fats: 28.7g; Protein: 14.2g; Carbs: 16.8g

116. Banana Curry

Preparation Time: 15 minutes   **Cooking Time: 15 minutes**
Servings: 3

Ingredients:

- 2 tablespoons olive oil
- 2 yellow onions, chopped
- 8 garlic cloves, minced
- 2 tablespoons curry powder
- 1 tablespoon ground ginger
- 1 tablespoon ground cumin
- 1 teaspoon ground turmeric
- 1 teaspoon ground cinnamon
- 1 teaspoon red chili powder
- Salt and ground black pepper, to taste
- 2/3 cup soy yogurt
- 1 cup tomato puree
- 2 bananas, peeled and sliced
- 3 tomatoes, chopped finely
- ¼ cup unsweetened coconut flakes

Directions: Take a large pan and heat the oil over medium heat and sauté onion for about 4–5 minutes.
Add the garlic, curry powder, and spices, and sauté for about 1minute.
Add the soy yogurt and tomato sauce and bring to a gentle boil.
Stir in the bananas and simmer for about 3 minutes. Add tomatoes and simmer for about 1–2 minutes.
Stir in the coconut flakes and immediately remove from the heat. Serve hot.

Nutrition: Calories: 381.9; Fats: 17.9g; Carbs: 52.8g; Protein: 9.2g

117. Pumpkin Orange Spice Hummus

Preparation Time: 30 minutes   **Cooking Time: 30 minutes**

Servings: 3

Ingredients:

- 1 cup canned, unsweetened pumpkin puree
- 1 16-ounce can garbanzo beans, rinsed and drained
- 1 tablespoon apple cider vinegar
- 1 tablespoon maple syrup
- ¼ cup tahini
- 1 tablespoon fresh orange juice
- ½ teaspoon orange zest and additional zest for garnish 1/8 teaspoon ground cinnamon
- 1/8 teaspoon ground ginger
- 1/8 teaspoon ground nutmeg
- ¼ teaspoon salt

Directions: Pour the pumpkin puree and garbanzo beans into a food processor and pulse to break up.
Add the vinegar, syrup, tahini, orange juice and orange zest pulse a few times.
Add the cinnamon, ginger, nutmeg and salt and process until smooth and creamy.
Serve in a bowl sprinkled with more orange zest with wheat crackers alongside.

Nutrition: Protein: 13.2g; Fats: 32.8g; Carbs: 54.9g

118. Banana Chips

Preparation Time: 10 minutes

Cooking Time: 1 hour

Servings: 6

Ingredients:

- 5 burro bananas, peeled and cut into ¼-inch-thick slices

Directions: Preheat your oven to 250ºF. Line a large baking sheet with baking paper.
Place the banana slices onto the prepared baking sheet in a single layer.
Bake for approximately 1 hour.

Nutrition: Calories: 87.9; Fats: 0.1g; Carbs: 22.3g; Protein: 1.3g

119. Sesame Seed Bread

Preparation Time: 15 minutes

Cooking Time: 1 hour

Servings: 10

Ingredients:

- 4½ cups spelt flour
- 2 teaspoons sea salt
- ¼ cup agave nectar
- 2 cups spring water
- 1 tablespoon sesame seeds

Directions: Take a bowl of a stand mixer, place 4 cups of spelt flour and salt and mix for 10 seconds.
Add the agave nectar and mix until well combined. Lightly coat the dough hook with a little grapeseed oil.
Add the spring water, 1 cup at a Time and mix until well combined.
Now, mix on medium speed for about 5 minutes.
Add remaining ½ cup of flour and mix until a non-sticky dough forms.
Add the sesame seeds and stir to combine. Place dough into a lightly greased and floured loaf pan.
Cover the loaf pan and set aside for about 1 hour. Preheat your oven to 350ºF.
Bake for approximately 52–60 minutes or until a wooden skewer inserted in the center of loaf comes out clean.
Remove from oven and place the baking sheet onto a wire rack to cool for at least 10 minutes.
Carefully invert the bread onto the rack to cool completely before serving.
With a knife, cut the bread loaf into desired-sized slices and serve.

Nutrition: Calories: 244.8; Fats: 0.1g; Carbs: 45.9g; Protein: 7.4g

120. Spelt and Raisin Cookies

Preparation Time: 10 minutes

Cooking Time: 18 minutes

Servings: 2

Ingredients:

- 1 cup spelt flour
- 1/3 cup raisins
- ½ cup dates, pitted
- 3 ½ tablespoons, applesauce homemade or pureed apples
- 2/3 tablespoon spring water
- Extra:
- 1/16 teaspoon sea salt
- 2 tablespoons agave syrup
- 1 ¾ tablespoon grapeseed oil

Directions: Switch on the oven, then set it to 350 degrees F and let it preheat.
Meanwhile, place flour in a food processor, add dates and salt in it, and then pulse until well blended.
Transfer flour mixture into a medium bowl, add remaining ingredients, and then stir until well mixed.
Divide the mixture into parts, each part about 2 tablespoons of the mixture, and then shape each part into a ball.
Place the cookie ball on a cookie sheet lined with parchment sheet, flatten it slightly by using a fork and then bake for 18 minutes until done. Let cookies cool for 10 minutes and then serve.

Nutrition: Calories: 148.7; Fats: 3.9g; Protein: 3.2g; Carbs: 54.9g

121. Taro Chips

Preparation Time: 5 minutes   **Cooking Time: 15 minutes**
Servings: 2

Ingredients:
- 4 tbsp. Cooking oil spray (coconut, sunflower, or safflower)
- 128 g thinly sliced taro (see Ingredient Tip)
- 2 tbsp. Sea salt

Directions: Drizzle the air fryer basket with oil and set aside. Place the sliced taro in the air fryer basket, spreading the pieces out as much as possible, and spray with oil. Fry for about 4 minutes. Remove the air fryer basket, shake (so that the chips cook evenly), and spray again with oil. Fry for another 4 minutes. If any chips are browned or crisp, remove them now. Remove the air fryer basket, shake again, spray again, and sprinkle lightly with salt to taste. Fry for another 3 to 4 minutes. Remove all of the chips that are done, and cook any remaining underdone chips for another minute, or until crisp. Please note that they may crisp up a tiny bit more as they sit at room temperature for a few minutes, but some may need extra time in the air fryer. You'll get the hang of how to test for doneness after you make a few batches.

Nutrition: Calories: 74.9; Fats: 0.9g; Carbs: 3.9g; Protein: 1.1g

122. Caramel Popcorn

Preparation Time: 10 minutes   **Cooking Time: 5-10 minutes**
Servings: 8

Ingredients:
- 1kg of popcorn
- 1 vegan butter tablet
- 128 g of sugar
- 96 g whipped cream

Directions: Put a quantity of corn in a pan in put it into the air fryer. Drizzle with a little olive oil.
Set the temperature at 2400F for 5 minutes.
When the popcorn is ready, put it in a large bowl and set aside while preparing the sauce.
Mix vegan butter, sugar and cream and heat over medium heat, stirring constantly. In a few minutes the sauce should be boiling, continue boiling until the mixture reaches the soft ball stage 2400F.
Remove mixture from heat and pour over popcorn, stirring until all popcorn is well coated. Be sure to serve it right away.

Nutrition: Calories: 109.9; Fats: 4.1g; Carbs: 11.2g; Protein: 1.3g

123. Spicy Beet Chips

Preparation Time: 10 minutes   **Cooking Time: 12 minutes**
Servings: 2

Ingredients:
- 7 oz beets
- 1 teaspoon chili flakes
- ½ teaspoon red pepper
- 1 teaspoon olive oil
- ¼ teaspoon sage

Directions: Wash the beet carefully and slice into the chips.
Sprinkle the beet chips with the chili flakes, red pepper, olive oil, and sage.
Mix up the beet chips carefully. Preheat the air fryer to 360 F.
Put the beet chips in the air fryer basket in one layer and cook for 10 minutes.
Then shake the chips gently and cook for 2 minutes more.

When the beet chips are cooked – let them chill till the room temperature and serve.

Nutrition: Calories: 64.9; Fats: 0.4g; Carbs: 6.9g; Protein: 0.5g

124.<u>Paprika Cucumber Chips</u>

Preparation Time: 10 minutes   **Cooking Time: 11 minutes**
Servings: 10

Ingredients:
- 453 g cucumber
- 1 teaspoon salt
- 1 tablespoon smoked paprika
- ½ teaspoon garlic powder

Directions: Wash the cucumbers carefully and slice them into chips.
Sprinkle the chips with salt, smoked paprika, and garlic powder.
Preheat the air fryer to 370 F. Place the cucumber slices in the air fryer rack.
Cook the cucumber chips for 11 minutes. Transfer the cucumber chips to a paper towel and allow to cool.
Serve the cucumber chips immediately or keep them in a paper bag.

Nutrition: Calories: 7.9; Fats: 0.3g; Carbs: 0.1g; Protein: 0.5g

125.<u>Coconut Banana Pot</u>

Preparation time: 10 minutes   **Cooking time: 15 minutes**
Servings: 4

Ingredients:
- 2 bananas, peeled and sliced
- ½ teaspoon cinnamon powder
- 1 cup yogurt
- 2 tablespoons sugar
- 2 tablespoons coconut flakes

Directions: In your instant pot, combine the bananas with the cinnamon and the remaining ingredients, cover and cook on High for 15 minutes. Release the pressure naturally for 10 minutes, divide the mix into bowls and serve.

Nutrition: Calories: 126.5; Fats: 1.7g; Fiber: 1.6g; Carbs: 23.9g; Protein: 4.3g

126.<u>Sweet Potatoes Vanilla Pudding</u>

Preparation time: 10 minutes   **Cooking time: 20 minutes**
Servings: 4

Ingredients:
- 1 cup sweet potatoes, peeled and grated
- 1 egg, whisked
- 2 cups coconut milk
- 3 tablespoons sugar
- 1 cup coconut cream
- 1 teaspoon vanilla extract
- 1 teaspoon saffron powder
- ½ teaspoon cardamom, ground

Directions: In your instant pot, combine the potatoes with the egg and the other ingredients, whisk, cover and cook on High for 20 minutes.
Release the pressure naturally for 10 minutes, divide the pudding into bowls and serve.

Nutrition: Calories: 296.8; Fats: 17.9g; Carbs: 29.1g; Protein: 7.6g

127.<u>Vegetable Wontons</u>

Preparation Time: 35 minutes   **Cooking Time: 20 minutes**
Servings: 12

Ingredients:
- 30 Wonton of Wrappers
- 3/4 cup of Grated Cabbage
- 64 g of Grated White Onion
- 64 g of Grated Carrot
- 64 g of Finely Chopped Mushrooms
- 3/4 cup Finely Chopped Red Pepper
- 1 tablespoon Chili Sauce
- 1 teaspoon of Garlic Powder
- 1/2 teaspoon of White Pepper
- Pinch of Salt
- 32 g of Water (for sealing wontons)
- Spray Olive Oil

Directions: In a hot skillet or medium-heat wok throw all your vegetables in. Cook until all the mushroom and onion moisture has released and cooked out of the saucepan.

Remove from heat and add salt, garlic powder, white pepper and chili sauce. Let the mixture cool before having your wontons assembled.

Remove from basket place once cooked and let cool before consuming. Serve alongside with duck sauce or soy! Place a wonton wrapper onto your work surface. Add 1 spoonful of your veggie mixture to the wonton wrapper center.

Dip your finger in 32 g of water and run your finger along the square wrapper's exposed top half to wet it. Push the bottom half carefully up and over the mixture making the corners rest offset.

Spray your palm again, and spray the wonton's lower corners. Fold gently over the wonton's bottom corners so that one sits on top of the other and exerts slight pressure to seal it. Make sure the seals along your wonton are not open. Do another 29 times. Remove from basket place once cooked and let cool before consuming. Serve alongside with duck sauce or soy! Preheat your air-fryer for 3 minutes to 320 degrees. While spritzing your wontons with a little olive oil preheats them.

Nutrition: Calories: 140.8; Fats: 4.1g; Carbs: 12.3g; Protein: 2.1g

Vegetables And Sides

128. Steamed Broccoli with Sesame

Preparation Time: 15 minutes
Servings: 2

Cooking Time: 5 minutes

Ingredients:
- 1 ½ lb. fresh broccoli florets
- ½ cup sesame oil
- 4 tbsps. sesame seeds
- Salt and ground pepper to taste

Directions: Put broccoli florets in your steamer basket above boiling water. Cover and steam for about 4 to 5 minutes. Remove from steam and place broccoli in serving the dish.
Season with the salt and pepper, and drizzle with sesame oil; toss to coat. Sprinkle with sesame seeds and serve immediately.

Nutrition: Calories: 53.8; Carbs: 4.8g; Fats: 1.9g; Protein: 3.2g

129. Balsamic Zucchini Bowls

Preparation Time: 10 minutes
Servings: 8

Cooking Time: 3 hours

Ingredients:
- 3 zucchinis, thinly sliced
- Salt and black pepper to the taste
- 2 tbsps. olive oil
- 1 tsp. turmeric powder
- 1 tsp. coriander, ground
- 2 tbsps. balsamic vinegar

Directions: Spread the zucchini on a lined baking sheet and mix it with the other ingredients. Toss and bake at 360°F for 3 hours. Divide into bowls and serve as a snack.

Nutrition: Calories: 99.8; Fats: 2.9g; Carbs: 2.7g; Protein: 4.7g

130. Vegan Fat Bombs

Preparation Time: 15 minutes

Servings: 8

Ingredients:
- 8-oz cream cheese, softened to room temperature
- 1 tsp. kosher salt
- 1 cup keto-friendly dark chocolate chips
- ½ cup keto-friendly peanut butter
- ¼ cup coconut oil, + 2 tbsps

Directions: With parchment paper, line a baking sheet. Mix well salt, coconut oil, peanut butter, and cream cheese in a bowl until combined thoroughly.
Put in the freezer for 15 minutes to firm up. Then with a spoon, roll into golf ball-sized balls. In a microwave-safe cup, melt chocolate in 30-second intervals until melted fully.
With a fork, drizzle melted chocolate all over each ball. Put in a tightly lidded container in the fridge and enjoy as a snack.

Nutrition: Calories: 312.8; Protein: 7.4g; Carbs: 12.1g; Fats: 26.8g

131. Carrot Cake Balls

Preparation Time: 15 minutes

Servings: 15

Ingredients:
- ½ cup coconut flour
- ½ cup + 1 tbsp. water
- 2 tbsps. unsweetened applesauce
- ½ tsp. vanilla extract
- 1 tsp. cinnamon
- 4 tbsps. Lakanto Classic Monkfruit Sweetener

- 1 medium carrot, finely chopped or shredded
- 4 tbsps. reduced-fat shredded coconut

Directions: In a mixing bowl, whisk well vanilla extract, applesauce, water, and coconut flour. Stir in shredded carrots, Lakanto, and cinnamon. Mix well.

Store dough in the fridge for 15 minutes. Place shredded coconut in a bowl. Evenly divide the dough into 15 equal parts and roll into balls.

Roll balls in a bowl of shredded coconut. Store in lidded containers and enjoy as a snack.

Nutrition: Calories: 23.9; Protein: 1.2g; Carbs: 2.8g; Fats: 0.9g

132. Avocado and Tempeh Bacon Wraps

Preparation Time: 10 minutes
Servings: 4

Cooking Time: 8 minutes

Ingredients:
- 2 tbsps. extra-virgin olive oil
- 8 oz. tempeh bacon, homemade or store-bought
- 4 (10-inch) soft flour tortillas or lavash flatbread
- ¼ cup vegan mayonnaise, homemade or store-bought
- 4 large lettuce leaves
- 2 ripe Hass avocados, pitted, peeled, and cut into ¼-inch slices
- 1 large ripe tomato, cut into ¼-inch slices

Directions: Heat-up the oil in a large skillet over medium heat. Add the tempeh bacon and cook until browned on both sides, about 8 minutes. Remove from the heat and set aside.

Place 1 tortilla on a work surface. Spread with some of the mayonnaise and one-fourth of the lettuce and tomatoes.

Thinly slice the avocado and place the slices on top of the tomato. Add the reserved tempeh bacon and roll up tightly. Repeat with remaining ingredients and serve.

Nutrition: Calories: 314.8; Carbs: 21.9g; Fats: 19.9g; Protein: 14.2g

133. Peppers and Hummus

Preparation Time: 15 minutes

Servings: 4

Ingredients:
- One 15 oz. can chickpeas, drained and rinsed
- Juice of 1 lemon, or 1 tbsp. prepared lemon juice
- ¼ cup tahini
- 3 tbsps. extra-virgin olive oil
- ½ tsp. ground cumin
- 1 tbsp. water
- ¼ tsp. paprika
- 1 red bell pepper, sliced
- 1 green bell pepper, sliced
- 1 orange bell pepper, sliced

Directions: Combine chickpeas, lemon juice, tahini, 2 tablespoons of the olive oil, the cumin, and water in a food processor. Process on high speed until blended for about 30 seconds. Scoop the hummus into a bowl and drizzle with the remaining tablespoon of olive oil. Sprinkle with paprika and serve with sliced bell peppers.

Nutrition: Calories: 169.9; Carbs: 12.8g; Fats: 11.8g; Protein: 4.2g

134. Mixed Vegetable

Preparation Time: 5 minutes
Servings: 2

Cooking Time: 20 minutes

Ingredients:
- 1 stick (½ cup) unsalted butter, divided
- 1 large potato, cut into ½-inch dice
- 1 onion, chopped
- ½ tbsp. minced garlic
- 1 cup green beans, chopped
- 2 ears fresh sweet corn, kernels removed
- 1 red bell pepper, seeded and cut into strips
- 2 cups sliced white mushrooms
- Salt
- Freshly ground black pepper

Directions: Warm half of the butter in a large nonstick skillet over medium-high heat. When the butter is frothy, add the potato and cook, stirring frequently, for 15 minutes, until golden. Lower the heat down slightly if the butter begins to burn. Add the rest butter, turn down the heat to medium, and add the onion, garlic, green beans, and corn. Cook, stirring frequently, for 5 minutes.

Add the red bell pepper and mushrooms. Cook for another 5 minutes, and the mushrooms have browned but are still plump. Add more butter, if necessary. Remove from heat and season with pepper and salt. Serve hot.

Nutrition: Calories: 687.9; Fats: 47.9g; Carbs: 62.8g; Fiber: 10.9g; Sugar: 10.9g; Protein: 11.2g

135. Indonesian-Style Spicy Fried Tempeh Strips

Preparation Time: 5 minutes   **Cooking Time: 20 minutes**
Servings: 4

Ingredients:
- *1 cup sesame oil, or as needed*
- *1 (12 oz.) package tempeh, cut into narrow 2-inch strips*
- *2 medium onions, sliced*
- *1 ½ tbsps. tomato paste*
- *3 tsps. tamari or soy sauce*
- *1 tsp. dried red chili flakes*
- *½ tsp. brown sugar*
- *2 tbsps. lime juice*

Directions: Heat the sesame oil in a large wok or saucepan over medium-high heat. Add more sesame oil as needed to raise the level to at least 1 inch.
When the oil is hot, put the tempeh slices and cook, stirring frequently, for 10 minutes.
Add the onions and stir for another 10 minutes, until the tempeh and onions are brown and crispy.
Use a slotted spoon to remove and and add to a large bowl lined with several sheets of paper towel.
While the tempeh and onions are cooking, whisk together the tomato paste, tamari or soy sauce, red chili flakes, brown sugar, and lime juice in a small bowl.
Remove the paper towel from the large bowl and pour the sauce over the tempeh strips. Mix well to coat.

Nutrition: Calories: 316.9; Fats: 22.8g; Carbs: 14.7g; Sugar: 3.9g; Protein: 16.9g

136. Pomegranate Flower Sprouts

Preparation Time: 15 minutes   **Cooking Time: 15 minutes**
Servings: 2

Ingredients:
- *3 tbsp. Pomegranate molasses*
- *150 g Flower sprouts*
- *Vegetable oil for deep-frying*
- *A pinch Sea salt flakes*
- *A pinch Pul Biber*

Directions: Heat the oil in the pan and when enough heat, add flower sprouts
Just fry them for 30 seconds. Add them into the bowl with other ingredients and mix 4. Serve right away.

Nutrition: Calories: 201.8; Fats: 10.9g; Protein: 3.2g; Carbs: 18.7g

137. Sherry Roasted King Trumpet

Preparation Time: 10 minutes   **Cooking Time: 20 minutes**
Servings: 4

Ingredients:
- *1 ½ pounds king trumpet mushrooms, cleaned and sliced in half lengthwise.*
- *2 tablespoons olive oil*
- *4 cloves garlic, minced or chopped*
- *1/2 teaspoon dried rosemary*
- *1/2 teaspoon dried thyme*
- *1/2 teaspoon dried parsley flakes*
- *1 teaspoon Dijon mustard*
- *1/4 cup dry sherry*
- *Sea salt and freshly ground black pepper, to taste*

Directions: Start by preheating your oven to 390 degrees F. Line a large baking pan with parchment paper.
Take a mixing bowl and mix the mushrooms with the remaining ingredients until well coated on all sides.
Place the mushrooms in a single layer on the prepared baking pan.
Roast the mushrooms for approximately 20 minutes, tossing them halfway through the cooking. Bon appétit!

Nutrition: Calories: 137.9; Fats: 7.9g; Carbs: 11.9g; Protein: 6.2g

138. Garlic and Herbs Mushrooms Skillet

Preparation Time: 10 minutes   **Cooking Time: 10 minutes**
Servings: 4

Ingredients:

- 4 tablespoons vegan butter
- 1 ½ pounds oyster mushrooms halved
- 3 cloves garlic, minced
- 1 teaspoon dried oregano
- 1 teaspoon dried rosemary
- 1 teaspoon dried parsley flakes
- 1 teaspoon dried marjoram
- 1/2 cup dry white wine
- Kosher salt and ground black pepper, to taste

Directions: In a sauté pan, heat the olive oil over a moderately high heat.
Now, sauté the mushrooms for 3 minutes or until they release the liquid. Add in the garlic and continue to cook for 30 seconds more or until aromatic.
Stir in the spices and continue sautéing an additional 6 minutes, until your mushrooms are lightly browned.

Nutrition: Calories: 206.8; Fats: 14.8g; Carbs: 11.8g; Protein: 9.1g

139. Baked Brussel Sprouts

Preparation Time: 10 minutes   **Cooking Time: 40 minutes**
Servings: 4

Ingredients:

- 1 pound Brussels sprouts
- 2 teaspoons extra-virgin olive or canola oil
- 4 teaspoons minced garlic (about 4 cloves)
- 1 teaspoon dried oregano
- ½ teaspoon dried rosemary
- ½ teaspoon salt
- ¼ teaspoon freshly ground black pepper
- 1 tablespoon balsamic vinegar

Directions: Preheat the oven to 400ºF.
Cover a rimmed baking sheet with parchment paper. Trim and halve the brussels sprouts. Transfer to a large bowl. Toss with the olive oil, garlic, oregano, rosemary, salt, and pepper to coat well.
Transfer to the prepared baking sheet.
Bake for 35-40 minutes, shaking the pan occasionally to help with even browning, until crisp on the outside and tender on the inside. Take out of oven then, transfer to a large bowl.
Stir in the balsamic vinegar.
Divide the brussels sprouts evenly among 4 single-serving containers. Let it cool before sealing the lids

Nutrition: Calories: 76.8; Fats: 2.8g; Carbs: 11.8g; Protein: 4.1g

140. 3-Ingredient Flatbread

Preparation Time: 10 minutes   **Cooking Time: 25 minutes**
Servings: 5

Ingredients:

- 1 cup tri-color quinoa
- 1½ cups water
- 1 tsp. onion powder

Directions: Before starting, preheat the oven to 400°F.
In a blender, all ingredients. Blend until smooth with no lumps.
Line a baking pan with parchment paper (make sure the pan has a small lip).
Evenly spread the quinoa blend on the baking sheet and put in the oven for 20-25 minutes.
Remove from oven and allow to cool.
Lift the bread out of the pan using the parchment paper and carefully peel bread from paper.

Nutrition: Protein: 17.2g; Fats: 20.8g; Carbs: 61.7

141. Grape Tomatoes and Zucchini

Preparation Time: 5 minutes   **Cooking Time: 10 minutes**
Servings: 2

Ingredients:

- Zucchini, one large cut in spirals

- Basil, fresh, chopped, one tablespoon
- Black pepper, one teaspoon
- Rosemary, one teaspoon
- Salt, one half teaspoon
- Lemon juice, one tablespoon
- Crushed red pepper flakes, one quarter teaspoon
- Grape tomatoes, one cup cut in half
- Garlic, minced, two tablespoons
- Olive oil, one tablespoon

Directions: Fry the minced garlic in the olive oil for one minute. Pour in the pepper, salt, red pepper flakes, and the tomatoes and mix well, then turn the heat lower.
Simmer this mix for fifteen minutes.
Add in the basil, rosemary, and the zucchini spiral noodles and turn the heat back up and cook for two minutes, stirring constantly. Drizzle the lemon juice over all of it and serve.

Nutrition: Calories: 329.8; Fats: 13.9g; Carbs: 24.9g; Protein: 4.2g; Fiber: 9.9g

142. Tofu & Asparagus Stir Fry

Preparation Time: 20 minutes
Servings: 3

Cooking Time: 10 minutes

Ingredients:
- 1 tablespoon ginger, peeled & grated
- 8 ounces firm tofu, chopped into slices
- 4 green onions, sliced thin
- Toasted sesame oil to taste
- 1 bunch asparagus, trimmed & chopped
- 1 handful cashew nuts, chopped & toasted
- 2 tablespoons hoisin sauce
- 1 lime, juiced & zested
- 1 handful mint, fresh & chopped
- 1 handful basil, fresh & chopped
- 3 cloves garlic, chopped
- 3 handfuls spinach, chopped
- Pinch sea salt

Directions: Get out a wok and heat up your oil. Add in your tofu, cooking for a few minutes.
Put your tofu to the side, and then sauté your red pepper flakes, ginger, salt, onions and asparagus for a minute.
Mix in your spinach, garlic, and cashews, cooking for another two minutes.
Add your tofu back in, and then drizzle in your lime juice, lime zest, hoisin sauce, cooking for another half a minute.
Remove it from heat, adding in your mint and basil.

Nutrition: Calories: 279.9; Fats: 7.9g; Carbs: 23.8g; Protein: 22.3g; Fiber:13.7g

143. Asparagus Spears

Preparation Time: 25 minutes
Servings: 4

Cooking Time: 25 minutes

Ingredients:
- 1 bunch asparagus spears (about 12 spears)
- ¼ cup nutritional yeast
- 2 tablespoons hemp seeds
- 1 teaspoon garlic powder
- ¼ teaspoon paprika (or more if you like paprika)
- 1/8 teaspoon ground pepper
- ¼ cup whole-wheat breadcrumbs
- Juice of ½ lemon

Directions: Prepare the oven to 350 degrees, Fahrenheit. Line a baking sheet with parchment paper.
Wash the asparagus, snapping off the white part at the bottom. Save it for making vegetable stock.
Mix together the nutritional yeast, hemp seed, garlic powder, paprika, pepper and breadcrumbs.
Place asparagus spears on the baking sheets giving them a little room in between and sprinkle with the mixture in the bowl. Bake for up to 25 minutes, until crispy.
Serve with lemon juice if desired.

Nutrition: Protein: 30.2g; Fats: 27.9g; Carbs: 41.7g

144. Oregano Tomato and Radish

Preparation time: 10 minutes

Servings: 4

Ingredients:
- 1 cup radishes, halved
- 1 pound cherry tomatoes, halved
- 1 tablespoon lime juice
- 1 tablespoon oregano, chopped
- Salt and black pepper to the taste
- 2 tablespoons parsley, chopped
- 2 tablespoons olive oil
- 1/3 cup black olives, pitted and halved
- Salt and black pepper to the taste

Directions: In a bowl, combine the tomatoes with the radishes and the other ingredients, toss and serve.

Nutrition: Calories: 89.7; Fats: 3.8g; Carbs: 11.8g; Protein: 8.2g; Fiber: 8.8g

145.Pepper & Tomato Bake

Preparation Time: 15 minutes　　　　　　　　　　　　　　　**Cooking Time: 35 minutes**
Servings: 6

Ingredients:

- Herb Sauce
- 4 garlic cloves, chopped
- ½ cup fresh parsley, chopped
- ½ cup fresh basil, chopped
- 3 tablespoons avocado oil
- 2 tablespoons fresh key lime juice
- ½ teaspoon ground cumin
- ½ teaspoon cayenne powder
- Sea salt, as needed
- Veggies
- 2 large red bell peppers, seeded and sliced
- 2 large yellow bell peppers, seeded and sliced
- 1 pound plum tomatoes, cut into 8 wedges
- 2 tablespoons avocado oil

Directions: Preheat your oven to 350ºF. Lightly grease a large shallow baking dish.
For sauce: Add all Ingredients: in a food processor and pulse on high speed until smooth.
In a large bowl, add the bell peppers, sauce, and herb sauce and gently toss to coat.
Place the bell pepper mixture into the prepared baking dish and drizzle with oil.
With a large piece of foil, cover the baking dish. Bake for approximately 35 minutes.
Uncover the baking dish and bake for approximately 20–30 minutes more. Serve hot.

Nutrition: Calories: 60.8; Fats: 0.3g; Carbs: 10.6g; Protein: 2.1g

146.Red Rose Potato Toasts

Preparation Time: 10 minutes　　　　　　　　　　　　　　　**Cooking Time: 15 minutes**
Servings: 7

Ingredients:

- 1 tablespoon avocado oil
- 2 red rose potatoes, sliced
- 1 teaspoon salt

Directions: Prepare the oven to 425 F and line a baking sheet with parchment paper.
Place potato slices on the parchment paper with spaces in between and grease with avocado oil on both sides.
Add salt on top. Cook for 5 minutes, flip and bake for 5 more minutes.

Nutrition: Calories: 103.8; Fats: 7.9g; Carbs: 7.9g; Protein: 2.7g

147.Zucchini Fries

Preparation Time: 5 minutes　　　　　　　　　　　　　　　**Cooking Time: 20 minutes**
Servings: 2

Ingredients:

- 4 medium zucchinis
- 1 teaspoon onion powder
- 1 teaspoon sea salt
- 1 red bell pepper, seeded, diced
- ½ sweet white onion, chopped
- ¼ cup vegetable broth
- ½ cup mushrooms, sliced

Directions: In a medium-sized microwave-safe bowl, microwave the 4 zucchinis for about 4 minutes or until soft. Allow zucchinis to cool.
Add the broth into a large non-stick pan over medium heat, add the red bell pepper and onion. Sauté your vegetables for 5 minutes.
While the vegetables are cooking, slice your zucchinis into quarters.
Add the mushrooms, onion powder, salt, and zucchinis to the pan. Cook your mixture for about 10 minutes or until the zucchinis are crisp. Serve and Enjoy!

Nutrition: Calories: 336.9; Fats: 0.7g; Carbs: 74.2g; Protein: 9.5g

148. Brussels Sprouts & Carrots

Preparation Time: 10 minutes   **Cooking Time: 5 minutes**
Servings: 6

Ingredients:
- 1 ½ lb. Brussels sprouts, trimmed and cut in half
- 4 carrots, peel, and cut in thick slices
- 1 tsp olive oil
- ½ cup filtered alkaline water
- 1 tbsp. dried parsley
- ¼ tsp garlic, chopped
- ¼ tsp pepper
- ¼ tsp sea salt

Directions: Put the ingredients into the instant pot and stir well.
Seal pot with lid and cook on manual high pressure for 2 minutes.
When finished, release pressure using the quick-release method than open the lid. Stir well and serve.

Nutrition: Calories: 72.8; Fats: 1.0g; Carbs: 14.2g; Protein 4.5g

149. Tofu Curry

Preparation Time: 10 minutes   **Cooking Time: 4 hours**
Servings: 4

Ingredients:
- 1 cup firm tofu, diced
- 2 tsp garlic cloves, minced
- 1 onion, chopped
- 8 oz. tomato puree
- 2 cups bell pepper, chopped
- 1 tbsp. garam masala
- 2 tbsp. olive oil
- 1 tbsp. curry powder
- 10 oz. coconut milk
- 1 ½ tsp sea salt

Directions: Add all ingredients except tofu in a blender and blend until smooth.
Pour blended mixture into the instant pot. Add tofu to a pot and stir well to coat.
Seal the pot with the lid and select slow cook mode and set the timer for 4 hours. Stir well and serve.

Nutrition: Calories: 325.8; Fats: 26.8g; Carbs: 18.2g; Protein: 9.2g

150. Rosemary Sweet Potato Chips

Preparation Time: 5 minutes   **Cooking Time: 12 minutes**
Servings: 2

Ingredients:
- 1 teaspoon Cooking oil spray (coconut, sunflower, or safflower)
- 1 small-medium sweet potato, unpeeled, thinly sliced (about 1 cup)
- ¼ teaspoon dried rosemary
- Dash sea salt

Directions: Spray the air fryer basket with oil. Place the sweet potato slices in the basket, spreading them out as much as possible. Spray the tops with oil. Fry for 4 minutes.
Remove the air fryer basket, spray again with oil, and sprinkle the rosemary and sea salt on top of the potato slices. Spray again with oil and fry for another 4 minutes.
Remove the air fryer basket, shake, spray with oil, and fry for another 4 minutes, or until the pieces are lightly browned. Chips may cook at slightly different rates, due to varying thicknesses, so remove any that are done before others that need more time. Also, they will usually crisp up once removed to a plate at room temperature for a minute, so if they look lightly browned, they're probably done. (Better to under-cook at this point—you can always pop them back in the air fryer if they don't crisp up at room temperature.) Continue to cook, checking often, until all of the pieces are browned. Once crisp, you can serve—and continue cooking subsequent batches if you like.

Nutrition: Calories: 80.9; Fats: 0.7g; Carbs: 3.6g; Protein: 0.9g

151. Sunflower Seed Bread

Preparation Time: 15 minutes   **Cooking Time: 18-20 minutes**
Servings: 4

Ingredients:
- 168 g whole wheat flour
- 168 g plain flour
- 96 g sunflower seeds
- 128 g lukewarm water
- ½ sachet instant yeast
- 1 teaspoon salt

Directions: Preheat the Air fryer to 390 o F and grease a cake pan.
Mix together flours, sunflower seeds, yeast and salt in a bowl. Add water slowly and knead for about 5 minutes until a dough is formed.
Cover the dough with a plastic wrap and keep in warm place for about half an hour. Arrange the dough into a cake pan and transfer into an Air fryer basket. Cook for about 18 minutes and dish out to serve warm.

Nutrition: Calories: 127.9; Fat: 1.3g; Carbs: 12.4g; Protein: 4.1g

152. Cheesy Fennel

Preparation Time: 10 minutes   **Cooking Time: 10 minutes**
Servings: 4

Ingredients:
- 2 fennel bulbs, cut into quarters
- 3 tablespoons olive oil
- 1 tbsp Salt and dark pepper to the taste
- 1 garlic clove, minced
- 1 red bean stew pepper, hacked
- 96 g veggie stock
- Juice from ½ lemon
- 32 g white wine
- 32 g parmesan, ground

Directions: Heat up a container that fits the air fryer cooker with the oil over medium high heat, put in garlic and stew pepper, mix and cook for 2 minutes.
Add fennel, salt, pepper, stock, wine, lemon juice, and parmesan, hurl to cover, present in the air fryer cooker and bake at 350 Deg. Fahrenheit for 6 minutes.
Divide among plates and serve immediately. Enjoy the recipe!

Nutrition: Calories: 160.8; Fats: 1.1g; Carbs: 7.2g; Protein: 10.2g

153. Sweetened Onions

Preparation Time: 10 minutes   **Cooking Time: 20 minutes**
Servings: 2

Ingredients:
- 2 large white onions
- 1 tablespoon raw agave
- 1 teaspoon water
- 1 tablespoon paprika

Directions: Peel the onions and using a knife, make cuts in the shape of a cross.
Then combine the raw agave and water; stir. Add the paprika and stir the mixture until smooth.
Place the onions in the air fryer basket and sprinkle them with the agave mixture.
Cook the onions for 16 minutes at 380° F. When the onions are cooked, they should be soft.
Transfer the cooked onions to serving plates and serve.

Nutrition: Calories: 50.8; Fats: 3.2g; Carbs: 1.3g; Protein: 3.4g

154. Baked Vegetables with Cheese and Olives

Preparation Time: 15 minutes   **Cooking Time: 15-20 minutes**
Servings: 4

Ingredients:
- ½ kg cauliflower, cut into 1-inch florets
- ¼ kg zucchini, cut into 1-inch chunks
- 1 red onion, sliced
- 2 bell pepper, cut into 1-inch chunks
- 2 tablespoons extra virgin olives
- 128 g dry white wine vinegar
- 1 teaspoon dried rosemary
- 1 tbsp Salt and pepper to taste
- ½ teaspoon dried basil
- 64 g tomato, pureed
- 64 g cashew cheese
- 100g kalamata olives pitted and halved

Directions: Prepare your Air Fryer to 390 degrees F
Toss vegetables with olive oil, vinegar, rosemary, salt, pepper, and basil until coated

Add pureed tomatoes to a lightly greased baking dish, spread to cover the bottom of the baking dish
Add vegetables and top with cashew cheese, scatter kalamata olives on top
Transfer to Air Fryer and cook for 20 minutes, making sure to shake halfway through

Nutrition: Calories: 190.8; Fats: 2.8g; Carbs: 8.2g; Protein: 4.2g

155. Hasselback Zucchini

Preparation Time: 10 minutes   **Cooking Time: 20 minutes**
Servings: 3

Ingredients:
- Three medium zucchinis
- Three tablespoons olive oil
- Four tablespoons coconut cream
- One tablespoon lemon juice
- Salt and pepper to taste
- Three slices bacon, fried and crumbled

Directions: The air fryer should preheat at 3500F for 5 minutes.
Line up chopsticks on both facets of the zucchini and slice thinly till you hit the stick. Brush the zucchinis with olive
Place the zucchini in the air fryer. Bake for 20 minutes at 3500F.
Meanwhile, combine the coconut cream and lemon juice in a mixing bowl. Season with salt and pepper to taste.
Once the zucchini is cooked, scoop the coconut cream mixture and drizzle on top.
Sprinkle with bacon bits. Serve and enjoy!

Nutrition: Calories: 126.8; Fats: 5.1g; Carbs: 12.5g; Protein: 6.3g

156. Saffron Avocado Cream

Preparation Time: 5 minutes   **Cooking Time: 10 minutes**
Servings: 4

Ingredients:
- 2 avocados, peeled, pitted and cut into wedges
- 1 teaspoon saffron powder
- 1 cup heavy cream
- 2 tablespoons lime juice
- 3 tablespoons sugar

Directions: In your instant pot, mix the avocados with the saffron and the other ingredients, whisk, cover and cook on High for 10 minutes.
Release the pressure fast for 5 minutes, blend the mix using an immersion blender, divide into bowls and serve.

Nutrition: Calories: 209.8; Fats: 10.8; Fiber: 2.1g; Carbs; 8.2g; Protein: 2.7g

157. Turmeric Artichokes

Preparation Time: 5 minutes   **Cooking Time: 15 minutes**
Servings: 4

Ingredients:
- 10 ounces canned artichoke hearts, drained and halved
- A pinch of salt and black pepper
- 2 tablespoons ghee, melted
- 1 teaspoon turmeric powder
- ½ teaspoon cumin, ground
- ½ teaspoon fenugreek leaves, dried

Directions: Set the instant pot on Sauté mode, add the ghee, heat it up, add the artichokes and sauté for 2 minutes. Add the rest of the ingredients, put the lid on and cook on High for 13 minutes.
Release the pressure fast for 5 minutes, divide the artichokes mix between plates and serve.

Nutrition: Calories: 93.8; Fats: 6.5g; Carbs: 8.1g; Protein: 2.8g

158. Garam Masala Asparagus

Preparation Time: 5 minutes   **Cooking Time: 10 minutes**
Servings: 4

Ingredients:
- 1 tablespoon vegetable oil

- ½ teaspoon pepper flakes, crushed
- 1 bunch asparagus, trimmed and halved
- 2 tablespoons almonds, chopped
- ½ tablespoon chili powder
- ½ teaspoon garam masala
- ½ teaspoon coriander, ground
- A pinch of salt and black pepper
- 1 cup vegetarian stock

Directions: Set the instant pot on Sauté mode, add the oil, heat it up, add the pepper flakes, almonds, chili powder, garam masala and the coriander, stir and cook for 2 minutes.
Add the remaining ingredients, toss, put the lid on and cook on High for 8 minutes.
Release the pressure fast for 5 minutes, divide the asparagus between plates and serve.

Nutrition: Calories: 55.9; Fats: 5.1g; Carbs: 1.9g; Protein: 1.5g

159. Walnuts Allspice Bell Peppers

Preparation Time: 10 minutes   **Cooking Time: 20 minutes**
Servings: 4

Ingredients:
- 1 pound red bell peppers, cut into wedges
- ½ cup coconut cream
- ½ teaspoon dry mango powder
- ½ teaspoon allspice, ground
- ½ teaspoon turmeric powder
- 1 bay leaf
- 1 tablespoon walnuts, chopped

Directions: In your instant pot, mix the bell peppers with the cream, mango powder and the rest of the ingredients, cover and cook on High for 20 minutes.
Release the pressure naturally for 10 minutes, divide the mix into bowls and serve.

Nutrition: Calories: 92.8; Fats: 8.2g; Carbs: 4.3g; Protein: 1.7g

160. Gold Potato Masala

Preparation Time: 10 minutes   **Cooking Time: 25 minutes**
Servings: 4
Ingredients:
- 1 pound gold potatoes, peeled and roughly cubed
- 1 teaspoon garam masala
- ½ teaspoon turmeric powder
- ½ teaspoon coriander, ground
- 1 tablespoon ghee, melted
- 4 garlic cloves, minced
- 1 cup seitan stock
- A pinch of salt and black pepper
- 1 tablespoon coriander, chopped

Directions: Set your instant pot on Sauté mode, add the ghee, heat it up, add the garlic, garam masala, turmeric and the ground coriander, stir and cook for 5 minutes.
Add the potatoes and the rest of the ingredients, put the lid on and cook on High for 20 minutes more.
Release the pressure naturally for 10 minutes, divide the mix between plates and serve.

Nutrition: Calories: 112.9; Fats: 3.2g; Carbs: 19.2g; Protein: 2.5g

161. Coriander Broccoli and Onions

Preparation Time: 10 minutes   **Cooking Time: 20 minutes**
Servings: 4

Ingredients:
- 1 pound broccoli florets
- 1 tablespoon sunflower oil
- 1 yellow onion, chopped
- 2 spring onions, chopped
- 1 teaspoon turmeric powder
- ½ teaspoon chili powder
- ½ teaspoon garam masala
- 2 garlic cloves, minced
- 1 cup vegetarian stock
- A pinch of salt and black pepper
- 1 tablespoon coriander, chopped

Directions: Set the instant pot on Sauté mode, add the oil, heat it up, add the onion and spring onions, stir and sauté for 5 minutes.
Add the broccoli, turmeric and the rest of the ingredients except the dill, put the lid on and cook on High for 15 minutes. Release the pressure naturally for 10 minutes, divide the mix between plates and serve.

Nutrition: Calories: 90.8; Fats: 4.1g; Carbs: 11.7g; Protein: 4.2g

162. Cinnamon Potato

Preparation Time: 10 minutes
Servings: 4

Cooking Time: 20 minutes

Ingredients:

- 1 yellow onion, chopped
- 2 tablespoons vegetable oil
- 3 garlic cloves, minced
- 2 pounds gold potatoes, peeled and cubed
- 1 tablespoon cinnamon powder
- ½ teaspoon garam masala
- ½ teaspoon dried mango powder
- A pinch of salt and black pepper
- 1 cup vegetarian stock
- 1 tablespoon cilantro, chopped

Directions: Set the instant pot on Sauté mode, add the oil, heat it up, add the onion, garlic, garam masala and mango powder, stir and sauté for 5 minutes.
Add the potatoes and the rest of the ingredients, put the lid on and cook on High for 15 minutes.
Release the pressure naturally for 10 minutes, divide the mix between plates and serve.

Nutrition: Calories: 209.9; Fats: 5.1g; Carbs: 7.2g; Protein: 4.8g

163. Ginger Zucchinis and Carrots

Preparation Time: 5 minutes
Servings: 4

Cooking Time: 20 minutes

Ingredients:

- 1 pound carrots, sliced
- 2 zucchinis, sliced
- 1 cup vegetarian stock
- ½ teaspoon dried mango powder
- 1 teaspoon chili powder
- 1 teaspoon sweet paprika
- ½ teaspoon ginger, grated
- 3 garlic cloves, minced
- 2 tablespoons ghee, melted
- 1 yellow onion, chopped
- 1 teaspoon cardamom, ground
- A pinch of salt and black pepper

Directions: Set the instant pot on sauté mode, add the ghee, heat it up, add the onion, garlic, mango powder, chili powder and the paprika, and sauté for 5 minutes.
Add the rest of the ingredients, cover and cook on High for 15 minutes.
Release the pressure fast for 5 minutes, stir the mix, divide between plates and serve.

Nutrition: Calories: 99.8; Fats: 5.4g; Carbs: 8.4g; Protein: 1.9g

164. Chinese Orange Tofu

Preparation Time: 20 minutes
Servings: 4

Cooking Time: 10-15 minutes

Ingredients:

- 453 g of extra-firm tofu, drained and pressed (or use super-firm tofu)
- 1 Tablespoon of tamari
- 1 Tablespoon of cornstarch, (or arrowroot powder)
- For the sauce:
- 1 teaspoon of orange zest
- 96 g of orange juice
- 64 g of water
- 2 teaspoons of cornstarch, (or arrowroot powder)
- 1/4 teaspoon of crushed red pepper flakes
- 1 teaspoon of fresh ginger, minced
- 1 teaspoon of fresh garlic, minced
- 1 Tablespoon of pure maple syrup

Directions: Cut the cubed tofu. Place the cubes of tofu in a plastic quarter size storage bag. Place the tamari in and seal the jar. Shake the bag until the tamari is all filled with tofu.
Add the cornstarch spoonful to the bag. Again, shake until coated with tofu. Place the tofu aside to marinate for 15 minutes or more.
In the meantime, add all the ingredients in the sauce to a small bowl and mix with a spoon. Deposit aside. Place the tofu into a single layer in the air fryer. This is probably going to have to be done in two batches.
Cook the tofu for 10 minutes at 390 degrees, and shake after 5 minutes.
Once the tofu batches have been prepared, add them all to a skillet over medium-high heat. Give a stir to the sauce, and pour over the tofu. Remove tofu and sauce until the sauce has thickened, and heat the tofu through.
Serve with rice and steamed vegetables immediately, if you so wish.

Nutrition: Calories: 150.9; Fats: 1.1g; Carbs: 11.5g; Protein: 1.9g

165. Baked Root Vegetables

Preparation Time: 20 minutes   **Cooking Time: 45 minutes**
Servings: 6

Ingredients:
- 32 g olive oil
- 1 head broccoli, cut into florets
- 1 tablespoon dry onion powder
- 2 sweet potatoes, peeled and cubed
- 4 carrots, cut into chunks - 4 zucchinis, sliced thickly
- 1 tbsp salt and pepper to taste

Directions: Prepare the air fryer to 400 F.
In a baking dish that can fit inside the air fryer, mix all the ingredients and bake for 45 minutes and the sides have browned.

Nutrition: Calories: 205.9; Fats: 2.9g; Carbs: 12.1g; Protein: 8.5g

166. Quinoa and Black Bean Lettuce Wraps

Preparation Time: 30 minutes   **Cooking Time: 15 minutes**
Servings: 6

Ingredients:
- 2 tablespoons avocado oil (optional)
- ¼ cup deseeded and chopped bell pepper
- ½ onion, chopped
- 2 tablespoons minced garlic
- 1 teaspoon salt (optional)
- 1 teaspoon pepper (optional)
- ½ cup cooked quinoa
- 1 cup cooked black beans
- ½ cup almond flour
- ½ teaspoon paprika
- ½ teaspoon red pepper flakes
- 6 large lettuce leaves

Directions: Warm 1 tablespoon of the avocado oil (if desired) in a skillet over medium-high heat.
Add the bell peppers, onions, garlic, salt (if desired), and pepper.
Sauté for 5 minutes or until the bell peppers are tender.
Turn off the heat and allow to cool for 10 minutes, then pour the vegetables in a food processor. Add the quinoa, beans, flour. Sprinkle with paprika and red pepper flakes. Pulse until thick and well combined.
Line a baking pan with parchment paper, then shape the mixture into 6 patties with your hands and place on the baking pan.
Put the pan in the freezer for 5 minutes to make the patties firm.
Heat the remaining avocado oil (if desired) in the skillet over high heat.
Add the patties and cook for 6 minutes or until well browned on both sides. Flip the patties halfway through.
Arrange the patties in the lettuce leaves and serve immediately.

Nutrition: Calories: 199.8; Fats: 10.4g; Carbs: 40.2g; Protein: 9.7g; Fiber: 8.1g

167. Pico de Gallo

Preparation Time: 5 minutes   **Servings: 6**

Ingredients:
- 1/2 of a medium red onion, peeled, chopped
- 2 cups diced tomato
- 1/2 cup chopped cilantro
- 1 jalapeno pepper, minced
- 1/8 teaspoon salt
- 1/4 teaspoon ground black pepper
- 1/2 of a lime, juiced
- 1 teaspoon olive oil

Directions: Take a large bowl, place all the ingredients in it and then stir until well mixed.
Serve the Pico de Gallo with chips.

Nutrition: Calories: 789.8; Fats: 6.2g; Protein: 25.8g; Carbs: 195.1g; Fiber: 35.1g

Soups, Stews and Salads

168. Creamy Cauliflower Pakora Soup

Preparation Time: 20 minutes

Cooking Time: 20 minutes

Servings: 8

Ingredients:

- 1 huge head cauliflower, cut into little florets
- 5 medium potatoes, stripped and diced
- 1 huge onion, diced
- 4 medium carrots, stripped and diced
- 2 celery ribs, diced
- 1 container (32 oz.) vegetable stock
- 1 tsp. garam masala
- 1 tsp. garlic powder
- 1 tsp. ground coriander
- 1 tsp. ground turmeric
- 1 tsp. ground cumin
- 1 tsp. pepper
- 1 tsp. salt
- ½ tsp. squashed red pepper chips
- Water or extra vegetable stock
- New cilantro leaves
- Lime wedges, discretionary

Directions: In a Dutch stove over medium-high warmth, heat the initial 14 fixings to the point of boiling. Cook and mix until vegetables are delicate, around 20 minutes. Expel from heat; cool marginally. Procedure in groups in a blender or nourishment processor until smooth. Modify consistency as wanted with water (or extra stock). Sprinkle with new cilantro. Serve hot, with lime wedges whenever wanted.

Stop alternative: Before including cilantro, solidify cooled soup in cooler compartments. To utilize, in part defrost in cooler medium-term.

Warmth through in a pan, blending every so often and including a little water if fundamental. Sprinkle with cilantro. Whenever wanted, present with lime wedges.

Nutrition: Calories: 247.9; Carbs: 6.9g; Protein: 1.2g; Fats: 18.7g

169. Tomato Gazpacho

Preparation Time: 30 minutes

Cooking Time: 55 minutes

Servings: 6

Ingredients:

- 2 tbsps. + 1 tsp. red wine vinegar, divided
- ½ tsp. pepper
- 1 tsp. sea salt
- 1 avocado
- ¼ cup basil, fresh & chopped
- 3 tbsps. + 2 tsps. olive oil, divided
- 1 clove garlic, crushed
- 1 red bell pepper, sliced & seeded
- 1 cucumber, chunked
- 2 ½ lbs. large tomatoes, cored & chopped

Directions: Place half of your cucumber, bell pepper, and ¼ cup of each tomato in a bowl, covering. Set it in the fried.

Puree your remaining tomatoes, cucumber, and bell pepper with garlic, three tablespoons oil, two tablespoons of vinegar, black pepper and sea salt into a blender, blending until smooth. Transfer it to a bowl, and chill for two hours.

Chop the avocado, add it to your chopped vegetables, adding your remaining oil, vinegar, salt, pepper, and basil. Ladle your tomato puree mixture into bowls, and serve with chopped vegetables as a salad.

Interesting Facts: Avocados themselves are ranked within the top five of the healthiest foods on the planet, so you know that the oil produced from them is too. It is loaded with healthy fats and essential fatty acids. Like race bran oil it is perfect to cook with as well! Bonus: Helps in the prevention of diabetes and lowers cholesterol levels.

Nutrition: Calories: 200.9; Protein: 23.1g; Fats: 3.8g; Carbs: 2.1g

170. Cauliflower Asparagus Soup

Preparation Time: 10 minutes

Cooking Time: 30 minutes

Servings: 4

Ingredients:

- 20 asparagus spears, chopped
- 4 cups vegetable stock
- ½ cauliflower head, chopped
- 2 garlic cloves, chopped
- 1 tbsp. coconut oil
- Pepper
- Salt

Directions: In a saucepan, warm coconut oil over medium heat.
Add garlic and sauté until softened. Add cauliflower, vegetable stock, pepper, and salt. Stir well and bring to boil.
Lower heat and cook for 20 minutes and, put chopped asparagus and cook until softened.
Blend the soup using an immersion blender. Stir well and serve warm.

Nutrition: Calories: 297.9; Carbs: 25.8g; Protein: 20.9g; Fats: 8.8g

171. Chickpea and Noodle Soup

Preparation Time: 10 minutes   **Cooking Time: 20 minutes**
Servings: 1 cup

Ingredients:

- 1 freshly diced celery stalk
- ¼ cup of 'chicken' seasoning
- 1 cup of freshly diced onion
- 3 cloves of freshly crushed garlic
- 2 cups of cooked chickpeas
- 4 cups of vegetable broth
- Freshly chopped cilantro
- 2 freshly cubed medium-size potatoes
- Salt
- 2 freshly sliced carrots
- ½ tsp. of dried thyme
- Pepper
- 2 cups of water
- 6 oz. of gluten-free spaghetti

Chicken Seasoning:

- 1 tbsp. of garlic powder
- 2 tsps. of sea salt
- 1 ⅓ cups of nutritional yeast
- 3 tbsps. of onion powder
- 1 tsp. of oregano
- ½ tsp. of turmeric
- 1 ½ tbsps. of dried basil

Directions: Put a pot on medium heat and sauté the onion. It will soften within 3 minutes.
Add celery, potato, and carrots and sauté for another 3 minutes
Add the 'chicken' seasoning to the garlic, thyme, water, and vegetable broth.
Simmer the mix on medium-high heat. Cook the veggies for about 20 minutes until they soften.
Add the cooked pasta and chickpeas. Add salt and pepper to taste.
Put the fresh cilantro on top and enjoy the fresh soup!

Nutrition: Calories: 404.9; Carbs: 0.9g; Protein: 19.2g; Fats: 37.9g

172. Kale and Cauliflower Salad

Preparation Time: 10 minutes   **Cooking Time: 15 minutes**
Servings: 1 portion

Ingredients:

- 6 oz. of Lacinato kale
- 8 oz. of cauliflower florets
- 1 lemon
- 1 tbsp. of Italian spice
- 2 radishes
- 1 oz. of butter beans
- Olive oil
- ¼ cup of walnuts
- ¼ cup of vegan Caesar dressing
- Pepper
- Salt

Directions: Preheat the oven to 400°F. Place the cauliflower florets on a baking sheet, toss them with olive oil and spices, and add salt. Roast the cauliflower until it is brown. It will be done within 15-20 minutes.
De-stem the kale and slice the leaves. Slice the radishes. Both kale and radish should be sliced thinly. Cut the lemon in half.
Place the kale in a large bowl and add the lemon juice and salt along with the pepper. Massage the kale so that it is properly covered with seasoning. The leaves will soon turn dark green. Mix the radishes.
Rinse the butter beans and pat them dry with a towel. On medium-high heat, put a large skillet, add some olive oil, and sauté the butter beans in a layer. Sprinkle some salt on top and shake the pan. The butter beans will be brown in places within 7 minutes.
Take two large plates and divide both the kale and beans equally. Put the walnuts and roasted cauliflower on top.
Add the Caesar dressing on top and enjoy the amazing salad.

Nutrition: Calories: 377.9; Carbs: 10.9g; Protein: 18.2g; Fats: 26.9g

173. Spinach Soup with Dill and Basil

Preparation Time: 10 minutes
Servings: 8

Cooking Time: 25 minutes

Ingredients:
- 1 lb. peeled and diced potatoes
- 1 tbsp. minced garlic
- 1 tsp. dry mustard
- 6 cups vegetable broth
- 20 oz. chopped frozen spinach
- 2 cups chopped onion
- 1 ½ tbsps. salt
- ½ cup minced dill
- 1 cup basil
- ½ tsp. ground black pepper

Directions: Whisk onion, garlic, potatoes, broth, mustard, and salt in a pan and cook it over medium flame.
When it starts boiling, low down the heat and cover it with the lid and cook for 20 minutes.
Add the remaining ingredients in it and blend it and cook it for a few more minutes and serve it.

Nutrition: Carbs: 11.9g; Protein: 13.2g; Fats: 0.9g; Calories: 164.8

174. Cauliflower Spinach Soup

Preparation Time: 30 minutes
Servings: 5

Cooking Time: 25 minutes

Ingredients:
- ½ cup unsweetened coconut milk
- 5 oz fresh spinach, chopped
- 5 watercress, chopped
- 8 cups vegetable stock
- 1 lb. cauliflower, chopped
- Salt

Directions: Add stock and cauliflower in a large saucepan and bring to boil over medium heat for 15 minutes.
Add spinach and watercress and cook for another 10 minutes.
Take off the heat then, blend the soup using a blender until smooth.
Add coconut milk and stir well. Season with salt.
Stir well and serve hot.

Nutrition: Calories: 270.9; Fats: 3.5g; Carbs: 53.8g; Protein: 6.7g

175. Zucchini Soup

Preparation Time: 10 minutes
Servings: 8

Cooking Time: 15 minutes

Ingredients:
- 2 ½ lbs. zucchini, peeled and sliced
- ⅓ cup basil leaves
- 4 cups vegetable stock
- 4 garlic cloves, chopped
- 2 tbsps. olive oil
- 1 medium onion, diced
- Pepper
- Salt

Directions: Warm olive oil over medium-low heat in a pan.
Add zucchini and onion and sauté until softened. Add garlic and sauté for a minute.
Put vegetable stock and simmer for 15 minutes.
Remove from heat. Stir in basil and puree the soup using a blender until smooth and creamy. Season with pepper and salt. Stir well and serve.

Nutrition: Calories: 433.8; Fats: 34.9g; Carbs: 26.8g; Protein: 6.9g

176. Vegetable Stew

Preparation Time: 5 minutes
Servings: 4

Cooking Time: 60 minutes

Ingredients:
- 2 tbsps. olive oil
- 1 medium red onion, chopped
- 1 medium carrot, cut into ¼-inch slices
- ½ cup dry white wine
- 3 medium new potatoes, unpeeled and cut into 1-inch pieces
- 1 medium red bell pepper, cut into ½-inch dice
- 1 ½ cups vegetable broth
- 1 tbsp. minced fresh savory or 1 tsp. dried
- 1 cup frozen peas
- 1 zucchini

- 1 yellow squash
- 1 cup tomatoes
- ½ tsp. black pepper
- ½ tsp. salt
- 1 frozen corn kernels
- 2 tbsps. fresh parsley, chopped
- 1 tsp. dried basil

Directions: Heat the oil over medium heat in a saucepan. Add the onion and carrot, cover, and cook until softened, 7 minutes. Stir in wine and let cook, uncovered, for 5 minutes. Stir in the potatoes, bell pepper, and broth and bring to a boil. Lower heat to medium and simmer for 15 minutes.
Add the zucchini, yellow squash, and tomatoes. Season with black pepper and salt to taste, cover, and simmer until the vegetables are tender, 20 to 30 minutes. Stir in the corn, peas, basil, parsley, and savory. Taste, adjusting seasonings if necessary. Simmer to blend flavors, about 10 minutes more. Serve immediately.

Nutrition: Calories: 218.7; Fats: 4.2g; Carbs: 38.1g; Protein: 6.5g

177.Egg Avocado Salad

Preparation Time: 10 minutes   **Servings: 4**

Ingredients:
- 1 avocado
- 6 hard-boiled eggs, peeled and chopped
- 1 tbsp. mayonnaise
- 2 tbsps. freshly squeezed lemon juice
- ¼ cup celery, chopped
- 2 tbsps. chives, chopped
- Salt and pepper to taste

Directions: Add the avocado to a large bowl. Mash the avocado using a fork.
Stir in the egg and mash the eggs. Add the mayo, lemon juice, celery, chives, salt, and pepper.
Chill in the freezer for at least 30 minutes before serving.

Nutrition: Calories: 223.8; Fats: 17.9g; Carbs: 5.8g; Fiber: 3.4g; Protein: 10.8g

178.Marinated Veggie Salad

Preparation Time: 4 hours and 30 minutes   **Servings: 6**

Ingredients:
- 1 zucchini, sliced
- 4 tomatoes, sliced into wedges
- ¼ cup red onion, sliced thinly
- 1 green bell pepper, sliced
- 2 tbsps. fresh parsley, chopped
- 2 tbsps. red-wine vinegar
- 2 tbsps. olive oil
- 1 clove garlic, minced
- 1 tsp. dried basil
- 2 tbsps. water
- Pine nuts, toasted and chopped

Directions: In a bowl, combine the zucchini, tomatoes, red onion, green bell pepper, and parsley.
Pour the vinegar and oil into a glass jar with a lid.
Add the garlic, basil, and water. Close the jar then shake well to mix.
Pour the dressing into the vegetable mixture. Cover the bowl.
Marinate in the refrigerator for 4 hours. Garnish with the pine nuts before serving.

Nutrition: Calories: 64.8; Fats: 4.3g; Carbs: 5.1g; Fiber 1.1g; Protein: 1.1g

179.Southwest Style Salad

Preparation Time: 10 minutes   **Servings: 3**

Ingredients:
- ½ cup dry black beans
- ½ cup dry chickpeas
- ⅓ cup purple onion, diced
- 1 red bell pepper, pitted, sliced
- 4 cups mixed greens, fresh or frozen, chopped
- 1 cup cherry tomatoes, halved or quartered
- 1 medium avocado, peeled, pitted, and cubed
- 1 cup sweet kernel corn, canned, drained
- ½ tsp. chili powder
- ¼ tsp. cumin
- ¼ tsp. Salt
- ¼ tsp. pepper
- 2 tsp. olive oil
- 1 tbsp. vinegar

Directions: Prepare the black beans and chickpeas according to the method.
Put all of the ingredients into a large bowl.
Toss the mix of veggies and spices until combined thoroughly.
Store, or serve chilled with some olive oil and vinegar on top!

Nutrition: Calories: 634.8; Fats: 19.7g; Carbs: 95.1g; Fiber: 27.9g; Protein: 24.5g

180. Arugula with Fruits and Nuts

Preparation Time: 10 minutes   Servings: 1

Ingredients:

- ½ cup arugula
- ½ peach
- ½ red onion
- ¼ cup blueberries
- 5 walnuts, chopped
- 1 tablespoon extra-virgin olive oil
- 2 tablespoons red wine vinegar
- 1 spring of fresh basil

Directions: Halve the peach and remove the seed. Heat a grill pan and grill it briefly on both sides. Cut the red onion into thin half-rings. Roughly chop the pecans.
Heat a pan and roast the pecans in it until they are fragrant.
Place the arugula on a plate and spread peaches, red onions, blueberries and roasted pecans over it.
Add the ingredients for the dressing in a food processor and mix to an even dressing. Drizzle the dressing over the salad.

Nutrition: Calories: 159.8; Fats: 6.8g; Carbs: 24.9g; Protein: 3.2g

181. Brussels Sprouts and Ricotta Salad

Preparation Time: 15 minutes   Servings: 2

Ingredients:

- 1 (½) cup Brussels sprouts, thinly sliced
- 1 green apple cut "à la julienne"
- ½ red onion
- 8 walnuts, chopped
- 1 teaspoon extra-virgin olive oil
- 1 tablespoon lemon juice
- 1 tablespoon orange juice
- 4 ounces ricotta cheese

Directions: Put the red onion in a cup and cover it with boiling water. Let it rest 10 minutes, then drain and pat with a kitchen paper. Slice Brussels sprouts and cut the apple à la julienne (sticks).
Mix Brussels sprouts, onion and apple, and season them with oil, salt, pepper, lemon juice and orange juice, and spread it on a serving plate.
Spread a small spoonful of ricotta cheese over Brussels sprouts mixture and top with chopped walnuts.

Nutrition: Calories: 352.9; Fats: 4.6g; Carbs: 27.8g; Protein: 28.5g

182. Endive Salad

Preparation Time: 10 minutes   Servings: 1

Ingredients:

- 1/2 red endive
- 1 orange
- 1 tomato
- 1/2 cucumber
- 1/2 red onion
- Olive oil and fresh lemon juice to taste

Directions: Cut off the hard stem of the endive and remove the leaves.
Peel the orange and cut the pulp into wedges. Cut the tomato and cucumber into small pieces. Cut the red onion into thin half-rings.
Place the endive boats on a plate; spread the orange wedges, tomato, cucumber and red onion over the boats.
Sprinkle some olive oil and fresh lemon juice and serve.

Nutrition: Calories: 111.8; Fats: 10.8g; Carbs: 1.9g; Protein: 0g

183. Moroccan Leeks Snack Salad

Preparation Time: 10 minutes   Servings: 4

Ingredients:

- 1 bunch radishes, sliced
- 3 cups leeks, chopped
- 1 (½) cup olive, pitted and sliced
- A pinch of turmeric powder
- 1 cup parsley, chopped
- 2 tablespoons extra-virgin olive oil
- Black pepper to taste

Directions: In a bowl, mix radishes with leeks, olives and parsley. Add black pepper, oil and turmeric, toss to coat and serve.

Nutrition: Calories: 134.9; Fats: 0.9g; Carbs: 17.9g; Protein: 9.2g

184. Roasted Butternut and Chickpeas Salad

Preparation Time: 10 minutes   **Cooking Time: 30 minutes**
Servings: 4

Ingredients:
- 1 cup chickpeas, drained
- 1 pound butternut squash
- 2 cups kale
- 2 tablespoons olive oil
- ½ lemon, juiced
- 2 cloves of garlic
- 2 green apples
- ½ teaspoon honey
- A pinch of salt and pepper

Directions: Heat the oven to 400°F.
Cut the squash into medium cubes, put them in a baking tray, add drained chickpeas, garlic, 1 tablespoon oil, salt and pepper and mix. Cook for 25 minutes.
Mix the kale with the dressing: salt, pepper, lemon, olive oil and honey so that while the squash is cooking, it becomes softer and more pleasant to eat.
When squash and chickpeas are done, put them aside for 10minutes, and in the meantime, chop the apples and mix them with kale. Add squash and chickpeas on top and serve warm.

Nutrition: Calories: 352.8; Fats: 4.5g; Carbs: 27.9g; Protein: 28.5g

185. Sprouts and Apples Snack Salad

Preparation Time: 10 minutes   **Servings: 4**

Ingredients:
- 1 pound Brussels sprouts, shredded
- 1 cup walnuts, chopped
- 1 apple, cored and cubed
- 1 red onion, chopped
- 3 tablespoons red vinegar
- 1 tablespoon mustard
- ½ cup olive oil
- 1 garlic clove, crushed
- Black pepper to taste

Directions: In a salad bowl, mix sprouts with apple, onion and walnuts.
In another bowl, mix vinegar with mustard, oil, garlic and pepper, whisk well, add this to your salad, toss well and serve as a snack.

Nutrition: Calories: 119.8; Fats: 1.9g; Carbs: 7.9g; Protein: 6.2g

186. Avocado with Raspberry Vinegar Salad

Preparation Time: 25 minutes   **Servings: 2**

Ingredients:
- 4 ounces raspberries
- 3 ounces red wine vinegar
- 1 teaspoon extra-virgin olive oil
- 2 firm-ripe avocados
- ¼ cup radicchio

Directions: Place half the raspberries in a bowl. Heat the vinegar in a saucepan until it starts to bubble and then pour it over the raspberries, then leave too steep for 5 minutes.
Strain the raspberries, pressing the fruit gently to extract all the juices but not the pulp.
Whisk the strained raspberry vinegar together with the oils and seasonings and then set aside.
Carefully halve each avocado and twist out the stone.
Remove the skin and cut the flesh straight into the dressing.
Stir gently until the avocados are entirely covered in the dressing.
Cover tightly and then chill in the fridge for 2 hours.
Meanwhile, separate the radicchio leaves, rinse and drain them, and then dry them on kitchen paper. Store in the fridge in a polythene bag. To serve, place a few radicchios leaves on individual plates.
Spoon on the avocado, stir and trim with the remaining raspberries.

Nutrition: Calories: 162.8; Fats: 3.9g; Carbs: 14.8g; Protein: 14.2g

187. Cannellini Pesto Spaghetti

Preparation Time: 5 minutes   **Cooking Time: 10 minutes**
Servings: 4

Ingredients:

- 12 ounces whole-grain spaghetti, cooked, drained and
- kept warm, ½ cup cooking liquid reserved
- 1 cup pesto
- 2 cups cooked cannellini beans, drained and rinsed

Directions: Put the cooked spaghetti in a large bowl and add the pesto.
Add the reserved cooking liquid and beans and toss well to serve.

Nutrition: Calories: 548.8; Protein: 18.5g; Carbs: 44.9g; Fats: 34.8g

188. Kale and Lemon Salad

Preparation Time: 15 minutes   **Cooking Time: 10 minutes**
Servings: 4

Ingredients:

- 5 cups of chopped kale
- 1 teaspoon of minced garlic
- ½ a tablespoon of maple syrup
- 2 tablespoons of lemon juice, freshly squeezed

Directions: Combine the garlic, maple syrup and lemon juice in a large bowl and whisk to combine.
Add the kale and massage the dressing into it for two minutes before serving.

Nutrition: Calories: 215.8; Fats: 11.9g; Carbs: 66.2g; Protein: 6.8g

189. Cauliflower Carrot Soup

Preparation Time: 10 minutes   **Cooking Time: 25 minutes**
Servings: 8

Ingredients:

- 1 cauliflower head, chopped
- 8 cups vegetable broth
- 1 onion, diced
- 4 carrots, shredded
- ½ tsp turmeric powder
- ½ tbsp ginger, grated
- 5 oz coconut milk
- 1 tbsp olive oil
- 1 tbsp curry powder
- Pepper
- Salt

Directions: Warm oil in a saucepan over medium heat.
Add onion and sauté for 5 minutes. Add cauliflower, carrots, and broth and bring to boil.
Turn heat to medium-low and simmer until vegetables are softened.
Add curry powder, turmeric, and ginger and stir well. Puree the soup using a blender until smooth.
Add coconut milk and stir well. Season with pepper and salt.

Nutrition: Calories: 124.8; Fats: 7.2g; Carbs: 8.5g; Fiber: 2.5g; Sugar: 4.1g; Protein: 6.7g

190. Creamy Potato Soup

Preparation Time: 5 minutes   **Cooking Time: 15 minutes**
Servings: 6-7

Ingredients:

- 4-5 medium potatoes, peeled and diced
- 2 carrots, chopped
- 1 zucchini, chopped
- 1 celery rib, chopped
- 5 cups water
- 3 tbsp olive oil
- ½ tsp dried rosemary
- Salt and black pepper, to taste
- 1/2 cup fresh parsley, finely cut

Directions: In a deep soup pot, heat olive oil over medium heat and sauté the vegetables and rosemary for 2-3 minutes. Add in 4 cups of water and bring the soup to a boil then lower heat and cook until all the vegetables are tender. Blend soup in a blender until smooth. Serve warm, seasoned with black pepper and fresh parsley sprinkled over each serving.

Nutrition: Calories: 259.8; Fats: 7.9g; Carbs: 34.8g; Protein: 9.2g; Fiber:8.7g

191. Lemony Capers, Kale and Nuts Salad

Preparation Time: 10 minutes   **Servings: 4**

Ingredients:

- 1 tablespoon capers, drained and chopped
- 2 cups baby kale
- 1 tablespoon balsamic vinegar
- 1 teaspoon lemon zest, grated
- 1 tablespoon lemon juice
- 2 tablespoons walnuts, chopped
- 2 tablespoons almond, chopped
- 1 tablespoon olive oil
- 1 teaspoon parsley, chopped
- Salt and black pepper to the taste

Directions: In a salad bowl, combine the kale with the capers, lemon zest and juice and the other ingredients, toss and serve.

Nutrition: Calories: 139.8; Fats: 8.8g; Carbs: 11.8g; Protein: 8.1g; Fiber: 9.8g

192. Chickpeas & Squash Stew

Preparation Time: 15 minutes
Servings: 4

Cooking Time: 1¼ hours

Ingredients:

- 2 tablespoons avocado oil
- 1 large white onion, chopped
- 4 garlic cloves, minced
- ½ tablespoon cayenne powder
- 4 large plum tomatoes, seeded and chopped finely
- 1 pound butternut squash; peeled, seeded, and chopped
- 1½ cups spring water
- 1 cup cooked chickpeas
- 2 tablespoons fresh key lime juice
- Sea salt, as needed
- 2 tablespoons fresh parsley, chopped

Directions: In a soup pan, heat the avocado oil over medium heat and sauté the onion for about 4–6 minutes.
Add the garlic and cayenne powder and sauté for about 1 minute.
Add the tomatoes and cook for about 2–3 minutes. Put the squash and water then, bring to a boil.
Now, adjust the heat to low and simmer, covered for about 50 minutes.
Add the chickpeas and cook for about 10 minutes.
Stir in lime juice and salt and remove from heat.
Serve hot with the garnishing of parsley.

Nutrition: Calories: 149.8; Fats: 0.3g; Carbs: 21.3g; Protein 5.4g

193. Quinoa & Veggie Stew

Preparation Time: 15 minutes
Servings: 4

Cooking Time: 1 hour

Ingredients:

- 2 tablespoons grapeseed oil
- 1 large onion, chopped
- Sea salt, as needed
- 2 cups butternut squash, peeled and cubed
- 3 garlic cloves, minced
- 1 teaspoon ground cumin
- 1 teaspoon cayenne powder
- 2½ cups plum tomatoes, chopped finely
- ½ cup dry quinoa, rinsed
- 3 cups spring water
- 3 cups fresh kale, tough ribs removed and chopped
- 1 tablespoon fresh key lime juice

Directions: In a soup pan, heat the grapeseed oil over medium heat and cook the onion with few pinches of salt for about 4–5 minutes, stirring occasionally. Add the butternut squash and cook for about 3–4 minutes.
Combine the spices and garlic and cook for about 1 minute.
Stir in the tomatoes, quinoa, and water and bring to a boil. Now, adjust the heat to low and simmer, covered for about 35 minutes.
Stir in the kale and cook for about 10 minutes.

Nutrition: Calories: 236.8; Fats: 0.8g; Carbs: 35.8g; Protein: 7.1g

194. Millet Tabbouleh, Lime and Cilantro

Preparation Time: 15 minutes
Servings: 6

Cooking Time: 20 minutes

Ingredients:

- ½ cup lime juice
- ½ cup Cilantro (chopped)
- 5-6 drops Hot sauce (Tabasco)
- ¼ cup Olive oil (and 2 teaspoons divided)

- *2 tomatoes (diced)*
- *2 bunches green onions*
- *2 cucumber (peeled, seeded and juiced)*
- *1 cup millet (rinsed and drained)*

Directions: Put oil in a saucepan and heat up over medium heat.

Add the millet and fry until it begins to smell fragrant (this takes between 3 to 4 minutes).

Put about 6 cups of water and bring to boil.

Wait for about 15 minutes. Turn off the heat, wash and rinse under cold water.

Drain the millet and transfer it to a large bowl.

Add cucumbers, tomatoes, lime juice, cilantro, green onions, the ¼ cup oil, and hot sauce.

Season with pepper and salt to taste.

Nutrition: Calories: 199.8; Fats: 7.9g; Carbs: 7.9g; Protein: 6.2g

195. Grilled Lettuce Salad

Preparation Time: 10 minutes
Servings: 4

Cooking Time: 10 minutes

Ingredients:
- *2 small heads of romaine lettuce, cut in half*
- *1 tablespoon chopped basil*
- *1 tablespoon chopped red onion*
- *¼ teaspoon onion powder*
- *½ tablespoon agave syrup*

Extra:
- *½ teaspoon salt*
- *¼ teaspoon cayenne pepper*
- *2 tablespoons olive oil*
- *1 tablespoon key lime juice*

Directions: Take a large skillet pan, place it over medium heat and when warmed, arrange lettuce heads in it, cut-side down, and then cook for 4 to 5 minutes per side until golden brown on both sides.

When done, transfer lettuce heads to a plate and then let them cool for 5 minutes.

Meanwhile, prepare the dressing and for this, place remaining ingredients in a small bowl and then stir until combined. Drizzle the dressing over lettuce heads.

Nutrition: Calories: 129.8; Fats: 1.8g; Protein: 2.1g; Carbs: 23.8g

196. Scallion and Mint Soup

Preparation Time: 5 minutes
Servings: 4
Ingredients:

Cooking Time: 15 minutes

- *6 cups vegetable broth*
- *¼ cup fresh mint leaves, roughly chopped*
- *¼ cup chopped scallions, white and green parts 3 garlic cloves, minced*
- *3 tablespoons freshly squeezed lime juice*

Directions: Mix the mint, scallions, broth, garlic and lime juice in a stockpot. Bring to a boil over medium-high heat. Cover and lower the heat then, bake for 15 minutes and serve.

Nutrition: Calories: 54.8; Protein: 5.2g; Carbs: 4.9g; Fats: 1.9g

197. Rainbow Mango Salad

Preparation Time: 10 minutes

Servings: 2

Ingredients:
- *1 mango, peeled, destoned, cubed*
- *¼ of onion, chopped*
- *½ cup cherry tomatoes halved*
- *½ of cucumber, deseeded, sliced*
- *½ of green bell pepper, deseeded, sliced*

Extra:
- *1/3 teaspoon salt*
- *¼ teaspoon cayenne pepper*
- *¼ of key lime, juiced*

Directions: Take a medium bowl, place the mango pieces in it, add onion, tomatoes, cucumber, and bell pepper, and then drizzle with lime juice.

Season with salt and cayenne pepper, toss until combined, and let the salad rest in the refrigerator for a minimum of 20 minutes.

Nutrition: Calories: 107.9; Fats: 0.4g; Protein: 1.2g; Carbs: 27.9g

198. Dandelion Salad

Preparation Time: 10 minutes   **Cooking Time: 7 minutes**
Servings: 2

Ingredients:
- ½ of onion, peeled, sliced
- Five strawberries, sliced
- 2 cups dandelion greens, rinsed
- 1 tablespoon key lime juice
- 1 tablespoon grapeseed oil

Extra:
- ¼ teaspoon salt

Directions: Take a medium skillet pan, place it over medium heat, add oil and let it heat until warm.
Add onion, season with 1/8 teaspoon salt, stir until mixed and then cook for 3 to 5 minutes until tender and golden brown. Meanwhile, take a small bowl, place slices of strawberries in it, drizzle with ½ tablespoon lime juice and then toss until coated.
When onions have turned golden brown, stir in remaining lime juice, stir until mixed, and then cook for 1 minute. Remove pan from heat, transfer onions into a large salad bowl, add strawberries and juices and dandelion greens, and then sprinkle with the remaining salt. Toss until mixed and then serve.

Nutrition: Calories: 203.9; Fats: 15.9g; Protein: 7.2g; Carbs: 10.2g

199. Amaranth Tabbouleh Salad

Preparation Time: 5 minutes   **Cooking Time: 10 minutes**
Servings: 2

Ingredients:
- 1 small white onion, peeled, chopped
- 1 cup cooked amaranth
- ½ of cucumber, deseeded, chopped
- 1 cup cooked chickpeas
- ½ of medium red bell pepper, chopped

Extra:
- 1/3 teaspoon sea salt
- 1/8 teaspoon cayenne pepper
- 2 tablespoons key lime juice

Directions: Take a small bowl, place lime juice in it, add salt and stir until combined.
Place remaining Ingredients: in a salad bowl, drizzle with lime juice mixture, toss until mixed, and then serve.

Nutrition: Calories: 213.8; Fats: 4.2g; Protein: 6.7g; Carbs: 36.8g

200. Cherry Tomato & Kale Salad

Preparation Time: 10 minutes   **Servings: 2**

Ingredients:
- 2 tbsps. Ranch dressing
- 2 cups organic baby tomatoes
- 1 bunch kale, stemmed, leaves washed and chopped

Directions: Put the ingredients in a bowl. Divide the salad equally into two servings dishes. Serve.

Nutrition: Calories: 57.9; Fats: 6.5g; Carbs: 1.4g; Protein: 1.3g

201. Avocado Power Salad

Preparation Time: 10 minutes   **Servings: 2**

Ingredients:
- 1 cubed avocado
- 1 cup cooled cooked quinoa
- 1 tbsp. freshly squeezed Seville orange juice
- 1 tsp. sea salt
- 1 tbsp. onion powder
- 1 tbsp. onion powder
- 1/4 cup chopped cilantro
- 1 cup peeled and diced cucumber
- 1 cup halved cherry tomatoes
- 5oz. fresh and roughly chopped kale

Directions: Mix all the ingredients. Keep the mixture in the fridge to chill for about 15 minutes. Serve.

Nutrition: Calories: 432.8; Fats: 14.6g; Carbs: 63.4g; Protein: 13.9g

202. Warm Kale Salad

Preparation Time: 5 minutes
Servings: 2

Cooking Time: 2 minutes

Ingredients:
- 1 tbsp. sesame oil
- 1/2 cup toasted and chopped coconuts
- 6 oz. package baby Kale leaves
- 1 cup chopped shiitake mushrooms
- 1 tsp. sea salt
- 1 tbsp. cider vinegar
- Water

Directions: In a bowl, mix the coconuts and Kale.
In a saucepan set over medium heat, mix in the sesame oil, mushrooms, salt, and cider vinegar.
Cook for 5 minutes then add water as it is absorbed.
Drizzle the mushroom dressing over the Kale then toss to mix them. Serve.

Nutrition: Calories: 270.9; Fats: 19.2g; Carbs: 20.1g; Protein: 10.5g

203. Creamy Asparagus Soup

Preparation Time: 10 minutes
Servings: 6

Cooking Time: 40 minutes

Ingredients:
- 2 lbs. fresh asparagus, cut off woody stems
- ¼ tsp lime zest
- 2 tbsp. lime juice
- 14 oz. coconut milk
- 1 tsp dried thyme
- ½ tsp oregano
- ½ tsp sage
- 1 ½ cups filtered alkaline water
- 1 cauliflower head, cut into florets
- 1 tbsp. garlic, minced
- 1 leek, sliced
- 3 tbsp. coconut oil
- Pinch of Himalayan salt

Directions: Prepare the oven to 400 F/ 200 C.
Line baking tray with parchment paper and set aside.
Arrange asparagus spears on a baking tray. Drizzle with 2 tablespoons of coconut oil and sprinkle with salt, hyme, oregano, and sage. Bake in preheated oven for 20-25 minutes.
Add remaining oil in the instant pot and set the pot on sauté mode.
Add garlic and leek to the pot and sauté for 2-3 minutes. Add cauliflower florets and water in the pot and stir well.
Seal pot with a lid and select steam mode and set timer for 4 minutes.
When finished, release pressure using the quick-release method.
Add roasted asparagus, lime zest, lime juice, and coconut milk and stir well.
Blend the soup using an immersion blender until smooth. Serve and enjoy.

Nutrition: Calories: 264.9; Fats: 22.7g; Carbs: 14.5g; Protein: 6.3g

204. Apple & Kale Salad

Preparation Time: 15 minutes
Servings: 4

Cooking Time: 15 minutes

Ingredients:
- 3 large apples, cored and sliced
- 6 cups fresh baby kale
- ¼ cup walnuts, chopped
- 2 tablespoons olive oil
- 1 tablespoon agave nectar
- Sea salt, as needed

Directions: In a salad bowl, place all Ingredients: and toss to coat well. Serve immediately.

Nutrition: Calories: 259.9; Fats: 1.2g; Carbs: 38.1g; Protein: 5.4g

205. Zucchini & Tomato Salad

Preparation Time: 15 minutes
Servings: 4

Cooking Time: 15 minutes

Ingredients:
- Two medium zucchinis, sliced thinly
- 2 cups plum tomatoes, sliced
- 2 tablespoons olive oil
- 2 tablespoons fresh key lime juice

- *Pinch of sea salt*

Directions: In a salad bowl, place all Ingredients: and gently toss to combine. Serve immediately.

Nutrition: Calories: 92.8; Fats: 0.9g; Carbs: 6.5g; Protein: 2.1g

206. Chickpeas & Quinoa Salad

Preparation Time: 20 minutes   **Cooking Time: 20 minutes**
Servings: 8

Ingredients:
- *1¾ cups spring water*
- *1 cup quinoa, rinsed*
- *Sea salt, as needed*
- *2 cups cooked chickpeas*
- *1 medium red bell pepper, seeded and chopped*
- *1 medium green bell pepper, seeded and chopped*
- *2 large cucumbers, chopped*
- *½ cup onion, chopped*
- *3 tablespoons olive oil*
- *4 tablespoons fresh basil leaves, chopped*

Directions: In a pan, add the water over high heat and bring to a boil.
Add the quinoa and salt and cook until boiling.
Now, adjust the heat to low and simmer, covered for about 15–20 minutes or until all the liquid is absorbed.
Remove from the heat and set aside, covered for about 10 minutes.
Uncover and with a fork, fluff the quinoa.
In a salad bowl, place quinoa with the remaining Ingredients: and gently toss to coat. Serve immediately.

Nutrition: Calories: 214.8; Fats: 0.8g; Carbs: 30.2g; Protein: 7.6g

207. Basil and Avocado Salad

Preparation Time: 10 minutes   **Servings: 2**

Ingredients:
- *½ cup avocado, peeled, pitted, chopped*
- *½ cup basil leaves*
- *½ cup cherry tomatoes*
- *2 cups cooked spelt noodles*

Extra:
- *1 teaspoon agave syrup*
- *1 tablespoon key lime juice*
- *2 tablespoons olive oil*

Directions: Take a large bowl, place pasta in it, add tomato, avocado, and basil in it and then stir until mixed.
Take a small bowl, add agave syrup and salt in it, pour in lime juice and olive oil, and then whisk until combined.
Pour lime juice mixture over pasta, toss until combined, and then serve.

Nutrition: Calories: 386.8; Fats: 16.3g; Protein: 9.6g; Carbs: 54.1g

208. Dandelion and Strawberry Salad

Preparation Time: 10 minutes   **Cooking Time: 7 minutes**
Servings: 2

Ingredients:
- *½ of onion, peeled, sliced*
- *5 strawberries, sliced*
- *2 cups dandelion greens, rinsed*
- *1 tablespoon key lime juice*
- *1 tablespoon grapeseed oil*

Extra:
- *¼ teaspoon salt*

Directions: Take a medium skillet pan, place it over medium heat, add oil and let it heat until warm.
Add onion, season with 1/8 teaspoon salt, stir until mixed, and then cook for 3 to 5 minutes until tender and golden brown. Meanwhile, take a small bowl, place slices of strawberries in it, drizzle with ½ tablespoon lime juice and then toss until coated.
When onions have turned golden brown, stir in remaining lime juice, stir until mixed, and then cook for 1 minute. Remove pan from heat, transfer onions into a large salad bowl, add strawberries along with their juices and dandelion greens and then sprinkle with remaining salt. Toss until mixed and then serve.

Nutrition: Calories: 203.8; Fats: 15.9g; Protein: 7.2g; Carbs: 10.3g

209. Mango Salad

Preparation Time: 10 minutes   **Servings: 2**

Ingredients:
- 1 mango, peeled, destoned, cubed
- ¼ of onion, chopped
- ½ cup cherry tomatoes, halved
- ½ of cucumber, deseeded, sliced
- ½ of green bell pepper, deseeded, sliced

Extra:
- 1/3 teaspoon salt
- ¼ teaspoon cayenne pepper
- ¼ of key lime, juiced

Directions: Take a medium bowl, place the mango pieces in it, add onion, tomatoes, cucumber, and bell pepper and then drizzle with lime juice.
Season with salt and cayenne pepper, toss until combined, and let the salad rest in the refrigerator for a minimum of 20 minutes.

Nutrition: Calories: 107.9; Fats: 0.4g; Protein: 1.2g; Carbs: 27.9g

210. Corn and Egg Salad

Preparation Time: 60 minutes   **Cooking Time: 40 minutes**
Servings: 8

Ingredients:
- 6 flax Eggs
- 3 ears of Corn cut into smaller pieces
- 2 teaspoons of Canola or Vegetable Oil
- 1 tbsp Salt and Pepper to taste
- 32 g of sliced Red Onion
- 64 g of julienned Carrots
- 64 g of julienned Red Bell Pepper
- 64 g of julienned Green Pepper

Dressing:
- 128 g of Mayonnaise
- 1 tablespoon of Yellow or Dijon Mustard
- 1 teaspoon of Maple Syrup or Agave
- 1 tbsp Salt and Pepper to taste

Directions: Place the trivet in the basket of your air fryer. Stir the eggs in. Air-fry at 250 F for 20 minutes.
Submerge the eggs in an ice bath as soon as the fryer beeps, using tongs.
Then, cut and dice them into large chunks.
Cut the corn cobs into small pieces in the air fryer to fit them in.
Coat the corns in vegetable oil and sprinkle salt and pepper over them.
Fry air for 10 minutes at 400, then flip once.
Once the corn is finished and slightly cooled, the kernels are carefully cut out from the cob using a knife.
Combine the air-fried corn kernels, the diced eggs, sliced onions, and julienned carrots, red and green peppers, in a large bowl. Good shoot it. The mayonnaise, mustard, maple syrup, salt, and pepper are mixed in a small bowl. Whisk to merge. Attach egg and corn salad to the dressing and toss to blend properly.
Cover and let the flavors evolve for about an hour chill.
Serve with grilled meat as a hand. Refrigerate the leftovers right away.

Nutrition: Calories: 175.8; Fats: 4.2g; Carbs: 31.6g; Protein: 9.7g

211. Noodle Vegetable Salad

Preparation Time: 30 minutes   **Cooking Time: 20 minutes**
Servings: 3

Ingredients:
- 1 carrot, sliced thinly
- 128 g cabbage, sliced thinly
- 1 green bell pepper, sliced thinly
- 1 onion, sliced thinly
- 1 package wheat noodles
- 1 sprig coriander, chopped
- 1 tablespoon cooking oil
- 1 tablespoon lime juice
- 1 tablespoon red chili sauce
- 1 tablespoon tamari
- 1 tomato, chopped
- 1 tbsp salt to taste

Directions: In a big pot, boil water and add a teaspoon of salt. Bring the water to a boil and add the noodles. Boil the noodles until it is half-cooked. Drain.
In a mixing bowl, pour oil over the noodles and mix until the noodles are coated evenly.
Place a tin foil on the base of the air fryer basket and place the noodles inside.

Cook in a preheated air fryer at 3950F for 15 to 20 minutes or until crisp.

Meanwhile, mix together the tamari, red chili sauce, and lime juice. Season with salt and pepper to taste.

Once the noodles are cooked, assemble the salad by placing the air fried noodles in a bowl. Add the vegetables and pour over sauce.

Nutrition: Calories: 350.8; Fats: 4.7g; Protein: 11.3g; Carbs: 45.7g

212.Creamy Parsnip Soup

Preparation Time: 5 minutes   **Cooking Time: 30 minutes**
Servings: 4-5

Ingredients:
- Six slices bacon
- Five parsnips, peeled and chopped
- 1/2 onion, chopped
- One small celery stalk, chopped
- One small potato, peeled and chopped
- Two garlic cloves, minced
- 512 g vegetable broth
- 2 tbsp extra virgin olive oil
- 1 tsp salt
- 1 tbsp black pepper, to serve
- 1 tbsp fresh thyme leaves, to serve
- 128 g croutons, to serve

Directions: Cook bacon until crisp in a skillet. Drain on paper towels; put aside. Coarsely chop bacon and place it in a microwave-safe plate. Drizzle bacon with agave; cover with wrapping. Just before serving, cook within the microwave for 30 seconds.

Heat olive oil in air fryer and gently sauté the onion, celery, and garlic until fragrant. Stir in vegetable broth, parsnips and salt, and bring to the boil.

Reduce heat and simmer for 30 minutes. Set aside to cool and blend until smooth. Garnish with croutons, fresh thyme, and chopped bacon.

Nutrition: Calories: 250.7; Fats: 4.1g; Carbs: 13.9g; Protein: 21.6g

213.Mexican Bean Salad

Preparation Time: 15 minutes   **Servings: 8**

Ingredients:
- 1 (15 ounce) can black beans, rinsed and drained
- 1 tablespoon lemon juice
- 1 (15 ounce) can kidney beans, drained
- 2 tablespoons white sugar
- 1 (15 ounce) can cannellini beans, drained and rinsed
- 1 tablespoon salt
- 1 green bell pepper, chopped
- 1 clove crushed garlic
- 1 red bell pepper, chopped
- 1/4 cup chopped fresh cilantro
- 1 (10 ounce) package frozen corn kernels
- 1/2 tablespoon ground cumin
- 1 red onion, chopped
- 1/2 tablespoon ground black pepper
- 1/2 cup olive oil
- 1 dash hot pepper sauce
- 1/2 cup red wine vinegar
- 1/2 teaspoon chili powder
- 2 tablespoons fresh lime juice

Directions: Mix bell peppers, red onion, beans, and frozen corn in a large bowl.

In a other bowl, whisk together lime juice, sugar, olive oil, cilantro, black pepper, lemon juice, salt, garlic, cumin, and red wine vinegar. Season with hot sauce and chili powder.

Pour olive oil dressing over vegetables; mix well. Chill thoroughly, and serve cold.

Nutrition: Calories: 333.2; Carbs: 41.5g; Fats: 14.5g; Protein: 11.4g

214.Roasted Potato Salad

Preparation Time: 30 minutes   **Cooking Time: 25-30 minutes**
Servings: 4

Ingredients:
- 2 kg tiny red or creamer potatoes, cut in half
- 1 tablespoon plus 42 g olive oil
- Pinch salt
- 1 tbsp Freshly ground black pepper
- 1 red bell pepper, chopped
- 2 green onions, chopped - 42 g lemon juice
- 3 tablespoons Dijon or yellow mustard

Directions: Set to 350 F. Roast. Place the potatoes in the air fryer basket and drizzle with 1 tablespoon of the olive oil. Sprinkle with salt and pepper.

Roast for 25 minutes, shaking twice during cooking time, until the potatoes are tender and light golden brown.

Meanwhile, place the bell pepper and green onions in a large bowl. In a small bowl, combine the remaining 42 g of olive oil, the lemon juice, and mustard, and mix well with a whisk. When the potatoes are ready, add them to the bowl with the bell peppers and top with the dressing. Toss gently to coat. Let cool for 20 minutes. Stir gently again and serve or refrigerate and serve later.

Nutrition: Calories: 116.8; Fats: 2.3g; Carbs: 9.1g; Protein: 2.2g

215. Avocado Salad

Preparation Time: 10 minutes   **Cooking Time: 5 minutes**
Servings: 4

Ingredients:
- 1 avocado, finely chopped
- 3 tablespoons boiled corn
- 1 tomato, thinly chopped
- 1 tablespoon extra-virgin olive oil
- Salt to taste
- 1 tablespoon lemon juice
- 3 green onions, chopped

Directions: In a large bowl, whisk in chopped avocado and lemon juice.
In the same bowl, mix it with other ingredients, except for tomato.
Serve on slices of bread with sliced tomatoes.

Nutrition: Calories: 163.9; Fats: 11.5g; Carbs: 11.3g; Protein: 5.6g

216. Cabbage Mango Slaw

Preparation Time: 10 minutes   **Serves: 6**

Ingredients:
- 3 cups cabbage, shredded
- 1 large mango, pitted and cubed
- ½ cup cilantro, chopped
- ¼ cup red onion, diced
- 1 jalapeño, chopped
- 2 teaspoons olive oil
- 1 orange, zest and juice
- 1 lime juice
- ½ teaspoon salt

Direction: Mix shredded cabbage with mango and the rest of the ingredients in a salad bowl. Serve.

Nutrition: Calories: 279.9; Fats: 7.9g; Carbs: 25.8g; Fiber: 0.8g; Sugar: 1.8g; Protein: 2.1g

217. Kohlrabi Slaw with Cilantro

Preparation Time: 10 minutes   **Servings: 6**

Ingredients:
- 6 cups kohlrabi, cut into matchsticks
- ½ cup cilantro, chopped
- ½ jalapeño, minced
- ¼ cup scallion, chopped
- Zest from 1 orange
- Juice from 1 orange
- Zest and juice from 1 lime
- Citrus Dressing:
- ¼ cup olive oil
- ¼ cup orange juice
- 1/8 cup lime juice
- ¼ cup honey
- ½ teaspoon kosher salt
- 1 tablespoon rice wine vinegar

Directions: Mix all the citrus dressing ingredients in a salad bowl.
Toss in kohlrabi and the rest of the ingredients, then mix well. Serve.

Nutrition: Calories: 333.8; Fats: 15.8g; Carbs: 2.8g; Fiber: 0.3g; Sugar: 2.9g; Protein: 3.5g

218. Butternut Squash Chickpea Stew

Preparation Time: 15 minutes   **Cooking Time: 21 minutes**
Servings: 6

Ingredients:
- 1 tablespoon olive oil
- 1 medium white onion, chopped
- 6 garlic cloves, minced
- 2 teaspoons cumin
- 1 teaspoon cinnamon
- 1 teaspoon ground turmeric
- ¼ teaspoon cayenne pepper
- 1 (28-ounce) can crushed tomatoes
- 2½ cups vegetable broth
- 1 (15-ounce) can chickpeas, rinsed
- 4 cups butternut squash, cubed
- 1 cup green lentils, rinsed
- ½ teaspoon salt
- Black pepper, to taste
- fresh juice of ½ lemon
- 1/3 cup cilantro, chopped

- *Basil leaves, chopped*

Direction: Sauté garlic and onion with oil in a suitable pot over medium high heat for 5 minutes.
Stir in cayenne, turmeric, cinnamon and cumin then sauté for 30 seconds.
Add black pepper, salt, lentils. Butternut squash, chickpeas, broth and tomatoes.
Cook to a boil, reduce its heat then cover and cook for 20 minutes.
Add basil, cilantro and lemon juice. Serve warm.

Nutrition: Calories: 323.9; Fats: 4.9g; Carbs: 30.8g; Fiber: 0.3g; Sugar: 0.9g; Protein: 5.9g

Legumes, Grains, Beans and Rice

219. Brown Lentil Bowl

Preparation Time: 10 minutes
Servings: 4

Cooking Time: 30 minutes

Ingredients:

- 1 cup brown lentils, soaked overnight, and drained
- 3 cups water
- 2 cups brown rice, cooked
- 1 zucchini, diced
- 1 red onion, chopped
- 1 tsp. garlic, minced
- 1 cucumber, sliced
- 1 bell pepper, sliced
- 4 tbsps. olive oil
- 1 tbsp. rice vinegar
- 2 tbsps. lemon juice
- 2 tbsps. soy sauce
- ½ tsp. dried oregano
- ½ tsp. ground cumin
- Sea salt and ground black pepper, to taste
- 2 cups arugula
- 2 cups Romaine lettuce, torn into pieces

Directions: Add the brown lentils and water to a saucepan and bring to a boil over high heat then, lower the heat and continue to cook for 20 minutes. Put the lentils in a salad bowl and let them cool completely.
Add in the remaining ingredients and toss to combine well. Serve at room temperature or well-chilled. Bon appétit!

Nutrition: Calories: 451.9; Fats: 16.4g; Carbs: 61.5g; Protein: 16.7g

220. Mom's Chili

Preparation Time: 10 minutes
Servings: 4

Cooking Time: 10 minutes

Ingredients:

- 1 lb. red black beans, soaked overnight and drained
- 3 tbsps. olive oil
- 1 large red onion, diced
- 2 bell peppers, diced
- 1 poblano pepper, minced
- 1 large carrot, trimmed and diced
- 2 cloves garlic, minced
- 2 bay leaves
- 1 tsp. mixed peppercorns
- Kosher salt and cayenne pepper, to taste
- 1 tbsp. paprika
- 2 ripe tomatoes, pureed
- 2 tbsps. tomato ketchup
- 3 cups vegetable broth

Directions: Cover the soaked beans with a fresh change of cold water and bring to a boil. Let it boil for about 10 minutes. Turn the heat to a simmer and continue to cook for 50 to 55 minutes or until tender.
Warm the olive oil over medium heat in a heavy-bottomed pot then, sauté the onion, peppers, and carrot.
Sauté the garlic for about 30 seconds or until aromatic.
Add in the remaining ingredients along with the cooked beans. Let it simmer, stirring periodically, for 25 to 30 minutes or until cooked through. Discard the bay leaves, ladle them into individual bowls and serve hot!

Nutrition: Calories: 454.9; Fats: 10.4g; Carbs: 68.4g; Protein: 24.9g

221. Middle Eastern Chickpea Stew

Preparation Time: 10 minutes
Servings: 4

Cooking Time: 10 minutes

Ingredients:

- 1 onion, chopped
- 1 chili pepper, chopped
- 2 garlic cloves, chopped
- 1 tsp. mustard seeds
- 1 tsp. coriander seeds
- 1 bay leaf
- ½ cup tomato puree
- 2 tbsps. olive oil
- 1 celery with leaves, chopped
- 2 medium carrots, trimmed and chopped
- 2 cups vegetable broth
- 1 tsp. ground cumin
- 1 small-sized cinnamon stick
- 16 oz. canned chickpeas, drained
- 2 cups Swiss chard, torn into pieces

Directions: In your blender or food processor, blend the onion, chili pepper, garlic, mustard seeds, coriander seeds, bay leaf, and tomato puree into a paste.

In a stockpot, heat the olive oil until sizzling. Now, cook the celery and carrots for about 3 minutes or until they've softened. Add in the paste and continue to cook for a further 2 minutes.

Then, add vegetable broth, cumin, cinnamon, and chickpeas; bring it to a gentle boil.

Turn the heat to simmer and let it cook for 6 minutes; fold in Swiss chard and continue to cook for 4 to 5 minutes more or until the leaves wilt. Serve hot and enjoy!

Nutrition: Calories: 304.9; Fats: 10.9g; Carbs: 38.4g; Protein: 12.9g

222. Middle Eastern Za'atar Hummus

Preparation Time: 10 minutes   **Cooking Time: 10 minutes**
Servings: 4

Ingredients:
- 10 oz. chickpeas, boiled and drained
- ¼ cup tahini
- 2 tbsps. extra-virgin olive oil
- 2 tbsps. sun-dried tomatoes, chopped
- 1 lemon, freshly squeezed
- 2 garlic cloves, minced
- Kosher salt and ground black pepper, to taste
- ½ tsp. smoked paprika
- 1 tsp. Za'atar

Directions: Blitz all the ingredients in your food processor until creamy and uniform.

Store in refrigerator until ready to serve. Bon appétit!

Nutrition: Calories: 139.8; Fats: 8.2g; Carbs: 12.3g; Protein: 4.2g

223. Anasazi Bean and Vegetable Stew

Preparation Time: 10 minutes   **Cooking Time: 10 minutes**
Servings: 4

Ingredients:
- 1 cup Anasazi beans, soaked overnight, and drained
- 3 cups roasted vegetable broth
- 1 bay laurel
- 1 thyme sprig, chopped
- 1 rosemary sprig, chopped
- 3 tbsps. olive oil
- 1 large onion, chopped
- 2 celery stalks, chopped
- 2 carrots, chopped
- 2 bell peppers, seeded and chopped
- 1 green chili pepper, seeded and chopped
- 2 garlic cloves, minced
- Sea salt and ground black pepper, to taste
- 1 tsp. cayenne pepper
- 1 tsp. paprika

Directions: In a saucepan, bring the Anasazi beans and broth to a boil then, turn the heat to a simmer. Add in the bay laurel, thyme, and rosemary; let it cook for about 50 minutes or until tender.

Meanwhile, in a heavy-bottomed pot, heat the olive oil over medium-high heat. Now, sauté the onion, celery, carrots, and peppers for about 4 minutes until tender.

Put the garlic and continue to sauté for 30 seconds more or until aromatic.

Add the sautéed mixture to the cooked beans. Season with black pepper, paprika, cayenne pepper, and salt.

Continue to simmer, stirring periodically, for 10 minutes more or until everything is cooked through. Bon appétit!

Nutrition: Calories: 443.9; Fats: 15.6g; Carbs: 58.1g; Protein: 20.6g

224. Black Bean and Corn Salad with Cilantro Dressing

Preparation Time: 5 minutes   **Servings: 4**

Ingredients:
- 2 cups frozen corn, thawed
- 3 cups cooked or 2 (15.5-ounce) cans black beans, rinsed and drained
- ½ cup chopped red bell pepper
- ¼ cup minced red onion
- 1 (4-ounce) can chopped mild green chiles, drained 2 garlic cloves, crushed
- ¼ cup chopped fresh cilantro
- 1 teaspoon ground cumin
- ½ teaspoon salt (optional)
- ¼ teaspoon freshly ground black pepper
- 2 tablespoons fresh lime juice
- 2 tablespoons water
- ¼ cup extra-virgin olive oil

Directions: Preparing the Ingredients

In a large bowl, mix the beans, onion, corn, bell pepper, and chiles. Set aside.

In a blender or food processor, mince the garlic. Add the cilantro, cumin, salt, and black pepper, then pulse to blend. Add the lime juice, water, and oil and process until well blended.

Pour the dressing over the salad and mix. Taste and adjust the seasonings, if necessary, then serve.

Nutrition: Protein: 16.2g; Fats: 19.8g; Carbs: 63.8g

225. Pecan Rice

Preparation Time: 10 minutes
Servings: 4

Cooking Time: 10 minutes

Ingredients:
- 1/4 cup chopped white onion
- 1/4 teaspoon ground ginger
- 1/2 cup chopped pecans
- 1/4 teaspoon salt
- 2 tablespoons minced parsley
- 1/4 teaspoon ground black pepper
- 1/4 teaspoon dried basil
- 2 tablespoons vegan margarine
- 1 cup brown rice, cooked

Directions: Take a skillet pan, place it over medium heat, add margarine and when it melts, add all the ingredients except for rice and stir until mixed.
Cook for 5 minutes, then stir in rice until combined and continue cooking for 2 minutes. Serve straight away.

Nutrition: Calories: 279.6g; Fats: 15.9g; Carbs: 30.8g; Protein: 4.5g; Fiber: 3.5g

226. Lentil and Wild Rice Soup

Preparation Time: 15 minutes
Servings: 4

Cooking Time: 40 minutes

Ingredients:
- 1/2 cup cooked mixed beans
- 12 ounces cooked lentils
- 2 stalks of celery, sliced 1 1/2 cup mixed wild rice, cooked
- 1 large sweet potato, peeled, chopped
- 1/2 medium butternut, peeled, chopped
- 4 medium carrots, peeled, sliced
- 1 medium onion, peeled, diced
- 10 cherry tomatoes
- 1/2 red chili, deseeded, diced
- 1 ½ teaspoon minced garlic
- 1/2 teaspoon salt
- 2 teaspoons mixed dried herbs
- 1 teaspoon coconut oil
- 2 cups vegetable broth

Directions: Take a large pot, place it over medium-high heat, add oil and when it melts, add onion and cook for 5 minutes.
Stir in garlic and chili, cook for 3 minutes, then add remaining vegetables, pour in the broth, stir and bring the mixture to a boil.
Switch heat to medium-low heat, cook the soup for 20 minutes, then stir in remaining ingredients and continue cooking for 10 minutes until soup has reached to desired thickness. Serve straight away.

Nutrition: Calories: 330.8; Fats: 1.9g; Carbs: 53.8g; Protein: 13.2g; Fiber: 11.9g

227. Broccoli and Rice Stir Fry

Preparation Time: 5 minutes
Servings: 8

Cooking Time: 10 minutes

Ingredients:
- 16 ounces frozen broccoli florets, thawed 3 green onions, diced
- ½ teaspoon salt
- ¼ teaspoon ground black pepper
- 2 tablespoons soy sauce
- 1 tablespoon olive oil
- 1 ½ cups white rice, cooked

Directions: Take a skillet pan, place it over medium heat, add broccoli, and cook for 5 minutes until tender-crisp.
Then add scallion and other ingredients, toss until well mixed and cook for 2 minutes until hot.
Serve straight away.

Nutrition: Calories: 186.9; Fats: 3.2g; Carbs: 32.8g; Protein: 6.5g; Fiber: 2.4g

228. Balsamic Black Beans with Parsnip

Preparation Time: 5 minutes
Servings: 6

Cooking Time: 11 minutes

Ingredients:

- 1 cup dried black beans, soaked in water overnight, rinsed and drained 1 teaspoon olive oil
- 2 cloves garlic, minced
- 1 cup diced parsnip
- ½ teaspoon ground coriander
- ½ teaspoon ground cardamom
- 2 cups water
- 2 tablespoons balsamic vinegar

Directions: In the Instant Pot, heat the oil on Sauté mode. Put the garlic and sauté for a minute or until soft, but not brown. Add the parsnip, coriander, and cardamom and sauté for 5 minutes.
Add the black beans and water. Stir to combine.
Secure the lid. Select Manual mode and set cooking time for 5 minutes on High Pressure.
When timer beeps, use a natural pressure release for 5 minutes, then release any remaining pressure.
Remove the lid and stir in 2 tablespoons of the balsamic vinegar. Serve immediately.

Nutrition: Protein: 16.2g; Fats: 3.1g; Carbs: 79.2g

229. Beluga Lentils with Lacinato Kale

Preparation Time: 15 minutes   **Cook Time: 40 minutes**
Servings: 6

Ingredients:

- ¼ cup olive oil, plus more for serving
- 2 shallots, diced
- 5 cloves garlic, minced
- ½ teaspoon red pepper flakes
- ½ teaspoon ground nutmeg
- 1 teaspoon fine sea salt
- 2 bunches (about 1 pound / 454 g) lacinato kale, stems
- discarded and leaves chopped into 1-inch pieces
- 2 large carrots, peeled and diced
- 2½ cups water
- 1 cup beluga lentils, rinsed

Directions: Select the Sauté setting on the Instant Pot, add the oil, and heat for 1 minute.
Put the garlic and shallots and sauté for about 4 minutes until the shallots soften.
Put the nutmeg, red pepper flakes, and salt and sauté for 1 minute more.
Stir in the kale and carrots and sauté for about 3 minutes, until the kale fully wilts.
Stir in the water and lentils, scraping down the sides of the pot to make sure the lentils are submerged.
Secure the lid. Select Bean/Chili setting and set the cooking time for 30 minutes at High Pressure.
When timer beeps, let the pressure release naturally for 10 minutes, then release any remaining pressure.
Open the pot and give the mixture a stir.
Ladle the lentils into serving dishes and drizzle with oil. Serve warm.

Nutrition: Protein: 7.2g; Fats: 71.8g; Carbs: 19.9g

230. Black Beans with Lime

Preparation Time: 10 minutes   **Cooking Time: 15 minutes**
Servings: 4

Ingredients:

- 2½ cups black beans, uncooked
- 1 medium white onion, peeled and chopped
- 2 teaspoons minced garlic
- 1 teaspoon chili flakes
- 1 teaspoon ground cumin
- 1 teaspoon dried mint
- 1 teaspoon ground coriander
- 3 cups vegetable broth
- 1 teaspoon salt
- 1 lime, juiced

Directions: Add all the ingredients, except for the lime juice, in the Instant Pot, stirring until mixed.
Secure Instant Pot, then press the Manual button, set cooking time for 25 minutes on High Pressure.
When timer beeps, do a natural pressure release for 10 minutes, then release any remaining pressure.
Carefully open the Instant Pot, stir the beans, drizzle with lime juice, and serve.

Nutrition: Protein: 21.3g; Fats: 3.8g; Carbs: 74.9g

231. Coconut Tofu Curry

Preparation Time: 5 minutes   **Cooking Time: 3 minutes**
Servings: 4

Ingredients:

- 1 (13.5-ounce / 383-g) can coconut milk
- ¼ cup red or green curry paste
- ¼ teaspoon salt
- ¼ cup water

- 1 (14-ounce / 397-g) package extra-firm tofu, pressed and
- cubed 2 teaspoons unrefined sugar
- 2 cups chopped fresh spinach

Directions: In the Instant Pot, combine the coconut milk, curry paste, salt, and water, stirring to mix well. Add the tofu. Close the lid, then select Manual mode and set cooking time for 3 minutes on High Pressure.
Once cooking is complete, quick release the pressure. Open the lid.
Stir in the sugar and spinach. Serve immediately.

Nutrition: Protein: 24.2g; Fats: 47.9g; Carbs: 26.9g

232. Green Beans with Balsamic Sauce

Preparation Time: 10 minutes
Servings: 6

Cooking Time: 15 minutes

Ingredients:
- 2 shallots, sliced
- 8 c. green beans, trimmed
- 2 tbsps. olive oil
- Salt and pepper to taste
- 2 tbsps. balsamic vinegar
- ¼ c. Parmesan cheese, grated

Direction: Preheat your oven to 425°F. Line you're baking with foil. In the pan, toss the shallots and beans in oil, salt, and pepper. Roast in the oven for 15 minutes. Drizzle with the vinegar and top with cheese.

Nutrition: Calories: 77.9g; Fiber: 0.5g; Protein: 2.2g

233. Cilantro and Avocado Lime Rice

Preparation Time: 5 minutes
Servings: 4

Cooking Time: 20 minutes

Ingredients:
- Avocado (2, Sliced)
- Brown Rice (5 C., Cooked)
- Cumin (1/2 t.)
- Cilantro (1/4 C., Chopped)
- Lime Juice (2 T.)
- Garlic Clove (1, Minced)
- Salt (to Taste)

Directions: For a rice recipe with a twist, you absolutely need to try this recipe! You will begin by taking out a mixing bowl and mashing down the avocado pieces until they are perfectly smooth.
Once the avocado is set, you will then add in your seasonings, cilantro, and then squeeze in the lime juice.
Stir the brown rice that has already been cooked and blend together well before serving.

Nutrition: Calories: 449.8g; Carbs: 59.8g; Fats: 14.9g; Proteins: 5.1g

234. Sweet Coconut Pilaf

Preparation Time: 5 minutes
Servings: 4

Cooking Time: 30 minutes

Ingredients:
- Coconut Oil (2 T.)
- Cinnamon Stick (1)
- Ground Cumin (1 t.)
- Cauliflower (1)
- Onion (1, Diced)
- Garlic Cloves (3)
- Bay Leaf (2)
- Ground Coriander (1 t.)
- Coconut Milk (1 C.)
- Ground Ginger (1 1/2 t.)
- Ground Cardamom (1 t.)
- Ground Turmeric (1 1/2 t.)
- Ginger (1 T., Grated)

Directions: Begin by heating your oven to 400.
Cut the cauliflower into bite-sized pieces and then carefully place them onto your baking pan. Once in place, drizzle some coconut oil over the cauliflower and dash with the salt, coriander, and cumin. When the cauliflower is set, pop the dish into the oven for about twenty-five minutes.
As the cauliflower cooks, take out a saucepan and begin heating
up another tablespoon of coconut oil over medium heat. Once warm, you can also add in the ginger, garlic, onion, coriander, and a bit of salt. You will cook these ingredients together for about five minutes.
With the garlic and onion cooked, add in the rest of the spices before also throwing in the quinoa, a half cup of water, cinnamon, coconut milk, and the bay leaves. Throw a lid on top and simmer the ingredients for fifteen minutes. When the quinoa is done, mix together the cauliflower and quinoa together, and your meal is set!

Nutrition: Calories: 149.8g; Carbs: 19.7g; Fats: 6.9g; Proteins: 5.2g

235. Millet Fritters

Preparation Time: 5 minutes
Servings: 4

Cooking Time: 20 minutes

Ingredients:
- Coconut Oil (2 T.)
- Psyllium Husk (1/3 C.)
- Chickpea Flour (1/2 C.)
- Millet (1 C.)
- Mustard Powder (1/8 t.)
- Pepper (to Taste)
- Onion Powder (1/2 t.)
- Paprika (1/2 t.)
- Dried Parsley (1 t.)
- Coriander (1/8 t.)
- Salt (to Taste)

Directions: To start this recipe, you will first want to cook your millet according to the directions on the package. Once this is cooked through, you will want to place the millet into a mixing bowl.
Next, you are going to add in the flour, psyllium husk, and all of the seasonings into your bowl and mix everything together well. Once you have a "dough" formed, use your hands to create patties from the ingredients and set on a plate to the side.
When you are set to bake the fritters, you will now want to take a medium skillet and throw it over an intermediate heat. As it warms up, place down some coconut oil and add your first batch of fritters into the pan. You will want to grill the fritters for nearly five minutes on either side or up until the fritter is a nice, golden color and crunchy on the outer surface.
Nutrition: Calories: 409.9g; Carbs: 49.8g; Fats: 14.7g; Proteins: 10.2g

236. Amaranth Porridge

Preparation Time: 30 minutes
Servings: 4

Cooking Time: 5 minutes

Ingredients:
- 3 cups water
- 1 cup amaranth
- 1/2 cup coconut milk
- 4 tablespoons agave syrup
- A pinch of kosher salt
- A pinch of grated nutmeg

Directions: Bring the water to a boil over medium-high heat; add in the amaranth and turn the heat to a simmer. Bake for 30 minutes, stirring periodically to prevent the amaranth from sticking to the bottom of the pan.
Stir in the remaining ingredients and continue to cook for 1 to 2 minutes more until cooked through.

Nutrition: Calories: 260.8g; Fats: 4.1g; Carbs: 48.8g; Protein: 7.1g

237. Millet Porridge with Sultanas

Preparation Time: 5 minutes
Servings: 3

Cooking Time: 20 minutes

Ingredients:
- 1 cup water
- 1 cup coconut milk
- 1 cup millet, rinsed
- 1/4 teaspoon grated nutmeg
- 1/4 teaspoon ground cinnamon
- 1 teaspoon vanilla paste
- 1/4 teaspoon kosher salt
- 2 tablespoons agave syrup
- 4 tablespoons sultana raisins

Directions: Place the water, milk, millet, nutmeg, cinnamon, vanilla, and salt in a saucepan; bring to a boil. Bring the heat to a simmer and let it cook for about 20 minutes; fluff the millet with a fork and spoon into individual bowls. Serve with agave syrup and sultanas.

Nutrition: Calories: 352.8; Fats: 5.2g; Carbs: 65.1g; Protein: 9.9g

238. Bulgur Wheat Salad

Preparation Time: 12 minutes
Servings: 4

Cooking Time: 13 minutes

Ingredients:
- 1 cup bulgur wheat
- 1 ½ cups vegetable broth
- 1 teaspoon sea salt
- 1 teaspoon fresh ginger, minced
- 4 tablespoons olive oil
- 1 onion, chopped
- 8 ounces canned garbanzo beans, drained
- 2 large roasted peppers, sliced
- 2 tablespoons fresh parsley, roughly chopped

91

Directions: In a deep saucepan, bring the bulgur wheat and vegetable broth to a simmer; let it cook, covered, for 12 to 13 minutes. Let it stand for about 10 minutes and fluff with a fork. Add the remaining ingredients to the cooked bulgur wheat; serve at room temperature or well-chilled. Bon appétit!

Nutrition: Calories: 358.7; Fats: 15.2g; Carbs: 47.9g; Protein: 10.3g

239. Aromatic Rice

Preparation Time: 5 minutes
Servings: 4

Cooking Time: 15 minutes

Ingredients:
- 3 tablespoons olive oil
- 1 teaspoon garlic, minced
- 1 teaspoon dried oregano
- 1 teaspoon dried rosemary
- 1 bay leaf
- 1 ½ cups white rice
- 2 ½ cups vegetable broth
- Sea salt and cayenne pepper, to taste

Directions: In a saucepan, heat the olive oil over a moderately high flame. Add in the garlic, oregano, rosemary, and bay leaf; sauté for about 1 minute or until aromatic.
Add in the rice and broth. Bring to a boil; immediately turn the heat to a gentle simmer.
Cook for 15 minutes. Fluff the rice with a fork, season with salt and pepper, and serve immediately.

Nutrition: Calories: 383.8; Fats: 11.2g; Carbs: 60.1g; Protein: 8.5g

240. Sweet Maize Meal Porridge

Preparation Time: 5 minutes
Servings: 2

Cooking Time: 10 minutes

Ingredients:
- 2 cups water
- 1/2 cup maize meal
- 1/4 teaspoon ground allspice
- 1/4 teaspoon salt
- 2 tablespoons brown sugar
- 2 tablespoons almond butter

Directions: In a saucepan, bring the water to a boil; then gradually add in the maize meal and turn the heat to a simmer. Add in the ground allspice and salt. Let it cook for 10 minutes.
Add in the brown sugar and almond butter and gently stir to combine.
Nutrition: Calories: 277.9; Fats: 12.5g; Carbs: 37.1g; Protein: 3.2g

241. Sweet Oatmeal

Preparation Time: 5 minutes
Servings: 4

Cooking Time: 15 minutes

Ingredients:
- 1 ½ cups steel-cut oats, soaked overnight
- 1 cup almond milk
- 2 cups water
- A pinch of grated nutmeg
- A pinch of ground cloves
- A pinch of sea salt
- 4 tablespoons almonds, slivered
- 6 dates, pitted and chopped
- 6 prunes, chopped

Directions: In a deep saucepan, bring the steel-cut oats, almond milk, and water to a boil.
Add in the nutmeg, cloves, and salt. Immediately turn the heat to a simmer, cover, and continue to cook for about 15 minutes or until they've softened.
Then, spoon the grits into four serving bowls; top them with the almonds, dates, and prunes.

Nutrition: Calories: 379.9; Fats: 10.9g; Carbs: 58.8g; Protein: 14.6g

242. Green Lentil Salad with Vinaigrette

Preparation Time: 15 minutes
Servings: 4 to 6

Cooking Time: 20 minutes

Ingredients:

Lentils:
- 1 cup green lentils, rinsed
- 3½ cups water, divided
- ½ teaspoon fine sea salt
- 1 large carrot, diced
- 1 red bell pepper, diced
- 2 ribs celery, diced
- ½ small red onion, diced
- ¼ cup chopped fresh flat-leaf parsley

Vinaigrette:
- 1 small shallot, minced
- 2 teaspoons Dijon mustard
- 1 teaspoon dried herbs de Provence
- ¼ cup fresh lemon juice
- 1½ teaspoons sugar
- ½ teaspoon fine sea salt
- ½ teaspoon freshly ground black pepper
- ½ cup olive oil

Directions: In a heatproof bowl, stir together the lentils, 1½ cups of water, and salt.

Pour the other 2 cups water into the Instant Pot and place a trivet in the pot. Put the bowl on the trivet.

Select Manual mode and set the cooking time for 20 minutes at High Pressure.

Meanwhile, in a bowl, combine the ingredients for the vinaigrette. Stir to mix well. Set aside.

When timer beeps, perform a quick pressure release. Open the pot and remove the bowl of lentils.

Drain the lentils in a colander, then return them to the bowl. While they are still warm, pour half of the vinaigrette over the lentils and stir gently. Let cool for 20 minutes.

In a serving bowl, toss the lentils, carrot, bell pepper, celery, onion, and parsley. Taste and add more vinaigrette as needed. Serve immediately.

Nutrition: Protein: 2.1g; Fats: 83.8g; Carbs: 12.8g;

243. Black Bean Taquitos

Preparation Time: 10 minutes
Servings: 12

Cooking Time: 20 minutes

Ingredients:
- Olive oil
- 1 onion
- 1 poblano chili pepper
- 1 jalapeño chili pepper
- 4 garlic cloves
- 1 can black beans
- ½ cup cilantro leaves
- 1 tsp. chili powder
- 1 tsp. cumin powder
- 1 tsp. sea salt
- 24 corn tortillas

Directions: Preheat your oven to 400°F.

Use a large baking pan and line it with parchment paper then grease with oil.

Chop your onion into quarters. Half both peppers and deseed them before chopping into quarters.

Using a food processor, add onion, poblano pepper, jalapeño pepper, and garlic. Use the chopping blade and pulse 3 times before adding the black beans, cilantro, chili powder, cumin, and salt.

Pulse another 3 times or until the mixture is finely chopped (you can pulse more if you want a smoother mix).

Put the tortillas on a pan and heat them in the oven for about a minute, or until soft and pliable.

Smear a large tablespoon of bean mixes across each tortilla. Tightly roll like a burrito with open edges and put on a baking pan with the edge facing down. Leave a smidge of space between each tortilla and cook for 20 minutes or until golden.

Nutrition: Protein: 9.2g; Fats: 13.9g; Carbs: 76.8g

244. Lima Bean Casserole

Preparation Time: 15 minutes
Servings: 5

Cooking Time: 30 minutes

Ingredients:
- Lima beans, canned two cups
- Lemon juice, two teaspoons
- Thyme, one half teaspoon
- Black pepper, one teaspoon
- Nutritional yeast, one half cup
- Olive oil, two tablespoons
- Dry mustard, two teaspoons
- Salt, one half teaspoon
- Cumin, one teaspoon

Directions: Heat oven to 375.

Drain the beans and save the liquid. Dump the drained beans into an eight by eight-inch baking pan.

Add the olive oil with the bean liquid to a skillet and heat until the warm.

Add in the pepper, salt, cumin, thyme, dry mustard, and lemon juice and stir together well.

Pour this mix over the beans in the baking pan and cover with the nutritional yeast. Bake for thirty minutes.

Nutrition: Calories: 289.8; Fats: 8.8g; Carbs: 33.9g; Protein: 18.2g; Fiber: 11.8g

245. Bean Bolognese

Preparation Time: 40 minutes
Servings: 4

Cooking Time: 20 minutes

Ingredients:
- White beans, one fourteen ounce can drain and rinse Fettuccini, whole-wheat, eight ounces
- Onion, one small chop
- Olive oil, two tablespoons
- Parsley, fresh, chopped, one-quarter cup divided Tomatoes, diced, one fourteen ounce can
- Balsamic vinegar, one half cup
- Celery, one quarter cup chop
- Carrot, one half cup chop
- Bay leaf, one
- Garlic, minced, two tablespoons
- Salt, one half teaspoon

Directions: Cook the pasta as directed on package.
Cook carrot, onion, celery, and garlic in the oil for ten minutes. Add in the bay leaf and salt and stir for one minute. Throw away the bay leaf. Pour in the balsamic vinegar and boil for five minutes. Add in the beans, tomatoes, and two tablespoons of the parsley to the skillet and simmer for five minutes, stirring often.
Spoon the pasta into four bowls. Top the pasta with the sauce mix from the skillet. Sprinkle on the remainder of the parsley and serve.

Nutrition: Calories: 349.9; Fats: 8.8g; Carbs: 37.9g; Protein: 6.2g; Fiber: 11.9g

246. Rice and Vegetables

Preparation Time: 15 minutes
Servings: 1

Cooking Time: 15 minutes

Ingredients:
- 1/3 cup Flavorful Brown Rice Pilaf
- 1/3 cup cannellini beans, drained
- ¼ cup diced Persian cucumbers
- ¼ cup diced fresh tomatoes
- ¼ cup chopped avocado
- ½ cup arugula
- Pinch onion powder
- Pinch garlic powder
- ½ tablespoon freshly squeezed lemon juice
- Pinch freshly ground black pepper

Directions: Take a large Mason jar with a cover, layer the rice, beans, cucumbers, tomatoes, avocado, and arugula and cover with the lid. To serve, add the lemon juice, garlic powder, and onion powder.
Cover and gently shake to season all the ingredients. Place the salad onto a plate or a bowl, and season with pepper. To save time, use microwavable rice.

Nutrition: Calories: 220.9; Fats: 5.9g; Carbs: 35.8g; Fiber: 6.9g; Protein: 9.2g

247. Black Bean Dip

Preparation Time: 1 hour and 30 minutes
Servings: 10

Cooking Time: 1 hour

Ingredients:
- 2 15-ounce cans black beans, rinsed and drained
- 1 jalapeno pepper, seeded and minced
- ½ of a red bell pepper, seeded and diced
- ½ of a yellow bell pepper, seeded and diced
- ½ of s small red onion, diced
- 1 cup fresh cilantro, finely chopped
- Zest of 1 lime
- Juice of 1 lime
- 1 10-ounce can Rotel, drained
- ½ teaspoon Kosher salt
- ¼ teaspoon ground black pepper

Directions: Put in a bowl the beans, garlic, onion, green onions, cilantro, jalapeno, red and yellow bell pepper, and mix together well.
Add the lime zest and juice, Rotel, salt and pepper and mix. Adjust seasoning to your own taste.
Refrigerate for at one hour, minimum, before serving, so the flavors have time to blend. Serve with wheat tortilla slices that have been crisped in the oven or with wheat or sesame crackers.

Nutrition: Protein: 21.3g; Fats: 3.9g; Carbs: 74.9g

248. Capers, Green Beans and Herbs Mix

Preparation Time: 10 minutes

Servings: 4

Ingredients:

- 2 tablespoons olive oil
- 1 tablespoon balsamic vinegar
- 2 tablespoons capers, drained
- 1-pound green beans, trimmed, halved and steamed
- 1 tablespoon chives, chopped
- 1 tablespoon coriander, chopped
- 1 tablespoons oregano, chopped
- Salt and black pepper to the taste
- 2 tablespoons parsley, chopped
- ¼ teaspoon red chili flakes
- 1 teaspoon hot paprika

Directions: In a bowl, mix green beans with the capers, the herbs and the other ingredients, toss and serve.

Nutrition: Calories: 89.8; Fats: 3.9g; Carbs: 10.9g; Protein: 8.2g; Fiber:11.8g

249.Chickpeas Curry

Preparation Time: 15 minutes   **Cooking Time: 25 minutes**
Servings: 6

Ingredients:

- 3 tablespoons avocado oil
- 1 medium onion, chopped finely
- 2 garlic cloves, minced
- 1 teaspoon ground cumin
- ½ teaspoon cayenne powder
- Sea salt, as needed
- 2 large plum tomatoes, chopped finely
- 3 cups cooked chickpeas
- 2 cups spring water
- ¼ cup fresh parsley, chopped

Directions: Warm the avocado oil over medium heat in a skillet, and sauté the onion and garlic for about 6–8 minutes. Stir in the spices and salt and cook for about 1–2 minutes.
Stir in the tomatoes, chickpeas, and water and bring to a boil over high heat.
Now, adjust the heat to medium and simmer for 10–15 minutes or until desired thickness.
Serve hot with a garnish of parsley.

Nutrition: Calories: 165.9; Fats: 0.4g; Carbs: 27.5g; Protein: 8.5g

250.Wild Rice and Black Lentils Bowl

Preparation Time: 10 minutes   **Cooking Time: 50 minutes**
Servings: 4

Ingredients:

- Wild rice
- 2 cups wild rice, uncooked
- 4 cups spring water
- ½ teaspoon salt
- 2 bay leaves
- Black lentils
- 2 cups black lentils, cooked
- 1 ¾ cups coconut milk, unsweetened
- 2 cups vegetable stock
- 1 teaspoon dried thyme
- 1 teaspoon dried paprika
- ½ of medium purple onion; peeled, sliced
- 1 tablespoon minced garlic
- 2 teaspoons creole seasoning
- 1 tablespoon coconut oil
- Plantains
- 3 large plantains, chopped into ¼-inch-thick pieces
- 3 tablespoons coconut oil
- Brussels sprouts
- 10 large brussels sprouts, quartered
- 2 tablespoons spring water
- 1 teaspoon sea salt
- ½ teaspoon ground black pepper

Directions: Prepare the rice: take a medium pot, place it over medium-high heat, pour in water, and add bay leaves and salt. Bring the water to a boil, then switch heat to medium, add rice, and then cook for 30–45 minutes or more until tender.
When done, discard the bay leaves from rice, drain if any water remains in the pot, remove it from heat, and fluff by using a fork. Set aside until needed.
While the rice boils, prepare lentils: take a large pot, place it over medium-high heat and when hot, put onion and cook for 5 minutes.
Stir garlic into the onion, cook for 2 minutes until fragrant and golden, then add remaining ingredients for the lentils and stir until mixed. Bring the lentils to a boil, then switch heat to medium and simmer the lentils for 20 minutes until tender, covering the pot with a lid.
When ready, remove the pot from heat and set aside until needed.
While rice and lentils simmer, prepare the plantains: chop them into ¼-inch-thick pieces.
Take a large skillet pan, place it over medium heat, add coconut oil and when it melts, add half of the plantain pieces and cook for 7–10 minutes per side or more until golden-brown.
When done, transfer browned plantains to a plate lined with paper towels and repeat with the remaining plantain pieces; set aside until needed. Prepare the sprouts: return the skillet pan over medium heat, add more oil if needed, and then add brussels sprouts.
Toss the sprouts until coated with oil, and then let them cook for 3–4 minutes per side until brown.

Drizzle water over sprouts, cover the pan with the lid, and then cook for 3–5 minutes until steamed.
Season the sprouts with salt and black pepper, toss until mixed, and transfer sprouts to a plate.
Assemble the bowl: divide rice evenly among four bowls and then top with lentils, plantain pieces, and sprouts.
Serve immediately.

Nutrition: Calories: 223.8; Carbs: 42.3g; Fats: 1.1g; Protein: 12.7g

251. Spanish-Style Saffron Rice with Black Beans

Preparation Time: 5 minutes
Servings: 4

Cooking Time: 25 minutes

Ingredients:
- 2 cups vegetable stock
- ¼ tsp. saffron threads (optional)
- 1 ½ tbsps. extra-virgin olive oil
- 1 small red or yellow onion, halved and thinly sliced
- 1 tbsp. minced garlic
- 1 tsp. turmeric
- 2 tsps. paprika
- 1 cup long-grain white rice, well-rinsed
- 1 (14 oz.) can black beans, drained and rinsed
- ½ cup green beans, halved or quartered
- 1 small red bell pepper, chopped
- 1 tsp. salt

Directions: In a small pot, heat the vegetable stock until boiling. Add the saffron and remove it from the heat and warm the olive oil in a nonstick skillet over medium heat.
Add the onion, garlic, turmeric, paprika, and rice and stir to coat.
Pour in the stock, and mix in the black beans, green beans, and red bell pepper.
Bring to a boil, lower the heat to medium-low, cover, and simmer for about 20 minutes. Stir in the salt and serve hot.

Nutrition: Calories: 331.8; Fats: 4.8g; Carbs: 62.9g; Fiber: 8.8g; Sugar: 1.9g; Protein: 11.3g

252. Green Beans

Preparation Time: 15 minutes
Servings: 8

Cooking Time: 20 minutes

Ingredients:
- 1 shallot, chopped
- 24 oz. green beans
- Salt and pepper to taste
- ½ tsp. smoked paprika
- 1 tsp. lemon juice
- 2 tsps. vinegar

Directions: Preheat your oven to 450°F.
Stir in the shallot and beans. Season with salt, pepper, and paprika.
Roast for 10 minutes. Drizzle with lemon juice and vinegar.
Roast for another 2 minutes.

Nutrition: Calories: 48.8; Fiber: 2.8g; Protein: 3.1g

253. Squash Risotto

Preparation Time: 10 minutes
Servings: 2

Cooking Time: 13 minutes

Ingredients:
- 1 small yellow onion, chopped
- A drizzle of olive oil - 1 garlic clove, minced
- ½ red bell pepper, chopped
- 128 g butternut squash, chopped
- 128 g Arborio rice
- 1 and ½ cups veggie stock
- 3 tablespoons dry white wine
- 112 g mushrooms, chopped
- A pinch of salt and black pepper
- A pinch of oregano, dried
- ¼ teaspoon coriander, ground
- 1 and ½ cups mixed kale and spinach
- 1 tablespoon nutritional yeast

Directions: Set your air fryer on sauté mode, add the oil and heat it up. Add onion, bell pepper, squash and garlic, stir and cook for 5 minutes.
Add rice, stock, wine, salt, pepper, mushrooms, oregano and coriander, stir, cover and cook on High for 5 minutes. Add mixed kale and spinach, parsley and yeast, stir and leave aside for 5 minutes.
Divide between 2 plates and serve as a side dish.

Nutrition: Calories: 268.8; Fats: 9.2g; Carbs: 29.4g; Protein: 4.7g

254.Zucchinis Cardamom Rice

Preparation Time: 10 minutes   **Cooking Time: 15 minutes**
Servings: 4

Ingredients:
- 2 cups zucchinis, grated
- 1 cup heavy cream
- 1 cup coconut milk
- ½ teaspoon saffron powder
- ½ teaspoon cardamom powder
- 4 tablespoons sugar
- 1 teaspoon vanilla extract

Directions: In your instant pot, mix the zucchinis with the cream, the coconut milk and with the other ingredients, cover and cook on High for 15 minutes.
Release the pressure naturally for 10 minutes, divide the mix into bowls and serve.

Nutrition: Calories: 251.9; Fats: 7.1g; Fiber: 1.9g; Carbs: 8.2g; Protein: 1.6g

255.Green Beans & Orange Sauce

Preparation Time: 5 minutes   **Cooking Time: 15 minutes**
Servings: 4

Ingredients:
- 1 pound green beans, trimmed and halved
- 2 teaspoons orange zest, grated
- 1 cup orange juice
- 1 teaspoon chili powder
- ½ teaspoon garam masala
- ½ teaspoon turmeric powder
- ½ teaspoon dried fenugreek leaves
- A pinch of salt and black pepper

Directions: In your instant pot, combine the green beans with the orange zest and the other ingredients and then, cover and cook on High for 15 minutes.
Release the pressure fast for 5 minutes, divide the mix between plates and serve.

Nutrition: Calories: 68.8; Fats: 0.3g; Carbs: 15.4g; Protein: 2.9g

256.Refried Beans

Preparation Time: 15 minutes   **Cooking Time: 8 hour**
Servings: 15

Ingredients:
- 1 onion, peeled and halved
- 5 teaspoons salt
- 3 cups dry pinto beans, rinsed
- 1 3/4 teaspoons fresh ground
- black pepper
- 1/2 fresh jalapeno pepper, seeded and chopped
- 1/8 teaspoon ground cumin,
- optional
- 2 tablespoons minced garlic
- 9 cups water

Directions: Place the pepper, salt, onion, rinsed beans, jalapeno, cumin, and garlic into a slow cooker. Add the water and stir to combine. Bake on High for 8 hours, adding more water as needed.
When the beans are cooked, drain them, and reserve the liquid. Crush the beans with a potato masher, adding the reserved water as needed to attain desired consistency.

Nutrition: Calories: 138.8; Carbs: 25.1g; Fats: 0.4g; Protein: 8.7g

257.Spanish Rice

Preparation Time: 10 minutes   **Cooking Time: 30 minutes**
Servings: 4

Ingredients:
- 2 tablespoons vegetable oil
- 2 cups water
- 1 cup uncooked white rice
- 1 (10 ounce) can diced tomatoes
- and green chiles
- 1 onion, chopped
- 2 teaspoons chili powder, or to taste
- 1/2 green bell pepper, chopped
- 1 teaspoon salt

Directions: Warm oil in a skillet over medium heat. Sauté onion, bell pepper, and rice until rice is browned and onions are tender.

Stir in water and tomatoes. Season with chili powder and salt. Cover and cook for about 30 minutes, or until rice is cooked and liquid is absorbed.

Nutrition: Calories: 269.9; Carbs: 45.6g; Fats: 7.4g; Protein: 4.9g

258. Chickpea Salad (2nd Version)

Preparation Time: 10 minutes   **Servings: 6**

Ingredients:
- 3 cups cooked garbanzo beans
- 1 red bell pepper, diced
- 1 yellow bell pepper, diced
- 1 cup vine tomatoes, chopped
- 1 cup cucumber, chopped
- 5 scallions, sliced
- 1 cup fresh mint, chopped
- 1 cup Italian parsley, chopped
- 1 garlic clove, minced
- Salt and black pepper, to taste
- ½ cup olive oil
- Zest of 1 lemon
- ¼ cup lemon juice
- 1 teaspoon sumac
- ½ teaspoon cayenne chili flakes

Direction: Mix beans with bell pepper, cucumber and the rest of the ingredients in a salad bowl. Serve.

Nutrition: Calories: 269.9; Fats: 13.9g; Carbs: 11.7g; Fiber: 0.2g; Sugar: 0.9g; Protein: 7.2g

259. Cannellini Bean and Bell Pepper Burger

Preparation Time: 15 minutes   **Cooking Time: 35 minutes**
Servings: 6

Ingredients:
- ¾ cup quinoa
- 1 ½ cups water
- 2 (15-ounce / 425-g) cans cannellini beans, rinsed and drained ½ cup ground flaxseeds
- 1 cup walnuts, finely chopped
- 1 tablespoon ground cumin
- 3 tablespoons Italian seasoning
- 1 tablespoon minced garlic
- 2 tablespoons almond butter
- 1 teaspoon salt (optional)
- ½ teaspoon freshly ground black pepper
- 3 tablespoons Dijon mustard
- 1 ½ tablespoons avocado oil (optional)
- 4 to 5 large red bell peppers cut into thirds

Topping:
- 1 cucumber, sliced
- 2 to 3 tomatoes, sliced
- ½ small red onion, sliced

Directions: In a saucepan, mix water and the quinoa. Bring to a boil over high heat, then cover and reduce heat to medium-low. Simmer for 20 minutes. Set aside.

On a large cutting board, spread out the beans. Pat dry with paper towels. Then press down firmly with the beans between the paper

towel and cutting board, using your knuckles to mash them. When you remove the paper towel, you should have a layer of semi-smashed beans. Using a chef's knife, chop the beans a little bit more, leaving a few larger chunks. Transfer the mashed beans to a medium bowl. Add the cooked quinoa, flaxseeds, walnuts, cumin, Italian seasoning, garlic, almond butter, salt (if desired), pepper, and mustard. Mix until well combined, then form 12 burger patties.

In a nonstick skillet, heat ½ tablespoon olive oil (if desired) over medium heat. Once hot, add 4 patties. Cook for 3 minutes, then flip to the other side and cook for 3 minutes more.

To serve, cutting bell peppers into thirds and sandwiching a burger patty between two pieces of pepper. Top with sliced cucumber, tomatoes, and onion.

Nutrition: Calories: 303.9; Fats: 15.8g; Carbs: 27.5g; Protein: 12.4g; Fiber: 11.5g

260. Chickpea Nuggets

Preparation Time: 10 minutes   **Cooking Time: 30 minutes**

Servings: 2

Ingredients:
- 2 cups cooked chickpeas
- ½ teaspoon salt
- 1 teaspoon onion powder
- 1/3 cup and 1 tablespoon bread crumbs

Directions: Switch on the oven, then set it to 350 degrees F and let it preheat.

Meanwhile, place chickpeas in a food processor and then pulse until crumbled.

Tip the chickpeas in a bowl, add remaining Ingredients: in it except for 1/3 cup of breadcrumbs and then stir until a chunky mixture comes together.

Shape the mixture into evenly sized balls, shape each ball into the nugget, arrange on a baking sheet greased with oil and then bake for 15 minutes per side until golden brown.

Nutrition: Calories: 291.4; Fats: 3.7g; Protein: 20.1g; Carbs: 26.5g

Sauces and Condiments

261. Green Cilantro Sauce

Preparation Time: 5 minutes
Servings: 10

Cooking Time: 20 minutes

Ingredients:
- Olive Oil (1 C.)
- Cilantro (1 C.)
- Water (5 T.)
- Garlic Cloves (4)
- Ground Cumin (1/4 t.)
- Sherry Vinegar (to Taste)

Directions: To begin this sauce, you will want to crush your garlic cloves and place it into a food processor and add the cilantro.
After you have processed these two ingredients together, slowly begin adding in your olive oil and blend everything together smoothly.
If you would like, feel welcome to combine as much or as little water as you would like, along with the sherry vinegar for some extra flavor. Finally, add in your ground cumin, stir, and the sauce will be prepared.

Nutrition: Calories: 199.8; Carbs: 3.9g; Fats: 19.7g; Proteins: 2.1g

262. Tartar Sauce

Preparation Time: 3 minutes
Servings: 4

Cooking Time: 3 minutes

Ingredients:
- 2 egg yolks
- 250ml groundnut oil
- 250ml olive oil
- 1 tsp. Dijon mustard
- juice of ½ a lemon
- 1 tbsp. chopped tarragon
- 1 tbsp. chopped gherkins
- 2 tbsp. chopped parsley
- 1 tbsp. rinsed capers

Directions: Start by preparing a mayonnaise of the 2 egg yolks, Dijon mustard, salt, and pepper. Slowly pour in the groundnut oil and olive oil in a steady stream and whisk. Pour in the lemon juice followed by tarragon, gherkins, capers, and parsley. Check for adequate seasoning at this point. Chill and serve.

Nutrition: Calories: 113.8; Fats: 6.5g; Carbs: 1.1g; Fiber: 0.2g; Protein: 11.7g

263. Sambal Sauce

Preparation Time: 10 minutes
Servings: 8

Cooking Time: 10 minutes

Ingredients:
- 2 pounds dried red or fresh jalapeños, stemmed and chopped very roughly
- 10 fresh Thai chilies, or 1 tablespoon red pepper flakes 1 cup minced garlic
- 1/4 cup canola oil
- 2 cups rice wine vinegar
- 1 teaspoon sugar
- 2 teaspoons salt

Directions: Take a medium pan and mix in the jalapenos, garlic, oil, and Thai chilies and cook on low heat until the ingredients are mixed in thoroughly. Once the mixture is reduced in half, slowly add the vinegar and cook it again on a slow flame.
Remove from heat and add the salt and sugar, then cool to room temperature. Move this mixture to a food processor, and pulse to an accepted texture. Store in the fridge in a jar till further use.

Nutrition: Calories: 577.9; Fats: 27.5g; Carbs: 85.9g; Fiber: 10.8g; Protein: 3.4g

264. Piri Sauce

Preparation Time: 6 minutes
Servings: 4

Cooking Time: 4 minutes

Ingredients:
- 4 to 8 fresh hot chilies, depending on the heat
- Juice of 1 lemon
- 2 garlic cloves, minced
- 1/2 to 1 cup extra-virgin olive oil, depending on how thin you want it
- Pinch of salt

Directions: Roughly chop up the peppers by discarding the stems, and place them in the food processor along with garlic, salt, lemon juice, and oil, and puree till your desired consistency. Serve or store in an air-tight jar for at least a week in the fridge.

Nutrition: Calories: 109.8; Fats: 11.7g; Carbs: 1.2g; Fiber: 0.1g; Protein: 0.3g

265. Hemp Falafel with Tahini Sauce

Preparation Time: 10 minutes
Servings: 6

Cooking Time: 10 minutes

Ingredients:
- 80g raw hemp hearts
- 4g chopped cilantro
- 4g chopped basil
- 2 cloves garlic, minced
- 2g ground cumin seeds
- 3g chili powder
- 14g flax meal + 30ml filtered water
- Sea salt and pepper, to taste
- Avocado or coconut oil, to fry

Sauce:
- 115g tahini
- 60ml fresh lime juice
- 115ml filtered water
- 30ml extra-virgin olive oil
- Sea salt, to taste
- A good pinch ground cumin seed

Directions: Mix flax with filtered water in a small bowl. Place aside for 10 minutes.
In the meantime, combine raw hemp hearts, garlic, cilantro, cumin, basil, chili, and seasonings in a food processor.
Process until it just comes together. Add the flax seeds mixture and process until finely blended and uniform.
Heat approximately 2 tablespoons of avocado oil in a skillet. Shape 1
tablespoon mixture into balls and fry for 3-4 minutes or until deep golden brown, then Take out of skillet and place on a plate lined with paper towels.
Make the sauce; combine all ingredients in a food blender. Blend until smooth and creamy.
Serve falafel with fresh lettuce salad and tahini sauce.

Nutrition: Calories: 346.9; Fats: 29.7g; Carbs: 7.1g; Fiber: 4.1g; Protein: 14.1g

266. Cranberry and Orange Sauce

Preparation Time: 15 minutes
Servings: 4

Cooking Time: 5 minutes

Ingredients:
- Zest and juice of an orange
- ½ cup maple syrup
- 1 bag (12 oz - 340 g) of fresh red cranberries
- 1 teaspoon cinnamon

Directions: In a small saucepan, add all the ingredients and let them boil, then reduce heat and cook for 15 minutes.
Put it to a bowl and refrigerate until it cools down, at least for an hour.

Nutrition: Calories: 239.8; Fats: 14.9g; Carbs: 3.8g Fiber: 9.9g; Protein: 18.2g

267. Alfredo Sauce

Preparation Time: 7 minutes

Servings: 4

Ingredients:
- 1 cup cashews, unsalted, soaked in warm water for 15 minutes 1 teaspoon minced garlic
- 1/4 teaspoon ground black pepper
- 1/3 teaspoon salt
- 1/4 cup nutritional yeast
- 2 tablespoons tamari
- 2 tablespoons olive oil
- 4 tablespoons water

Directions: Drain the cashews, transfer them into a food processor, add remaining ingredients in it, and pulse for 3 minutes until thick sauce comes together. Serve straight away.

Nutrition: Calories: 105.3; Fats: 5.1g; Carbs: 10.9g; Protein: 4.9g; Fiber: 1.9g

268.Coriander Tahini Sauce

Preparation Time: 10 minutes
Servings: 6

Cooking Time:10 minutes

Ingredients:
- 1/4 cup cashews, soaked overnight and drained 1/4 cup water
- 4 tablespoons tahini
- 1/4 cup fresh coriander leaves, roughly chopped 1 clove garlic, minced
- Kosher salt and cayenne pepper, to taste

Directions: Process the cashews and water in your blender until creamy and uniform.
Add in the remaining ingredients and continue to blend until everything is well incorporated.
Conserve in your refrigerator for up to a week. Bon appétit!

Nutrition: Calories: 90.8; Fat: 7.2g; Carbs: 4.3g; Protein: 3.2g

269.Tofu Hollandaise

Preparation Time: 10 minutes
Servings: 12

Cooking Time: 15 minutes

Ingredients:
- 1/4 cup vegan butter, at room temperature
- 1 cup silken tofu
- 1 cup unsweetened rice milk
- Sea salt and ground black pepper, to taste 1/4 cup nutritional yeast
- 1/2 teaspoon turmeric powder
- 2 tablespoons fresh lime juice

Directions: Minimize all the ingredients in a high-speed blender or food processor.
Then, heat the mixture in a small saucepan over low-medium heat; cook, stirring occasionally, until the sauce has reduced and thickened. Bon appétit!

Nutrition: Calories: 81.9; Fats: 4.7g; Carbs: 6.2g; Protein: 3.1g

270.Cranberry Sauce

Preparation Time: 10 minutes
Servings: 8

Cooking Time: 15 minutes

Ingredients:
- 1/2 cup brown sugar
- 1/2 cup water
- 8 ounces cranberries, fresh or frozen
- A pinch of allspice
- A pinch of sea salt
- 1 tablespoon crystallized ginger

Directions: In a heavy-bottomed saucepan, bring the sugar and water to a rolling boil.
Stir until the sugar has dissolved.
Add in the cranberries, followed by the remaining ingredients. Turn the heat to a simmer and continue to cook for 10 to 12 minutes or until the cranberries burst.
Let it cool at room temperature. Conserve in a glass jar in your refrigerator. Bon appétit!

Nutrition: Calories: 61.9; Fat: 0.5g; Carbs: 15.8g; Protein: 0.4g

271.Homemade Trail Mix

Preparation Time: 20 minutes
Servings: 2

Cooking Time: 20 minutes

Ingredients:
- ½ cup uncooked old-fashioned oatmeal
- ½ cup chopped dates
- 2 cups whole grain cereal
- ¼ cup raisins
- ¼ cup almonds
- ¼ cup walnuts

Directions: Mix all the ingredients in a large bowl. Place in an airtight container until ready to use.

Nutrition: Protein: 9.2g; Fats: 17.9g; Carbs: 72.8g

272.Mushroom Sauce

Preparation Time: 5 minutes　　　　　　　　　　　　　　**Cooking Time: 12 minutes**
Servings: 4

Ingredients:
- ¾ tablespoon spelt flour
- ¼ of onion, peeled, diced
- 4 ounces sliced mushrooms
- ½ cup walnut coconut milk, homemade
- 1 tablespoon chopped walnuts
- Extra:
- ¼ teaspoon salt
- 1/8 teaspoon cayenne pepper
- ½ teaspoon dried thyme
- 1 tablespoon grapeseed oil
- ¼ cup vegetable broth, homemade

Directions: Take a medium skillet pan, place it over medium heat, add oil and when hot, add onion and mushrooms, season with 1/16 teaspoon each of salt and cayenne pepper, and then cook for 4 minutes until tender.
Stir in spelt flour until coated, cook for 1 minute, slowly whisk in coconut milk and vegetable broth and then season with remaining salt and cayenne pepper.
Switch heat to low-level, cook for 5 to 7 minutes until sauce has thickened slightly and then stir in walnuts and thyme. Serve straight away with spelt flour bread.

Nutrition: Calories: 65.1; Fats: 1.5g; Protein: 3.7g; Carbs: 9.4g

273.Quinoa with Mushroom

Preparation Time: 15 minutes　　　　　　　　　　　　　**Cooking Time: 30 minutes**
Servings: 4

Ingredients:
- ½ tablespoon avocado oil
- 1 cup uncooked quinoa, rinsed
- 12 ounces fresh white mushrooms, sliced
- 3 garlic cloves, minced
- 1¾ cup spring water
- ¼ cup fresh cilantro, chopped
- ¼ teaspoon cayenne powder
- Sea salt, as needed

Directions: Ina medium pan, heat avocado oil over medium-high heat and sauté the garlic for about 30–40 seconds. Add the mushrooms and cook on for about 5–6 minutes, stirring frequently.
Stir in the quinoa and cook for about 2 minutes, stirring continuously.
Add the water, cayenne, and salt and bring to a boil.
Now, adjust the heat to low and simmer, covered for about 15–18 minutes or until almost all the liquid is absorbed. Serve hot with the garnishing of cilantro.

Nutrition: Calories: 180.9; Fats: 0.3g; Carbs: 30.8g; Protein: 9.1g

274.Vegetable Chili

Preparation Time: 5 minutes　　　　　　　　　　　　　　**Cooking Time: 30 minutes**
Servings: 6

Ingredients:
- 2 cups black beans, cooked
- 1 medium red bell pepper; deseeded, chopped
- 1 poblano chili; deseeded, chopped
- 2 jalapeño chilies; deseeded, chopped
- 4 tablespoons cilantro, chopped
- 1 large white onion; peeled, chopped
- 1 ½ tablespoon minced garlic
- 1 ½ teaspoon sea salt
- 1 ½ teaspoon cumin powder
- 1 ½ teaspoon red chili powder
- 3 teaspoons lime juice
- 2 tablespoons grapeseed oil
- 2 ½ cups vegetable stock

Directions: Get a large pot, place it over medium-high heat, add oil and when hot, add onion and bake for 4–5 minutes until translucent.

Add bell pepper, jalapeno pepper, poblano chili, and garlic and then cook for 3–4 minutes until veggies turn tender. Season the vegetables with salt, stir in cumin powder and red chili powder, then add chickpeas and pour in vegetable stock.

Bring the mixture to a boil, then change heat to medium-low and simmer the chili for 15–20 minutes until thickened slightly.

Then remove the pot from heat, ladle chili stew among six bowls, drizzle with lime juice, garnish with cilantro, and serve.

Nutrition: Calories: 223.9; Carbs: 42.3g; Fats: 1.1g; Protein: 12.7g

275. Mushroom Dip

Preparation Time: 10 minutes
Servings: 4

Cooking Time: 20 minutes

Ingredients:
- ¼ cup coconut cream
- 1 tsp. garlic powder
- 1 tsp. chili powder
- 1 tbsp. olive oil
- 1 tsp. oregano, dried
- 1 small yellow onion, chopped
- 24 oz. white mushroom caps
- Salt and black pepper to the taste
- 1 tsp. curry powder

Directions: Heat-up a pan with the oil over medium heat, add the onion, oregano, chili, curry, and garlic, and cook for 5 minutes. Put the mushrooms and cook for 5 minutes more.

Add the rest of the ingredients, cook the mix for 10 minutes, cool down a bit, blend with an immersion blender and serve as a party dip.

Nutrition: Calories: 223.9; Fats: 11.2g; Carbs: 6.9g; Protein: 11.2g

276. Cilantro, Lime Quinoa

Preparation time: 5 minutes
Servings: 6

Cooking time: 15 minutes

Ingredients:
- 1 cup quinoa, rinsed and drained
- ½ cup fresh cilantro, chopped
- 1 lime zest, grated
- 2 tbsp. fresh lime juice
- 1 ¼ cups filtered alkaline water
- Sea salt

Directions: Add quinoa and water to the instant pot and stir well.

Seal pot with a lid and select manual mode and set timer for 5 minutes.

When finished, allow releasing pressure naturally then open the lid.

Add in cilantro, lime zest, and lime juice. Season with salt and serve.

Nutrition: Calories: 104.8; Fats: 1.9g; Carbs: 18.2g; Protein: 4.2g

277. Mushroom Gravy

Preparation Time: 5 minutes
Servings: 2

Cooking Time: 12 minutes

Ingredients:
- ¾ tablespoon spelt flour
- ¼ of onion, peeled, diced
- 4 ounces sliced mushrooms
- ½ cup walnut coconut milk, homemade
- 1 tablespoon chopped walnuts
- Extra:
- ¼ teaspoon salt
- 1/8 teaspoon cayenne pepper
- ½ teaspoon dried thyme
- 1 tablespoon grapeseed oil
- ¼ cup vegetable broth, homemade

Directions: Take a medium skillet pan, place it over medium heat, add oil and when hot, add onion and mushrooms, season with 1/16 teaspoon each of salt and cayenne pepper, and then cook for 4 minutes until tender.

Stir in spelt flour until coated, cook for 1 minute, slowly whisk in coconut milk and vegetable broth and then season with remaining salt and cayenne pepper.

Switch heat to low-level, cook for 5 to 7 minutes until sauce has thickened slightly and then stir in walnuts and thyme. Serve straight away with spelt flour bread.

Nutrition: Calories: 65.1; Fats: 1.4g; Protein: 3.7g; Carbs: 9.4g

278.Spicy Tomato Chutney

Preparation Time: 10 minutes

Cooking Time: 6 minutes

Servings: 4

Ingredients:
- Four green tomatoes, chopped
- 1/2 tsp mustard seeds
- 1 tbsp brown sugar
-
- Two jalapeno pepper, chopped
- 1/2 tsp turmeric
- 1 tbsp olive oil
- 1 tsp salt

Directions: Add oil into the fryer of air fryer duo fresh and set pot on sauté mode.
Once the oil is hot, then put mustard seeds and let them pop.
Add remaining ingredients and stir well. Cook on high for 5 minutes.
Mash tomatoes mixture using a potato masher until getting the desired consistency.
Serve and enjoy.

Nutrition: Calories: 65.8; Fats: 3.7g; Carbs: 7.5g; Protein: 1.4g

279.Lemon Avocado Salad Dressing

Preparation Time: 5 minutes

Cooking Time: 5 minutes

Servings: 2-3

Ingredients:
- 2 tablespoons olive oil
- 1 garlic clove, minced
- 1/2 teaspoon seasoned salt
- 1 medium ripe avocado, peeled and mashed
- 1/4 cup water
- 2 tablespoons sour cream
- 2 tablespoons lemon juice
- 1 tablespoon minced fresh dill or 1 teaspoon dill weed
- 1/2 teaspoon agave
- Salad greens, cherry tomatoes, sliced cucumbers, and sweet red and yellow pepper strips

Directions: Mix the first nine ingredients in a blender; cover and process until blended.
Serve with tomatoes, peppers, salad greens, and cucumbers. Store in the refrigerator.

Nutrition: Calories: 37.9; Fats: 2.4g; Carbs: 3.5g; Protein: 0.9g

280.Red Salsa

Preparation Time: 35 minutes

Cooking Time: 15 minutes

Servings: 8

Ingredients:
- 4 Roma tomatoes, halved
- ¼ cup chopped cilantro
- 1 jalapeno pepper, seeded, halved
- ½ of a medium white onion, peeled, cut into quarters 3 cloves of garlic, peeled
- ½ teaspoon salt
- 1 tablespoon brown sugar
- 1 teaspoon apple cider vinegar

Directions: Switch on the oven, then set it to 425ºF and let it preheat.
Meanwhile, take a baking sheet, line it with foil and then spread tomato, jalapeno pepper, onion and garlic.
Bake the vegetables for 15 minutes until vegetables have cooked and begin to brown, and then let the vegetables cool for 3 minutes.
Transfer the roasted vegetables into a blender, add the remaining ingredients and then pulse until smooth.
Tip the salsa into a medium bowl and then chill it for 30 minutes before serving with vegetable sticks.

Nutrition: Calories: 239.8; Fats: 0g; Protein: 0g; Carbs: 47.9g; Fiber: 15.8

Gluten-Free Recipes

281. Peach Mango Crumble (Pressure Cooker)

Preparation Time: 10 minutes
Servings: 4-6

Cooking Time: 15 minutes

Ingredients:

- 3 cups chopped fresh or frozen peaches
- 3 cups chopped fresh or frozen mangos
- 4 tablespoons unrefined sugar or pure maple syrup, divided 1 cup gluten-free rolled oats
- ½ cup shredded coconut, sweetened or unsweetened 2 tablespoons coconut oil or vegan margarine

Directions: Preparing the Ingredients. In a 6- to 7-inch round baking dish, toss together the peaches, mangos, and 2 tablespoons of sugar.

In a food processor, mix the coconut, oats, coconut oil, and remaining 2 tablespoons of sugar. Pulse until combined. (If you use maple syrup, you'll need less coconut oil. Start with just the syrup and add oil if the mixture isn't sticking together.) Drizzle the oat mixture over the fruit mixture.

Cover the dish with aluminum foil. Put a trivet in the bottom of your electric pressure cooker's cooking pot and pour in a cup or two of water. Using a foil sling or silicone helper handles, lower the pan onto the trivet.

High pressure for 6 minutes. Cover and select High Pressure for 6 minutes.

Pressure Release. Once the cook time is complete, quick release the pressure. Unlock and remove the lid.

Allow to cool for a five minutes before carefully lifting out the dish with oven mitts or tongs. Scoop out portions to serve.

Nutrition: Calories: 320.9; Fats: 17.9g; Protein: 4.2g; Carbs: 31.8g

282. Ginger Spice Brownies

Preparation Time: 5 minutes
Servings: 6

Cooking Time: 35 minutes

Ingredients:

- 1¾ cups whole-grain flour
- 1 teaspoon baking powder
- 1 teaspoon baking soda
- ½ teaspoon salt
- 1 tablespoon ground ginger
- ½ teaspoon ground cinnamon
- ½ teaspoon ground allspice
- 3 tablespoons unsweetened cocoa powder
- ½ cup vegan semisweet chocolate chips
- ½ cup chopped walnuts
- ¼ cup canola oil
- ½ cup dark molasses
- ½ cup water
- 1/3 cup light brown sugar
- 2 teaspoons grated fresh ginger

Directions: Prepare the oven to 350°F. Grease an 8-inch square pan and set aside. In a large bowl, combine the flour, baking powder, baking soda, salt, ground ginger, cinnamon, allspice, and cocoa. Stir in the chocolate chips and walnuts and set aside.

In medium bowl, combine the oil, molasses, water, sugar, and fresh ginger, then mix well.

Put the wet ingredients into the dry ingredients and mix.

Scrape the dough into the prepared baking pan. Press the dough evenly into the pan.

Cook until a toothpick inserted in the center comes out clean, for 30-35 minutes. Cool on a wire rack 30 minutes before cutting. Store in an airtight container.

Nutrition: Calories: 421.8; Fats: 20.9g; Carbs: 57.9g; Protein: 4.2g

283. Cauliflower Wings

Preparation Time: 10 minutes
Servings: 6

Cooking Time: 40 minutes

Ingredients:

- 1 cup oat milk
- ¾ cup gluten-free or whole-wheat flour
- 2 teaspoons garlic powder
- 2 teaspoons onion powder
- ½ teaspoon paprika
- ¼ teaspoon freshly ground black pepper
- 1 head cauliflower, cut into bite-size florets

Directions: Preheat the oven to 425°F. Line a baking sheet with parchment paper.

Mix together the milk, flour, garlic powder, onion powder, paprika, and pepper. Put the cauliflower florets, and mix until the florets are completely coated.

Place the coated florets on the baking sheet in an even layer, and cook for 40 minutes, turning once halfway through the cooking process. Serve.

Nutrition: Calories: 95.8; Fats: 0.9g; Carbs: 19.8; Protein: 3.1g

284. Eggplant Parmesan

Preparation Time: 10 minutes
Servings: 1

Cooking Time: 15 minutes

Ingredients:

- ¼ cup nondairy milk
- ¼ cup bread crumbs or panko
- 2 tablespoons nutritional yeast (optional)
- ¼ teaspoon salt
- 4 (¼-inch-thick) eggplant slices, peeled if desired 1 tablespoon olive oil, plus more as needed
- 4 tablespoons Simple Homemade Tomato Sauce
- 4 teaspoons Parm Sprinkle

Directions: Put the milk in a shallow bowl. In another shallow bowl, stir together the bread crumbs, nutritional yeast (if using), and salt.

Dip one eggplant slice in the milk, making sure both sides get moistened. Dip it into the bread crumbs, flipping to coat both sides.

Transfer to a plate and repeat to coat the remaining slices and then, warm the olive oil in a large skillet over medium heat and add the breaded eggplant slices, making sure there is oil under each.

Bake for 5 to 7 minutes, until browned. Flip, adding more oil as needed. Top each slice with 1 tablespoon tomato sauce and 1 teaspoon Parm Sprinkle. Cook for 5 to 7 minutes more

Nutrition: Calories: 459.8; Fats: 30.8g; Carbs: 30.9g; Protein: 23.1g

285. Portobello Mushroom Stew

Preparation Time: 10 minutes
Servings: 5

Cooking Time: 8 hours

Ingredients:

- 8 cups vegetable broth
- 1 cup dried wild mushrooms
- 1 cup dried chickpeas
- 3 cups chopped potato
- 2 cups chopped carrots
- 1 cup corn kernels
- 2 cups diced white onions
- 1 tablespoon minced parsley
- 3 cups chopped zucchini
- 1 tablespoon minced rosemary
- 1 1/2 teaspoon ground black pepper
- 1 teaspoon dried sage
- 2/3 teaspoon salt
- 1 teaspoon dried oregano
- 3 tablespoons soy sauce
- 1 1/2 teaspoons liquid smoke
- 8 ounces tomato paste

Directions: Switch on the slow cooker, add all the ingredients in it, and stir until mixed.

Shut the cooker with lid and cook for 8 hours at a high heat setting until cooked.

Serve straight away.

Nutrition: Calories: 446.9; Fats: 35.8g; Carbs: 23.9g; Protein: 11.2g

286. Barley and Chickpea Soup

Preparation Time: 15 minutes
Servings: 2

Cooking Time: 1 hour 30 minutes

Ingredients:
- 1 cup pearl barley
- 1 (15-ounce) can chickpeas, rinsed and drained 2 large carrots, peeled and chopped
- 1 zucchini, chopped
- 2 celery stalks, chopped
- 1 red onion, chopped
- 2 cups tomatoes, chopped
- 1 teaspoon dried parsley, crushed
- 1 teaspoon curry powder
- 1 teaspoon paprika
- 3 bay leaves
- Salt and ground black pepper, to taste
- 5 cups homemade vegetable broth
- 4 cups water
- ½ cup fresh cilantro, chopped

Directions: In a large soup pan, mix all the ingredients (except parsley) over high heat and heat to a boil.
Reduce the heat to medium-low and cook, covered for about 1½ hours.
Remove from the heat and discard the bay leaves. Serve hot with the garnishing of cilantro.

Nutrition: Calories: 325.8; Fats: 4.9g; Protein: 16.9g; Carbs: 58.7g

287.Chili with Tofu

Preparation Time: 15 minutes
Servings: 4

Cooking Time: 1 hour 40 minutes

Ingredients:
- 3/4-pound cannellini beans, soaked overnight and drained 3 tablespoons olive oil
- 1 large onion, diced
- 1 cup turnip, chopped
- 1 carrot, chopped
- 1 bell pepper, sliced
- 1 sweet potato, chopped
- 3 cloves garlic, minced
- 2 ripe tomatoes, pureed
- 3 tablespoons tomato paste
- 2 cups vegetable broth
- 2 bay leaves
- 1 tablespoon red chili powder
- 1 tablespoon brown sugar
- Sea salt and cayenne pepper, to taste
- 12 ounces silken tofu, cubed

Directions: Cover the soaked beans with a fresh change of cold water and bring to a boil. Let it boil for about 10 minutes. Turn the heat to a simmer and continue to cook for 50 to 55 minutes or until tender and then, warm the olive oil over medium heat, in a heavy-bottomed pot.
Once hot, sauté the onion, turnip, carrot, bell pepper and sweet potato.
Sauté the garlic for about 1 minute or so.
Add in the tomatoes, tomato paste, vegetable broth, bay leaves, red chili powder, brown sugar, salt, cayenne pepper and cooked beans. Let it simmer, stirring periodically, for 25 to 30 minutes or until cooked through.
Serve garnished with the silken tofu. Bon appétit!

Nutrition: Calories: 604.8g; Fats: 19.8g; Carbs: 73.9g; Protein: 38.2g

288.Pineapple and Mango Oatmeal

Preparation Time: 5 minutes

Servings: 2

Ingredients:
- 2 cups unsweetened almond milk
- 2 cups rolled oats
- ½ cup pineapple chunks, thawed if frozen
- ½ cup diced mango, thawed if frozen
- 1 banana, sliced
- 1 tablespoon chia seeds
- 1 tablespoon maple syrup

Directions: Stir together the almond milk, oats, pineapple, mango, banana, chia seeds, and maple syrup in a large bowl until you see no clumps.
Cover and refrigerate to chill for at least 4 hours, preferably overnight.
Serve chilled with your favorite toppings.

Nutrition: Calories: 511.9; Fats: 21.9g; Carbs: 12.8g; Protein: 14.2g

289.Slow Cooker Butternut Squash Oatmeal

Preparation Time: 15 minutes   **Cooking Time: 6-8 hours**
Servings: 4

Ingredients:

- 1 cup steel-cut oats
- 3 cups water
- 2 cups cubed (½-inch pieces) peeled butternut squash ¼ cup unsweetened coconut milk
- 1 tablespoon chia seeds
- 1½ teaspoons ground ginger
- 2 teaspoons yellow (mellow) miso paste
- 1 tablespoon sesame seeds, toasted
- 1 tablespoon chopped scallion, green parts only

Directions: Mix together the oats, water, and butternut squash in a slow cooker.
Cover and bake on Low for 6 to 8 hours, or until the squash is tender when tested with a fork. Mash the cooked butternut squash with a potato masher or heavy spoon. Stir together the butternut squash and oats until well mixed.
Mix together the milk, chia seeds, ginger, and miso paste in a small bowl and stir to combine. Put this mixture to the squash mixture and stir well.
Ladle the oatmeal into bowls and serve hot topped with sesame seeds and scallion.

Nutrition: Calories: 228.8; Fats: 4.7g; Carbs: 39.5g; Protein: 7.3g

290.French Toast

Preparation Time: 5 minutes   **Cooking Time: 15 minutes**
Servings: 2

Ingredients:

- 1 tablespoon ground flax seeds
- 1 cup coconut milk
- 1/2 teaspoon vanilla paste
- A pinch of sea salt
- A pinch of grated nutmeg
- 1/2 teaspoon ground cinnamon
- 1/4 teaspoon ground cloves
- 1 tablespoon agave syrup
- 4 slices bread

Directions: In a mixing bowl, thoroughly mix the flax seeds, coconut milk, vanilla, salt, nutmeg, cinnamon, cloves and agave syrup.
Dredge each slice of bread into the milk mixture until well coated on all sides.
Preheat an electric griddle to medium heat and lightly oil it with a nonstick cooking spray.
Cook each slice of bread on the preheated griddle for about 3 minutes per side until golden brown.

Nutrition: Calories: 232.9; Fats: 6.3g; Carbs: 35.3g; Protein: 8.4g

Dessert and Smoothie

291.Chocolate Peanut Butter Bars

Preparation Time: 45 minutes   **Servings: 6-8**

Ingredients:
- 1 cup dates
- 1 cup raw cashews
- ¼ cup Dutch-process cocoa powder
- 1 tsp. vanilla extract
- 1½ cups crunchy peanut butter
- 2 cups dairy-free chocolate chips
- 1 cup all-natural smooth peanut butter
- 3 cups puffed rice cereal

Directions: Prepare an 8-inch square baking dish lined using parchment paper. Set aside. Soak the dates in a bowl of warm water for 10 minutes. Drain and pat dry.
In a food processor, Mix the dates, cocoa powder, cashews and vanilla extract and process to form a thick dough. Press into the baking dish. Cover with the crunchy peanut butter, spreading it into an even layer. Refrigerate for 5 minutes.
In a large microwave-safe bowl, mix the chocolate chips and smooth peanut butter. Microwave in 30-second increments, stirring in between, until smooth. Take out of microwave and stir in the puffed rice cereal, mixing to coat.
Pour the puffed rice mixture over the chunky peanut butter layer in the baking dish and press flat. Refrigerate for at least 30 minutes. Remove then cut into squares.

Nutrition: Calories: 976.8; Fats: 65.8g; Carbs: 82.9g; Protein: 26.1g

292.Apple Crumble

Preparation Time: 15 minutes   **Cooking Time: 25 minutes**
Servings: 6

Ingredients:

For the filling:
- 4 to 5 apples, cored and chopped (about 6 cups)
- ½ cup unsweetened applesauce, or ¼ cup water
- 2 to 3 tbsps. unrefined sugar (coconut, date, Sucanat, maple syrup)
- 1 tsp. ground cinnamon
- Pinch sea salt

For the Crumble:
- 2 tbsps. almond butter, or cashew or sunflower seed butter
- 2 tbsps. maple syrup
- 1½ cups rolled oats
- ½ cup walnuts, finely chopped
- ½ tsp. ground cinnamon
- 2 to 3 tbsps. unrefined granular sugar (coconut, date, Sucanat)

Directions: Preheat the oven to 350°F. Put the apples and applesauce in an 8-inch-square baking dish, and sprinkle with the sugar, cinnamon, and salt. Toss to combine.
In a medium bowl, mix together the nut butter and maple syrup until smooth and creamy. Add the oats, walnuts, cinnamon, and sugar and stir to coat, using your hands if necessary.
Sprinkle the topping over the apples, and put the dish in the oven. Cook for 25 minutes, or until the fruit is soft and the topping is lightly browned.

Nutrition: Calories: 355.9; Fats: 16.8g; Carbs: 48.7g; Protein: 7.1g

293.Chocolate and Peanut Butter Smoothie

Preparation Time: 5 minutes   **Servings: 4**

Ingredients:

- 1 tbsp. unsweetened cocoa powder
- 1 tbsp. peanut butter
- 1 banana
- 1 tsp. maca powder
- ½ cup unsweetened soy milk
- ¼ cup rolled oats
- 1 tbsp. flaxseeds
- 1 tbsp. maple syrup
- 1 cup water

Directions: Mix all the ingredients to a blender, then process until the mixture is smooth and creamy. Add water or soy milk if necessary. Serve immediately.

Nutrition: Calories: 473.8; Fats: 15.8g; Carbs: 26.8g; Fiber: 17.9g; Protein: 13.2g

294.Lime and Cucumber Drink

Preparation Time: 5 minutes   Servings: 4

Ingredients:

- ¼ cup chopped cucumber
- 1 tbsp. fresh lime juice
- 1 tbsp. apple cider vinegar
- 2 tbsps. maple syrup
- ¼ tsp. sea salt, optional
- 4 cups water

Directions: Mix all the ingredients in a glass. Stir to mix well. Refrigerate overnight before serving.

Nutrition: Calories: 113.9; Fats: 0.1g; Carbs: 28.7g; Fiber: 0.2g; Protein: 0.5g

295.Beet and Clementine Smoothie

Preparation Time: 10 minutes   Servings: 3

Ingredients:

- 1 small beet, peeled and chopped
- 1 clementine, peeled and broken into segments
- ½ ripe banana
- ½ cup raspberries
- 1 tbsp. chia seeds
- 2 tbsps. almond butter
- ¼ tsp. vanilla extract
- 1 cup unsweetened almond milk
- ⅛ tsp. fine sea salt, optional

Directions: Mix all the ingredients in a food processor, then pulse on high for 2 minutes or until glossy and creamy. Refrigerate for an hour and serve chilled.

Nutrition: Calories: 525.9; Fats: 25.1g; Carbs: 61.5g; Fiber: 17.2g; Protein: 20.8g

296.Hazelnut and Chocolate Milk

Preparation Time: 5 minutes   Servings: 2

Ingredients:

- 2 tbsps. cocoa powder
- 4 dates, pitted
- 1 cup hazelnuts
- 3 cups of water

Directions: Put the ingredients in the order in a food processor or blender and then pulse for 2 to 3 minutes at high speed until smooth. Pour the smoothie into two glasses and then serve.

Nutrition: Calories: 119.8; Fats: 4.8g; Carbs: 18.9g; Protein: 2.1g; Fiber: 0.8g

297.Sweet and Sour Juice

Preparation Time: 5 minutes   Servings: 2

Ingredients:

- 2 medium apples, cored, peeled, chopped
- 2 large cucumbers, peeled
- 4 cups chopped grapefruit
- 1 cup mint

Directions: Process all the ingredients in the order in a juicer or blender and then strain it into two glasses. Serve straight away.

Nutrition: Calories: 89.8; Fats: 0g; Carbs: 22.8g; Protein: 0g; Fiber: 8.8g

298. Banana Walnut Bread

Preparation Time: 5 minutes
Servings: 1

Cooking Time: 50 minutes

Ingredients:
- 1/2 cups whole wheat flour
- ¾ teaspoon baking soda
- 1 very ripe banana, mashed
- ½ cup maple syrup
- ¼ cup unsweetened applesauce
- 2 tablespoons aquafaba (the liquid from a can of chickpeas) 1 teaspoon vanilla extract
- 1 teaspoon pink Himalayan salt
- ¾ cup chopped walnuts

Directions: Prepare the oven to 180 C or 350 F. Line the pan using parchment paper or a silicone liner.
Sift the baking soda and flour together, in a mixing bowl.
In a separate container, combine the mashed bananas, maple syrup, applesauce, aquafaba, vanilla, and salt. Mix well. Mix well in the flour mixture. Gently stir the walnuts.
Transfer the combination into the arranged pan. Cook it for 40 to 50 minutes, until brown on the top and edges.
Enjoy right after it cools or store it in a reusable container at room temperature for up to 5 days.

Nutrition: Calories: 540.9; Fats: 16.9g; Carbs: 95.7g; Proteins: 12.3g; Fibers: 10.9g

299. Cranberry and Almond Muffins

Preparation Time: 10 minutes
Servings: 1

Cooking Time: 20 minutes

Ingredients:
- 1/2 cups whole wheat flour (or gluten-free flour) 1 teaspoon baking soda
- 1 teaspoon baking powder
- ½ teaspoon pink Himalayan salt 1/4 cup unsweetened plant-based milk
- 1/8 cup dried cranberries, soaked in water for 1 hour to soften 1/8 cup maple syrup
- 1/8 cup chopped almonds
- 1/8 cup unsweetened applesauce
- 1 tablespoon freshly squeezed lemon juice
- 1 tablespoons aquafaba (the liquid from a can of chickpeas) ½ teaspoon vanilla extract

Directions: Preheat the oven to 375ºF (190ºC). Insert silicone muffin cups into a muffin pan.
In a bowl, combine the flour, baking soda, baking powder, and salt and mix well.
In a separate bowl, combine the milk, cranberries, maple syrup, almonds, applesauce, lemon juice, aquafaba, and vanilla and mix well. Mix the wet and dry ingredients and mix well.
Fill each muffin cup a little more than half full with batter. Cook for 20 minutes, or until lightly browned and a toothpick inserted into the center of a muffin comes out clean. Enjoy as soon as they cool or store in a reusable container at room temperature.

Nutrition: Calories: 142.8; Fats: 1.9g; Carbs: 30.9g; Proteins: 3.2g; Fibers: 2.9g

300. Pineapple Coconut Macaroons

Preparation Time: 5 minutes
Servings: 1

Cooking Time: 20 minutes

Ingredients:
- 1/3 cups unsweetened coconut shreds
- ½ cup chopped pineapple
- ½ cup coconut sugar
- ½ banana
- 3 tablespoons wheat flour (or gluten-free flour)

Directions: Prepare the oven to 350ºF (180ºC). Line a pan with parchment paper or a silicone liner.
In a food processor, mix all the ingredients and process until almost smooth.
Use a tablespoon to make 10 heaping macaroons. Space them evenly on the pre-prepared baking sheet.
Bake for 20 minutes, or until the tops and bottoms are light browns.
Let cool on a wire rack for 10 minutes before serving. Store in a reusable container in the refrigerator for up to 5 days.

Nutrition: Calories: 89.9; Fats: 3.8g; Carbs: 14.9g; Proteins: 1.2g; Fibers: 0.9g

301.Chocolate Chip Banana Cookies

Preparation Time: 5 minutes   **Cooking Time: 10 minutes**
Servings: 1

Ingredients:
- 2 bananas
- 1 cup rolled oats
- 1 teaspoon ground flaxseed
- 1 teaspoon vanilla extract
- ¼ cup vegan mini chocolate chips
- ¼ cup chopped walnuts

Directions: Prepare the oven to 350ºF (180ºC). Line a pan with parchment paper or a silicone liner.
In a food processor, combine the bananas, oats, flaxseed, and vanilla and blend until very well combined. Use a spoon to mix in the chocolate chips and walnuts.
Scoop the batter into 9 cookies, spacing them out on the prepared baking sheet. Cook for 10 minutes, or until the bottoms are light brown. Enjoy right after they cool or store in a reusable container at room temperature.

Nutrition: Calories: 121.9; Fats: 4.8g; Carbs: 16.8g; Proteins: 2.3g; Fibers: 1.9g

302.Watermelon Strawberry Ice Pops

Preparation Time: 5 minutes   **Servings: 1**

Ingredients:
- 1 cup diced watermelon
- 1 strawberry, tops removed
- 1 tablespoon freshly squeezed lime juice

Directions: In a blender, mix the lime juice, strawberries, and watermelon. Blend for 1 to 2 minutes, or until well combined.
Pour evenly into 6 ice-pop molds, insert ice-pop sticks, and freeze for at least 6 hours before serving.

Nutrition: Calories: 61 Fats: 0g Carbs: 15g Proteins: 1g Fibers: 1g

303.Raspberry Muffins

Preparation Time: 10 minutes   **Cooking Time: 25 minutes**
Servings: 12

Ingredients:
- 1/2 cup and 2 tablespoons whole-wheat flour 1 (1/2) cups raspberries, fresh and more for decorating 1 cup white whole-wheat flour
- 1/8 teaspoon salt
- 3/4 cup of coconut sugar
- 2 teaspoons baking powder
- 1 teaspoon apple cider vinegar
- 1 1/4 cups water
- 1/2 cup olive oil

Directions: Switch on the oven, then set it to 400ºF and let it preheat.
Meanwhile, take a large bowl, place both flours in it, add salt and baking powder and then stir until combined.
Take a medium bowl, add oil to it and then whisk in the sugar until dissolved.
Whisk in vinegar and water until blended, slowly stir in flour mixture until smooth batter comes together, and then fold in berries.
Take a 12-cups muffin pan, grease it with oil, fill evenly with the prepared mixture and then put a raspberry on top of each muffin. Bake the muffins for 25 minutes until the top is golden brown and then serve.

Nutrition: Calories: 108.8; Fats: 3.2g; Protein: 2.3g; Carbs: 17.4g; Fiber: 0.9g

304.Chocolate Cake

Preparation Time: 15 minutes   **Cooking Time: 50 minutes**
Servings: 8

Ingredients:
- 1 (1/2) cup white whole-wheat flour
- 1 tablespoon flaxseed meal
- 2 (1/2) tablespoons cocoa powder
- 1/4 teaspoon salt
- 4 tablespoons chopped walnuts
- 1 teaspoon baking powder

- 2/3 cup coconut sugar
- 1/4 teaspoon baking soda
- 1 teaspoon vanilla extract, unsweetened
- 3 tablespoons peanut butter
- 1/4 cup olive oil
- 1 cup almond milk, unsweetened

Directions: Switch on the oven, then set it to 350ºF and let it preheat.

Meanwhile, take a medium bowl, place flour in it, add salt, baking powder and soda in it and then stir until mixed. Take a large bowl, pour in milk, add sugar, flaxseed meal, oil and vanilla, whisk until sugar has dissolved, and then whisk in flour mixture until smooth batter comes together.

Spoon half of the prepared batter in a medium bowl, add cocoa powder and then stir until combined.

Add peanut butter into the other bowl and then stir until combined.

Take a loaf pan, line it with a parchment sheet, spoon half of the chocolate batter in it, and then spread it evenly. Layer the chocolate batter with half of the peanut butter batter, cover with the remaining chocolate batter and then layer with the remaining peanut butter batter.

Make swirls into the batter with a toothpick, smooth the top with a spatula, sprinkle walnuts on top, and then bake for 50 minutes until done.

When done, let the cake rest in its pan for 10 minutes, then remove it to cool completely and cut it into slices. Serve straight away.

Nutrition: Calories: 298.8; Fat: 13.9g; Protein: 6.1g; Carbs: 38.7g; Fiber: 2.9g

305. Banana Muffins

Preparation Time: 10 minutes
Servings: 12

Cooking Time: 30 minutes

Ingredients:
- 1 (½) cup mashed banana
- 1 (½) cup and 2 tablespoons white whole-wheat flour, divided ¼ cup of coconut sugar
- ¾ cup rolled oats, divided
- 1 teaspoon ginger powder
- 1 tablespoon ground cinnamon, divided
- 2 teaspoons baking powder
- ½ teaspoon salt
- 1 teaspoon baking soda
- 1 tablespoon vanilla extract, unsweetened
- ½ cup maple syrup
- 1 tablespoon rum
- ½ cup of coconut oil

Directions: Switch on the oven, then set it to 350ºF and let it preheat.

Meanwhile, take a medium bowl, place 1 (½) cups flour in it, add ½ cup oats, ginger, baking powder and soda, salt and 2 teaspoons cinnamon and then stir until mixed.

Place ¼ cup of coconut oil in a heatproof bowl, melt it in the microwave oven and then whisk in maple syrup until combined.

Add mashed banana along with rum and vanilla, stir until combined and then whisk this mixture into the flour mixture until the smooth batter comes together.

Take a separate medium bowl, place the remaining oats and flour in it, add cinnamon, coconut sugar and coconut oil, and then stir with a fork until a crumbly mixture comes together.

Take a 12-cups muffin pan, fill evenly with prepared batter, top with oats mixture and then bake for 30 minutes until firm and the top turn golden brown.

Nutrition: Calories: 239.8; Fats: 9.1g; Protein: 2.9g; Carbs: 35.1g; Fiber: 1.9g

306. Baked Apples

Preparation Time: 5 minutes
Servings: 4

Cooking Time: 20 minutes

Ingredients:
- 6 medium apples, peeled, cut into chunks
- 1 teaspoon ground cinnamon
- 2 tablespoons melted coconut oil

Directions: Switch on the oven, then set it to 350ºF and let it preheat.

Take a medium baking dish and then spread apple pieces in it.

Get a small bowl, place coconut oil in it, stir in cinnamon, drizzle this mixture over apples and then toss until coated. Put the baking dish into the oven and then bake for 20 minutes or more until apples turn soft, stirring halfway. Serve straight away.

Nutrition: Calories: 170 Fat: 3.8g Protein: 0.5g Carbs: 31g Fiber: 5.5g

307.Banana Coconut Cookies

Preparation Time: 40 minutes   **Servings: 8**

Ingredients:
- 1 (½) cup shredded coconut, unsweetened
- 1 cup mashed banana

Directions: Switch on the oven, then set it to 350ºF and let it preheat.
Take a medium bowl, place the mashed banana in it and then stir in coconut until well combined.
Get a large baking sheet, line it with a parchment sheet and then scoop the prepared mixture on it, 2 tablespoons of mixture per cookie.
Place the baking sheet into the refrigerator and then let it cool for 30 minutes or more until harden.
Serve straight away.

Nutrition: Calories: 50.9; Fats: 2.8g; Protein: 0.4g; Carbs: 3.9g; Fiber: 0.9g

308.Butter Carrots

Preparation Time: 10 minutes   **Cooking Time: 10 minutes**
Servings: 4

Ingredients:
- 2 cups baby carrots
- 1 tablespoon brown sugar
- ½ tablespoon vegan butter, melted
- A pinch each salt and black pepper

Directions: Take a baking dish suitable to fit in your air fryer. Toss carrots with sugar, butter, salt and black pepper in the baking dish. Put the dish in the air fryer basket and seal the fryer.
Cook the carrots for 10 minutes at 350 degrees F on air fryer mode.

Nutrition: Calories: 269.8; Fats: 9.8g; Carbs: 24.6g; Protein: 5.4g; Fiber:3.5g

309.Parsley Potatoes

Preparation Time: 10 minutes   **Cooking Time: 10 minutes**
Servings: 4

Ingredients:
- 1-pound gold potatoes, sliced
- 2 tablespoons olive oil
- ¼ cup parsley leaves, chopped
- Juice from ½ lemon
- Salt and black pepper to taste

Directions: Take a baking dish suitable to fit in your air fryer.
Place the potatoes in it and season them liberally with salt, pepper, olive oil, and lemon juice.
Put the baking dish in the air fryer basket and seal it.
Cook the potatoes for 10 minutes at 350 degrees F on air fryer mode.
Serve warm with parsley garnishing. Devour.

Nutrition: Calories: 279.9; Fats: 4.7g; Carbs: 35.5g; Protein: 4.1g; Fiber 2.7g

310.Tomato Kebabs

Preparation Time: 10 minutes   **Cooking Time: 6 minutes**
Servings: 4

Ingredients:
- 3 tablespoons balsamic vinegar
- 24 cherry tomatoes
- 2 cups vegan feta cheese, sliced
- 2 tablespoons olive oil
- 3 garlic cloves, minced
- 1 tablespoon thyme, chopped
- Salt and black pepper to the taste

Ingredients For the Dressing:
- 2 tablespoons balsamic vinegar
- 4 tablespoons olive oil
- Salt and black pepper to taste

Directions: In a medium bowl combine oil, garlic cloves, thyme, salt, vinegar, and black pepper.
Mix well then add the tomatoes and coat them liberally.
Thread 6 tomatoes and cheese slices on each skewer alternatively.
Place these skewers in the air fryer basket and seal it.
Cook them for 6 minutes on air fryer mode at 360 degrees F.
Meanwhile, whisk together the dressing ingredients.
Place the cooked skewers on the serving plates. Pour the vinegar dressing over them. Enjoy.

Nutrition: Calories: 189.8; Fat: 5.9g; Carbs: 17.8g; Protein: 8.2g; Fiber: 5.8g

311.Fried Mustard Greens

Preparation Time: 10 minutes
Servings: 4

Cooking Time: 11 minutes

Ingredients:
- 2 garlic cloves, minced
- 1 tablespoon olive oil
- ½ cup yellow onion, sliced
- 3 tablespoons vegetable stock
- ¼ teaspoon dark sesame oil
- 1-pound mustard greens, torn
- Salt and black pepper to the taste

Directions: Take a baking dish suitable to fit in your air fryer.
Add oil and place it over the medium heat and sauté onions in it for 5minutes.
Stir in garlic, greens, salt, pepper, and stock. Mix well then place the dish in the air fryer basket.
Seal it and cook them for 6 minutes at 350 degrees F on air fryer mode.
Drizzle sesame oil over the greens. Devour.

Nutrition: Calories: 209.8; Fats: 7.9g; Carbs: 23.7g; Protein: 4.2g; Fiber: 9.8g

312.Mushroom Stuffed Tomatoes

Preparation Time: 10 minutes
Servings: 4

Cooking Time: 15 minutes

Ingredients
- 4 tomatoes, tops removed and pulp removed (reserve for filling) 1 yellow onion, chopped
- ½ cup mushrooms, chopped
- 1 tablespoon bread crumbs
- 1 tablespoon vegan butter
- ¼ teaspoon caraway seeds
- 1 tablespoon parsley, chopped
- 2 tablespoons celery, chopped
- 1 cup vegan cheese, shredded
- Salt and black pepper to the taste

Directions: Put a pan over medium heat, add butter.
When it melts, add onion and celery to sauté for 3 minutes.
Stir in mushrooms and tomato pulp. Cook for 1 minute then add crumbled bread, pepper, salt, cheese, parsley, and caraway seeds.
Cook while stirring for 4 minutes then remove from the heat. After cooling the mixture, stuff it equally in the tomatoes. Put the tomatoes in the air fryer basket and seal it. Cook them for 8 minutes at 350 degrees F on air fryer mode. Enjoy.

Nutrition: Calories: 279.9; Fats: 8.8g; Carbs: 34.9g; Protein: 11.2g; Fiber:10.8g

313. Banana Walnut Muffins

Preparation Time: 10 minutes   **Cooking Time: 18 minutes**
Servings: 12

Ingredients:
- 4 large pitted dates, boiled
- 1 cup almond milk
- 2 tablespoons lemon juice
- 2½ cups rolled oats
- 1 teaspoon baking powder
- 1 teaspoon baking soda
- 1 teaspoon cinnamon
- ¼ teaspoon nutmeg
- 1/8 teaspoon salt
- 1½ cups mashed banana
- ¼ cup maple syrup
- 1 tablespoon vanilla extract
- 1 cup walnuts, chopped

Directions: Preheat your oven to 350 degrees F.
Separately, whisk together the dry ingredients in one bowl and the wet ingredients in another bowl.
Beat the two mixtures together until smooth. Fold in walnuts and give it a gentle stir.
Line a muffin tray with muffin cups and evenly divide the muffin batter among the cups.
Bake for 18 minutes and serve.

Nutrition: Calories: 329.8; Fats: 3.8g; Carbs: 54.6g; Protein: 6.2g; Fiber:3.7g

314. Protein Fat Bombs

Preparation Time: 10 minutes   **Cooking Time: 1 hour**
Servings: 12

Ingredients:
- 1 cup coconut oil
- 1 cup peanut butter, melted
- ½ cup cocoa powder
- ¼ cup plant-based protein powder
- 1 pinch of salt
- 2 cups unsweetened shredded coconut

Directions: In a bowl, put all the ingredients except coconut shreds. Mix well then make small balls out of this mixture and place them into silicone molds. Freeze for 1 hour to set. Roll the balls in the coconut shreds. Serve.

Nutritional: Calories: 339.8; Fats: 13.9g; Carbs: 34.6g; Protein: 12.1g; Fiber: 2.9g

315. Chocolate Mint Grasshopper Pie

Preparation Time: 4 hours and 15 minutes   **Servings: 4**

Ingredients:

For the Crust:
- 1 cup dates, soaked in warm water for 10 minutes in
- water, drained 1/8 teaspoons salt
- 1/2 cup pecans
- 1 teaspoons cinnamon
- 1/2 cup walnuts

For the Filling:
- ½ cup mint leaves
- 2 cups of cashews, soaked in warm water for 10 minutes
- in water, drained 2 tablespoons coconut oil
- 1/4 cup and 2 tablespoons of agave
- 1/4 teaspoons spirulina
- 1/4 cup water

Directions: Prepare the crust, and for this, place all its ingredients in a food processor and pulse for 3 to 5 minutes until the thick paste comes together.
Take a 6-inch springform pan, grease it with oil, place crust mixture in it and spread and press the dough evenly in the bottom and along the sides, and freeze.
Prepare the filling and for this, place all its ingredients in a food processor, and pulse for 2 minutes until smooth.
Pour the filling into prepared pan, smooth the top, and freeze for 4 hours until set.
Cut pie into slices and then serve.

Nutrition: Calories: 339.8; Fats: 8.8g; Carbs: 44.8g; Protein: 4.1g; Fiber: 2.9g

316. Cold Lemon Squares

Preparation Time: 30 minutes   **Servings: 4**

Ingredients:
- 1 cup avocado oil+ a drizzle
- 2 bananas, peeled and chopped
- 1 tablespoon honey ¼ cup lemon juice
- A pinch of lemon zest, grated

Directions: In your food processor, mix the bananas with the rest of the ingredients, pulse well and spread on the bottom of a pan greased with a drizzle of oil.
Introduce in the fridge for 30 minutes, slice into squares and serve.

Nutrition: Calories: 135.9; Fats: 10.9g; Fiber: 0.2g; Carbs: 6.8g; Protein: 1.3g

317. Green Tea and Vanilla Cream

Preparation Time: 2 hours   **Servings: 4**

Ingredients:
- 14 ounces almond milk, hot
- 2 tablespoons green tea powder
- 14 ounces heavy cream
- 3 tablespoons stevia
- 1 teaspoon vanilla extract
- 1 teaspoon gelatin powder

Directions: In a bowl, combine the almond milk with the green tea powder and the rest of the ingredients, whisk well, cool down, divide into cups and keep in the fridge for 2 hours before serving.

Nutrition: Calories: 119.8; Fats: 2.9g; Fiber: 2.9g; Carbs: 6.8g; Protein: 4.2g

318. Strawberries Cream

Preparation Time: 10 minutes   **Cooking Time: 20 minutes**
Servings: 4

Ingredients:
- ½ cup stevia
- 2 pounds strawberries, chopped
- 1 cup almond milk
- Zest of 1 lemon, grated
- ½ cup heavy cream
- 3 egg yolks, whisked

Directions: Heat up a pan with the milk over medium-high heat, add the stevia and the rest of the ingredients, whisk well, simmer for 20 minutes, divide into cups and serve cold.

Nutrition: Calories: 151.8; Fats: 4.2g; Fiber: 5.2g; Carbs: 4.8g; Protein 1.2g

319. Power Smoothie

Preparation Time: 5 minutes   **Servings: 4**

Ingredients:
- 1 banana
- ¼ cup rolled oats, or 1 scoop plant protein powder 1 tablespoon flaxseed, or chia seeds
- 1 cup raspberries, or other berries
- 1 cup chopped mango (frozen or fresh)
- ½ cup non-dairy milk (optional)
- 1 cup water

Directions: Purée everything in a blender until smooth, adding more water (or non-dairy milk) if needed.
Add none, some, or all the bonus boosters, as desired. Purée until blended.

Nutrition: Calories: 549.8; Fats: 8.8g; Carbs: 11.3g; Fiber: 28.7g; Protein: 13.2g

320. Pink Panther Smoothie

Preparation Time: 5 minutes   **Servings: 3**

Ingredients:

- 1 cup strawberries
- 1 cup chopped melon (any kind)
- 1 cup cranberries or raspberries
- 1 tablespoon chia seeds
- ½ cup coconut milk or other non-dairy milk
- 1 cup water

Directions: Purée everything in a blender until smooth, add more water (or coconut milk) if needed. Add bonus boosters, as desired, and purée until blended.

Nutrition: Calories: 458.8; Fats: 29.9g; Carbs: 51.9g; Fiber: 18.7g; Protein: 8.1g

321.Tropical Smoothie

Preparation Time: 5 minutes   Servings: 4

Ingredients:

- 1 cup frozen mango chunks
- 1 cup frozen pineapple chunks
- 1 small tangerine, peeled and pitted
- 4 cups spinach leaves
- 1 cup coconut water
- ¼ teaspoon cayenne pepper, optional

Directions: Add all the ingredients to a food processor, then blitz until the mixture is smooth and combined well. Serve or chill in the refrigerator for 1 hour before serving.

Nutrition: Calories: 282.9; Fats: 1.7g; Carbs: 67.5g; Fiber: 10.2g; Protein: 6.5g

322.Pumpkin Smoothie

Preparation Time: 5 minutes   Servings: 2

Ingredients:

- ½ cup pumpkin purée
- 4 Medjool dates, pitted and chopped
- 1 cup unsweetened almond milk
- ¼ teaspoon vanilla extract
- ¼ teaspoon ground cinnamon
- ½ cup ice
- A pinch of ground nutmeg

Directions: Put the ingredients to a blender, then process until the mixture is glossy and well mixed. Serve immediately.

Nutrition: Calories: 416.9; Fats: 2.9g; Carbs: 94.6g; Fiber: 10.2g; Protein: 11.6g

323.Banana and Chia Smoothie

Preparation Time: 5 minutes   Servings: 3

Ingredients:

- 1 banana
- 1 cup alfalfa sprouts
- 1 tablespoon chia seeds
- ½ cup unsweetened coconut milk
- 1 to 2 soft Medjool dates, pitted
- ¼ teaspoon ground cinnamon
- 1 tablespoon grated fresh ginger
- 1 cup water
- A pinch of ground cardamom

Directions: Put the ingredients to a blender, then process until the mixture is smooth and creamy. Add water or coconut milk if necessary. Serve immediately.

Nutrition: Calories: 476.9; Fats: 40.9g; Carbs: 30.8g; Fiber: 13.9g; Protein: 8.2g

324.Pineapple, Banana & Spinach Smoothie

Preparation Time: 10 minutes   Servings: 1

Ingredients:

- ½ cup almond milk
- ¼ cup soy yogurt
- 1 cup spinach
- 1 cup banana
- 1 cup pineapple chunks
- 1 tbsp. chia seeds

Directions: Add all the ingredients in a blender. Blend until smooth.
Chill in the refrigerator before serving.

Nutrition: Calories: 296.8; Fats: 5.9g; Carbs 53.8g; Fiber: 9.9g; Protein: 13.2g

325.Pumpkin Chia Smoothie

Preparation Time: 5 minutes   Serves: 1

Ingredients:

- 3 Tablespoons Pumpkin Puree
- 1 Tablespoon MCT Oil
- ¾ Cup Coconut Milk, Full Fat
- ½ Avocado, Fresh
- 1 Teaspoon Vanilla, Pure
- ½ Teaspoon Pumpkin Pie Spice

Directions: Combine all ingredients together until blended.

Nutrition: Calories: 725.9; Protein: 5.6g; Fats: 69.7g; Carbs: 14.8g

326.Green Mango Smoothie

Preparation Time: 5 minutes   Serves: 1

Ingredients:

- 2 Cups Spinach
- 1-2 Cups Coconut Water
- 2 Mangos, Ripe, Peeled & Diced

Directions: Blend everything together until smooth.

Nutrition: Calories: 416.9; Protein: 7.4g; Fats: 2.6g; Carbs: 102.5g

327.Overnight Oatmeal

Preparation Time: 25 minutes + 6 hours   **Cooking Time: 20 minutes**
Servings: 4

Ingredients

- 1½ cups blueberries, frozen
- 4 tablespoons chia seeds, divided
- 2 cups rolled oats
- 3 cups almond milk
- 4 pitted dates
- 2 tablespoons peanut butter

Directions: Microwave blueberries in 1 tablespoon water for 2-3 minutes.
Stir in 2 tablespoon chia seed to the blueberries. Refrigerate for 20 minutes.
Put ½ cup oats and ½ tablespoon chia seeds into 4 jars. Blend milk, dates, and peanut butter. Pour it into the jars. Add blueberry chia jam to the jars. Refrigerate for 6-8 hours.

Nutrition: Calories: 289.8; Fats: 9.8g; Carbs: 34.7g; Protein: 13.2g; Fiber: 9.9g

328.Almond Flour Muffins

Preparation Time: 10 minutes   **Cooking Time: 30 minutes**
Servings: 12

Ingredients:

- 1 cup blanched almond flour
- 2 flax eggs
- 1 tablespoon agave nectar
- ¼ teaspoon baking soda
- ½ teaspoon apple cider vinegar

Directions: Mix soda and flour in a bowl. Mix flax eggs, nectar, and vinegar in a separate bowl.
Combine both mixtures and stir well.
Preheat the oven to 350 F, pour the mixture into muffin tins. Bake for 15 minutes.

Nutrition: Calories: 107.9; Fats: 49.9g; Carbs: 7.9g; Protein: 48.1g

329.Strawberry Ice Cream

Preparation Time: 15 minutes   **Cooking Time: 15 minutes**
Servings: 6

Ingredients:
- 5 frozen burro bananas
- 1 cup frozen strawberries
- ½ of avocado; peeled, pitted, and chopped
- ¼ cup unsweetened hemp coconut milk
- 1 tablespoon agave nectar

Directions: In a high-powered blender, put all Ingredients: and pulse until smooth.
Transfer the strawberry mixture into an airtight container and refrigerate for about 4–6 hours or until firm before serving.

Nutrition: Calories: 142.8; Fats: 0.7g; Carbs: 28.3g; Protein: 1.8g

330.Blackberry Pie

Preparation Time: 10 minutes   **Cooking Time: 10 minutes**
Servings: 4

Ingredients:
- 1 vanilla bean, cut lengthwise, deseeded
- ¼ teaspoon cinnamon
- 6 cups blackberry, sliced
- ¼ cup unsweetened coconut milk
- ½ cup orange juice, freshly squeezed

Directions: Combine all your ingredients.
In a medium-size skillet on medium-high heat, cook the fruit mixture. Cook the fruit mixture for 10 minutes.
Divide the fruit mixture among four serving dishes. Top with 1 tablespoon of coconut milk. Serve and Enjoy!

Nutrition: Calories: 108.8; Fats: 0.1g; Carbs: 28.4g; Protein: 0.3g

331.Cardamom Pears Smoothie

Preparation Time: 10 minutes   **Cooking Time: 15 minutes**
Servings: 4

Ingredients:
- 4 pears, cored, peeled and chopped
- 1 cup heavy cream
- 1 cup coconut milk
- 1 teaspoon cardamom, ground
- ½ teaspoon turmeric powder
- 1 teaspoon vanilla extract

Directions: In your instant pot, mix the pears with the cream and the rest of the ingredients, put the cover on and cook on High for 15 minutes.
Release the pressure naturally for 10 minutes, blend using an immersion blender, divide into bowls and serve.

Nutrition: Calories: 228.8; Fats: 5.1g; Fiber: 3.1g; Carbs: 11.2g; Protein: 5.9g

332.Pineapple Pudding

Preparation Time: 10 minutes   **Cooking Time: 20 minutes**
Servings: 4

Ingredients:
- 2 cups coconut milk
- 1 cup white rice
- ½ cup pineapple, peeled and cubed
- 1 teaspoon saffron powder
- ½ teaspoon cardamom powder
- ½ cup sugar
- ½ teaspoon vanilla extract

Directions: In your instant pot, mix the rice with the pineapple and the other ingredients, cover and cook on High for 20 minutes.
Release the pressure naturally for 10 minutes, divide the pudding into bowls and serve cold.

Nutrition: Calories: 261.8; Fats: 6.1g; Fiber: 1.9g; Carbs: 11.2g; Protein: 4.8g

333.Indian Almond Kulfi

Preparation Time: 10 minutes
Servings: 4

Cooking Time: 20 minutes

Ingredients:

- 1 quart coconut milk
- ½ teaspoon saffron powder
- ½ cup sugar
- 12 almonds, blanched and chopped
- 4 green cardamoms
- 2 tablespoons pistachios, chopped

Directions: In your instant pot, combine the coconut milk with the saffron and the other ingredients, mix, cover and cook on High for 20 minutes.
Release the pressure naturally for 10 minutes, divide the mix into molds and freeze before serving.

Nutrition: Calories: 249.8; Fats: 7.6g; Carbs: 38.8g; Protein: 9.5g

334.Wheat Cashew Kheer

Preparation Time: 10 minutes
Servings: 4

Cooking Time: 20 minutes

Ingredients:

- 1 cup broken wheat
- 1 tablespoon ghee, melted
- 1 tablespoon raisins
- 2 cardamom pods
- 1 tablespoon sugar
- ½ cup gram cashew nut
- ½ quart coconut milk

Directions: In your instant pot, combine the wheat with the ghee and the other ingredients, stir, cover and cook on High for 20 minutes.
Release the pressure naturally for 10 minutes, divide the mix into bowls and serve.

Nutrition: Calories: 226.8; Fats: 15.1g; Carbs: 16.1g; Protein: 7.8g

335.Saffron Zucchini Pudding

Preparation Time: 10 minutes
Servings: 4

Cooking Time: 20 minutes

Ingredients:

- 3 cups zucchinis, grated
- 1 cup caster sugar
- 2 eggs, whisked
- 2 tablespoons ghee, melted
- 1 cup coconut milk
- ½ teaspoon saffron powder

Directions: In your instant pot, combine the zucchinis with the sugar and the other ingredients, toss, cover and cook on High for 20 minutes.
Release the pressure naturally for 10 minutes, divide the pudding into bowls and serve cold.

Nutrition: Calories: 251.8; Fats: 5.2g; Carbs: 11.4g; Protein: 3.8g

336.Raisins Rice

Preparation Time: 10 minutes
Servings: 4

Cooking Time: 25 minutes

Ingredients:

- 1 cup grapes, halved
- ½ cup white rice
- 2 cups coconut milk
- ¼ cup raisins
- 2 tablespoons sugar
- ½ teaspoon lime juice
- 1 teaspoon vanilla extract

Directions: In your instant pot, combine grapes with the rice, coconut milk and the other ingredients, mix, cover and cook on High for 25 minutes.
Release the pressure naturally for 10 minutes, divide the mix into bowls and serve.

Nutrition: Calories: 261.9; Fats: 11.9g; Carbs: 11.2g; Protein: 3.7g

337.Carrots Sugary Pudding

Preparation Time: 10 minutes   **Cooking Time: 20 minutes**
Serving: 4

Ingredients:
- 1 pound carrots, grated
- 2 flax eggs, whisked
- 2 cups coconut milk
- ¾ cup sugar
- 1 teaspoon cinnamon powder
- 1 teaspoon turmeric powder
- ½ teaspoon saffron powder
- 1 cup water

Directions: In a bowl, mix the carrots with the eggs and the other ingredients except the water, whisk well and transfer to a pudding mold.
Add the water to the instant pot, add the steamer basket, put the pudding pan inside, cover and cook on High for 20 minutes. Release the pressure naturally for 10 minutes, cool the pudding down and serve.

Nutrition: Calories: 199.9; Fats: 8.3g; Carbs: 11.3g; Protein: 4.7g

338.Saffron Coconut Cream

Preparation Time: 10 minutes   **Cooking Time: 15 minutes**
Servings: 4

Ingredients:
- 1 cup heavy cream
- 1 cup coconut cream
- ½ teaspoon saffron powder
- 1 teaspoon vanilla extract
- 4 tablespoons sugar
- Zest of 1 lime, grated
- 1 tablespoon lime juice
- 1 cup water

Directions: In a bowl, mix the cream with the coconut cream and the other ingredients except the water, whisk well and divide into 4 ramekins.
Add the water to the instant pot, add the steamer basket, put the ramekins inside, cover and cook on High for 15 minutes. Release the pressure naturally for 10 minutes and serve the mix cold.

Nutrition: Calories: 291.8; Fats: 25.3g; Carbs: 17.1g; Protein: 2.1g

339.Masala Grapes and Bananas

Preparation Time: 5 minutes   **Cooking Time: 10 minutes**
Servings: 4

Ingredients:
- 1 cup grapes, halved
- 2 bananas, peeled and sliced
- Juice of ½ lemon
- 1 tablespoon lemon zest, grated
- 1 cup coconut cream
- ½ teaspoon turmeric powder
- ½ teaspoon chana masala
- ½ teaspoon vanilla extract

Directions: In your instant pot, mix grapes with the bananas and the other ingredients, toss, cover and cook on High for 10 minutes. Release the pressure fast for 5 minutes, divide the mix into bowls and serve.

Nutrition: Calories: 161.9; Fats: 4.1g; Carbs: 7.3g; Protein: 1.8g

340.Sugary Orange Cream

Preparation Time: 10 minutes   **Cooking Time: 20 minutes**
Servings: 4

Ingredients:
- Juice of 1 orange
- 1 pound orange, peeled and cut into segments
- 1 tablespoon lime zest, grated
- 4 tablespoons sugar
- 1 cup heavy cream

Directions: In your instant pot, mix the oranges with the orange juice and the remaining of the ingredients, cover and cook on High for 20 minutes. Release the pressure naturally for 10 minutes, blend the mix using an immersion blender, divide into bowls and serve cold.

Nutrition: Calories: 161.9; Fats: 8.9g; Carbs: 11.2g; Protein: 2.7g

341. Rhubarb Coconut Milk Quinoa

Preparation Time: 10 minutes   **Cooking Time: 15 minutes**
Servings: 4

Ingredients:
- 1 cup coconut milk
- ½ cup quinoa
- ½ teaspoon saffron powder
- 2 tablespoons sugar
- ½ teaspoon cardamom powder
- 2 cups rhubarb, chopped
- 1 teaspoon vanilla extract

Directions: In your instant pot, combine the coconut milk with the quinoa and the other ingredients, whisk, put the lid on and cook on High for 15 minutes.
Release the pressure naturally for 10 minutes, divide into bows and serve cold.

Nutrition: Calories: 147.9; Fats: 2.5g; Fiber: 2.5g; Carbs: 25.4g; Protein: 5.8g

342. Almond Chia Pudding

Preparation Time: 10 minutes   **Servings: 2**

Ingredients:
- 3 tablespoons almond butter
- 2 tablespoons maple syrup
- 1 cup almond milk
- ¼ cup plus 1 tablespoon chia seeds

Directions: In a sealable container, add everything and mix well.
Seal the container and refrigerate overnight. Serve with a splash of almond milk.

Nutrition: Calories: 211.8; Fats: 11.5g; Carbs: 14.5g; Fiber: 4.3g; Sugar: 7.9g; Protein: 7.5g

343. Strawberry and Banana Smoothie

Preparation Time: 5 minutes   **Servings: 1**

Ingredients:
- 1 cup sliced banana, frozen
- 2 tablespoons chia seeds
- 2 cups strawberries, frozen
- 2 teaspoons honey
- ¼ teaspoon vanilla extract, unsweetened
- 6 ounces coconut yogurt
- 1 cup almond milk, unsweetened

Directions: Put the ingredients in the jar of a food processor or blender, and then cover it with the lid.
Pulse until smooth and then serve.

Nutrition: Calories: 113.8; Fats: 1.9g; Protein: 3.8g; Carbs: 22.1g; Fiber: 3.5g

344. Banana Shake

Preparation Time: 5 minutes   **Servings: 1**

Ingredients:
- 3 medium frozen bananas
- 1 tablespoon cocoa powder, unsweetened
- 1 teaspoon shredded coconut
- 1 tablespoon maple syrup
- 1 tablespoon peanut butter
- 1 teaspoon vanilla extract, unsweetened
- 2 cups of coconut water
- 1 cup of ice cubes

Directions: Add banana in a food processor, add maple syrup and vanilla, pour in water and then add ice.
Pulse until smooth and then pour half of the smoothie into a glass.
Add butter and cocoa powder into the blender, pulse until smooth, and then add to the smoothie glass.
Sprinkle coconut over the smoothie and then serve.

Nutrition: Calories: 300.8; Fats: 9.1g; Protein: 6.9g; Carbs: 48.8g; Fiber: 1.6g

345.Easy Brownies

Preparation Time: 20 minutes
Servings: 12

Ingredients:

- 2 Tablespoons Coconut Oil, Melted
- ½ Cup Peanut Butter, Salted
- ¼ Cup Warm Water
- 2 Cups Dates, Pitted
- 1/3 Cup Dark Chocolate chips
- 1/3 Cup Cocoa Powder
- ½ Cup Raw Walnuts, Chopped

Directions: Heat the oven to 350, and then get out a loaf pan. Place parchment paper in it, and then get out a food processor. Blend your dates until it's a fine mixture. Add in some hot water, and blend well until the mixture become an as smooth batter.

Add in the coconut oil, cacao powder, and peanut butter. Blend more, and then fold in the chocolate and walnuts. Spread this into your loaf pan. Bake for fifteen minutes, and then chill before serving.

Nutrition: Calories: 49.9; Fats: 4.8g; Protein: 4.1g; Carbs: 5.8g; Fiber: 0g

Recipe Index

1-9

3-Ingredient Flatbread	61

A

Alfredo Sauce	101
Almond Chia Pudding	124
Almond Flour Muffins	120
Amaranth Banana Porridge	24
Amaranth Polenta with Wild Mushrooms	32
Amaranth Porridge	91
Amaranth Tabbouleh Salad	79
Anasazi Bean and Vegetable Stew	87
Apple & Kale Salad	80
Apple Cinnamon Smoothie	20
Apple Crumble	110
Apple Porridge	25
Aromatic Rice	92
Arugula Pesto Couscous	37
Arugula with Fruits and Nuts	74
Asparagus Spears	62
Avocado and Tempeh Bacon Wraps	59
Avocado Miso Chickpeas Toast	23
Avocado Power Salad	79
Avocado Salad	84
Avocado with Raspberry Vinegar Salad	75

B

Baked Apples	114
Baked Brussel Sprouts	61
Baked Parsnip and Potato	34
Baked Root Vegetables	69
Baked Vegetables with Cheese and Olives	65
Balsamic Black Beans with Parsnip	88
Balsamic Zucchini Bowls	58
Banana and Chia Smoothie	119
Banana Chips	54
Banana Coconut Cookies	115
Banana Curry	53
Banana Muffins	114
Banana Shake	124
Banana Walnut Bread	112
Banana Walnut Muffins	117

Banana-Nut Butter Boats	18
Barley and Chickpea Soup	107
Barley and Mushrooms with Beans	39
Basil and Avocado Salad	81
Basil Zucchini Noodles	50
Bean Bolognese	94
Beet and Clementine Smoothie	111
Bell Peppers and Masala Potatoes	47
Beluga Lentils with Lacinato Kale	89
Berries with Cream	20
Berry Compote Pancakes	23
Berry Ginger Zing Smoothie	21
Black and Veggie Tacos	37
Black Bean and Corn Salad with Cilantro Dressing	87
Black Bean Dip	94
Black Bean Taquitos	93
Black Beans with Lime	89
Blackberry Pie	121
Bowl with Root Vegetables	31
Breakfast Burritos	20
Broccoli and Rice Stir Fry	88
Brown Lentil Bowl	86
Brown Rice Lettuce Wraps	48
Brussels Sprouts & Carrots	64
Brussels Sprouts & Cranberries Salad	28
Brussels Sprouts and Ricotta Salad	74
Buffalo Cauliflower Dip	51
Bulgur Wheat Salad	91
Butter Carrots	115
Butternut Squash Chickpea Stew	84

C

Cabbage Mango Slaw	84
Caesar Vegan Salad	41
Cannellini Bean and Bell Pepper Burger	98
Cannellini Pesto Spaghetti	75
Capers, Green Beans and Herbs Mix	94
Caprese Stuffed Avocado	36
Caramel Popcorn	55
Cardamom Pears Smoothie	121
Carrot Cake Balls	58
Carrots Sugary Pudding	123
Cashew Mac and Cheese	48
Cauliflower Asparagus Soup	70
Cauliflower Carrot Soup	76

Cauliflower Fried Rice	28
Cauliflower Oatmeal	21
Cauliflower Popcorn	50
Cauliflower Spinach Soup	72
Cauliflower Steaks	43
Cauliflower Wings	106
Cheese Board	42
Cheese Broccoli Pasta	34
Cheese Pockets	36
Cheesy Fennel	65
Cherry Tomato & Kale Salad	79
Chia Seed Pudding	19
Chickpea and Noodle Soup	71
Chickpea Flour Quiche	33
Chickpea Nuggets	98
Chickpea Salad	27
Chickpea Salad (2nd Version)	98
Chickpeas & Quinoa Salad	81
Chickpeas & Squash Stew	77
Chickpeas Curry	95
Chickpeas Spread Sourdough Toast	24
Chili with Tofu	108
Chinese Orange Tofu	68
Chocolate Almond Bars	51
Chocolate and Peanut Butter Smoothie	110
Chocolate Cake	113
Chocolate Chip Banana Cookies	113
Chocolate Mint Grasshopper Pie	117
Chocolate Peanut Butter Bars	110
Chocolate Peanut Butter Protein Shake	18
Chocolate Strawberry Milkshake	20
Chocolate Zucchini Bread	22
Cilantro and Avocado Lime Rice	90
Cilantro, Lime Quinoa	104
Cinnamon and Almond Porridge	25
Cinnamon Potato	68
Coconut Banana Pot	56
Coconut Brussels Sprouts	29
Coconut Curry Lentils	40
Coconut milk Rice	35
Coconut Rice	39
Coconut Tofu Curry	89
Cold Lemon Squares	118
Coriander Broccoli and Onions	67
Coriander Tahini Sauce	102

Corn and Egg Salad	82
Corn Griddle Cakes with Tofu Mayonnaise	22
Cranberry and Almond Muffins	112
Cranberry and Orange Sauce	101
Cranberry Sauce	102
Creamy Asparagus Soup	80
Creamy Cauliflower Pakora Soup	70
Creamy Eggplants	47
Creamy Parsnip Soup	83
Creamy Potato Soup	76
Cucumber Bites with Chive and Sunflower Seeds	44

D

Dandelion and Strawberry Salad	81
Dandelion Salad	79
Dijon Maple Burgers	44
Dinner Rolls	46

E

Easy Brownies	125
Egg Avocado Salad	73
Eggplant Masala	35
Eggplant Parmesan	107
Eggplant Sandwich	24
Eggplant Stacks	47
Emmenthal Soup	42
Endive Salad	74

F

French Toast	109
Fried Mustard Greens	116
Fudgy Choco-Peanut Butter	52

G

Garam Masala Asparagus	66
Garlic and Herbs Mushrooms Skillet	61
Ginger Spice Brownies	106
Ginger Zucchinis and Carrots	68
Gold Potato Masala	67
Grape Tomatoes and Zucchini	61
Greek Salad with Tofu Feta	28
Green Beans	96
Green Beans & Orange Sauce	97
Green Beans with Balsamic Sauce	90
Green Cilantro Sauce	100

Green Lentil Salad with Vinaigrette 92
Green Mango Smoothie 120
Green Tea and Vanilla Cream 118
Grilled Eggplant Roll-Ups 31
Grilled Lettuce Salad 78
Grilled Peaches 45

H
Hasselback Zucchini 66
Hazelnut and Chocolate Milk 111
Hemp Falafel with Tahini Sauce 101
High Protein Toast 23
Homemade Trail Mix 102
Hot Roasted Peppers Cream 26

I
Indian Almond Kulfi 122
Indonesian-Style Spicy Fried Tempeh Strips 60

K
Kale and Black Olives 34
Kale and Cauliflower Salad 71
Kale and Lemon Salad 76
Kale Spread 52
Kale Wraps with Chili and Green Beans 45
Kohlrabi Slaw with Cilantro 84

L
Lemon Avocado Salad Dressing 105
Lemony Capers, Kale and Nuts Salad 76
Lentil and Wild Rice Soup 88
Lentil Vegetable Loaf 26
Lima Bean Casserole 93
Lime and Cucumber Drink 111

M
Mango Salad 82
Marinated Veggie Salad 73
Masala Grapes and Bananas 123
Mexican Bean Salad 83
Mexican Lentil Soup 38
Middle Eastern Chickpea Stew 86
Middle Eastern Za'atar Hummus 87
Millet Fritters 91
Millet Porridge with Sultanas 91
Millet Tabbouleh, Lime and Cilantro 77

Minty Masala Tomatoes	35
Mixed Vegetable	59
Mom's Chili	86
Moroccan Eggplant Stew	30
Moroccan Leeks Snack Salad	74
Mushroom Dip	104
Mushroom Gravy	104
Mushroom Sauce	103
Mushroom Soup	39
Mushroom Steaks	43
Mushroom Stuffed Tomatoes	116
Mushrooms and Chard Soup	30

N

Noodle Vegetable Salad	82
Nori Burritos	33
Nutmeg Okra	47

O

Oil-Free Mushroom and Tofu Burritos	48
Oregano Tomato and Radish	62
Overnight Oatmeal	120

P

Paprika Cucumber Chips	56
Parsley Potatoes	115
Pasta with Kidney Bean Sauce	39
Pasta with Mushroom Sauce	32
Pasta with Olives and White Beans	31
Peach Mango Crumble (Pressure Cooker)	106
Peanut Butter Protein Smoothie	20
Pecan Rice	88
Pepper & Tomato Bake	63
Peppers and Hummus	59
Pico de Gallo	69
Pineapple and Mango Oatmeal	108
Pineapple Coconut Macaroons	112
Pineapple Pudding	121
Pineapple Tofu Kabobs	49
Pineapple, Banana & Spinach Smoothie	119
Pineapple, Peach, and Mango Salsa	51
Pink Panther Smoothie	118
Piri Sauce	100
Plant-Strong Bowl	28
Pomegranate Flower Sprouts	60

Pomegranate Smoothie	21
Portobello Mushroom Stew	107
Power Smoothie	118
Protein Bars	21
Protein Fat Bombs	117
Pumpkin Chia Smoothie	120
Pumpkin Orange Spice Hummus	53
Pumpkin Smoothie	119
Pumpkin Spice Granola Bites	25

Q

Quinoa & Veggie Stew	77
Quinoa and Black Bean Lettuce Wraps	69
Quinoa and Parsley Salad	26
Quinoa Porridge with Amaranth	24
Quinoa with Mushroom	103

R

Rainbow Mango Salad	78
Raisins Rice	122
Raspberry Muffins	113
Red Pepper and Tomato Soup	38
Red Rose Potato Toasts	63
Red Salsa	105
Refried Beans	97
Rhubarb Coconut Milk Quinoa	124
Rice and Vegetables	94
Roasted Bell Peppers with Spicy Mayonnaise	46
Roasted Brussel Sprouts with Parmesan	34
Roasted Butternut and Chickpeas Salad	75
Roasted Butternut Squash Pasta	37
Roasted Potato Salad	83
Rosemary Sweet Potato Chips	64

S

Saffron Avocado Cream	66
Saffron Coconut Cream	123
Saffron Zucchini Pudding	122
Sambal Sauce	100
Sausage Links	46
Scallion and Mint Soup	78
Seed Crackers	53
Sesame Seed Bread	54
Sherry Roasted King Trumpet	60
Slow Cooker Butternut Squash Oatmeal	109

Smoky Red Pepper Hummus	49
Southwest Style Salad	73
Spaghetti Squash With Peanut Sauce	32
Spanish Rice	97
Spanish-Style Saffron Rice with Black Beans	96
Spelt and Raisin Cookies	54
Spicy Beet Chips	55
Spicy Hummus Quesadillas	27
Spicy Oats	19
Spicy Tomato Chutney	105
Spinach Soup with Dill and Basil	72
Sprout Wraps	43
Sprouts and Apples Snack Salad	75
Squash Risotto	96
Steamed Broccoli with Sesame	58
Strawberries Cream	118
Strawberry and Banana Smoothie	124
Strawberry Ice Cream	121
Strawberry Watermelon Ice Pops	51
Stuffed Peppers with Kidney Beans	40
Sugary Orange Cream	123
Sunflower Seed Bread	64
Sweet and Sour Juice	111
Sweet Coconut Pilaf	90
Sweet Maize Meal Porridge	92
Sweet 'n' Spicy Crunchy Snack Mix	52
Sweet Oatmeal	92
Sweet Potato Quesadillas	29
Sweet Potatoes Vanilla Pudding	56
Sweetened Onions	65

T

Tahini Braised Greens	18
Taro Chips	55
Tarragon Soup	38
Tartar Sauce	100
Tempeh Tikka Masala	40
Tex-Mex Tofu & Beans	27
Tofu & Asparagus Stir Fry	62
Tofu Cacciatore	29
Tofu Curry	64
Tofu Fries	19
Tofu Hollandaise	102
Tofu Sandwiches on Multigrain Bread	53
Tomato Gazpacho	70

Tomato Kebabs	115
Tropical Smoothie	119
Turmeric Artichokes	66
Turmeric Tofu Scramble	18
Turmeric Zucchinis	35

V
Vegan Fat Bombs	58
Vegan Taco Bowls	36
Vegetable Chili	103
Vegetable Fajitas	44
Vegetable Fajitas Tacos	33
Vegetable Stew	72
Vegetable Tacos	30
Vegetable Wontons	56
Vegetables with Wild Rice	42
Veggie Balls in Tomato Sauce	45

W
Walnuts Allspice Bell Peppers	67
Warm Kale Salad	80
Watermelon Strawberry Ice Pops	113
Wheat Cashew Kheer	122
Wild Rice and Black Lentils Bowl	95

Z
Zucchini & Tomato Salad	80
Zucchini Chips	50
Zucchini Fries	63
Zucchini Oatmeal	22
Zucchini Soup	72
Zucchinis Cardamom Rice	97

Made in United States
North Haven, CT
21 June 2022